Eurodélices

Meat and Poultry

EURODÉLICES

MEAT & POULTRY

DINE WITH EUROPE'S
MASTER CHEFS

KÖNEMANN

Acknowledgements

We want to thank the following people, restaurants and companies for their contribution to this book:
Ancienne Manufacture Royale, Aixe-sur-Vienne; Baccarat, Paris; Chomette Favor, Grigny; Christofle, Paris; Cristalleries de Saint-Louis, Paris; Grand Marnier, Paris; Groupe Cidelcem, Marne-la-Vallée; Haviland, Limoges; Jean-Louis Coquet, Paris; José Houel, Paris; Lalique, Paris; Les maisons de Cartier, Paris; Maîtres cuisiniers de France, Paris; Philippe Deshoulières, Paris; Porcelaines Bernardaud, Paris; Porcelaine Lafarge, Paris; Puiforcat Orfèvre, Paris; Robert Haviland et C. Parlon, Limoges; Société Caviar Petrossian, Paris; Villeroy & Boch, Garges-les-Gonesse; Wedgwood Dexam-International, Coye-la-Forêt.

A special thank you to: Lucien Barcon, Georges Laffon, Clément Lausecker, Michel Pasquet, Jean Pibourdin, Pierre Roche, Jacques Sylvestre and Pierre Fonteyne.

Skill ratings of the recipes:

★   easy
★★   medium
★★★   difficult

Photos: Studio Lucien Loeb, Maren Detering

Copyright © Fabien Bellahsen und Daniel Rouche

Original title: Eurodélices — Viandes, Volailles, Gibiers

Copyright © 1998 for the English edition:
Könemann Verlagsgesellschaft mbH
Bonner Str. 126, D-50968 Cologne

Translation and typesetting of the English edition:
Translate-A-Book, a division of Transedition Limited, Oxford, England
Coordinator for the English language edition: Tammi Reichel
Series project manager: Bettina Kaufmann
Assistance: Stephan Küffner
Production Manager: Detlev Schaper
Assistance: Nicola Leurs
Reproduction: Reproservice Werner Pees, Essen
Printing and binding: Neue Stalling, Oldenburg

Printed in Germany

ISBN 3-8290-1132-6

10 9 8 7 6 5 4 3

Contents

Foreword

The Eurodélices series brings a selection of European haute cuisine right into your kitchen. Almost 100 professional chefs, many of them recipients of multiple awards and distinctions, associated with renowned restaurants in 17 countries throughout Europe, joined forces to create this unique series. Here they divulge their best and their favorite recipes for unsurpassed hot and cold appetizers, fish and meat entrees, desserts, and pastry specialties.

The series as a whole, consisting of six volumes with over 1,900 pages, is not only an essential collection for gourmet cooks, but also a fascinating document of European culture that goes far beyond short-lived culinary trends. In a fascinating way, Eurodélices explores the common roots of the different "arts of cooking" that have developed in various geographic locations, as well as their abundant variety.

For eating is much more than the fulfillment of a basic bodily need; cooking is often elevated to the level of an art, especially in association with parties and celebrations of all kinds, in private life and in the public sphere. Young couples plan their futures over a special dinner at an elegant restaurant, partners gather at table to launch new business ventures, heads of state are wined and dined. Every conceivable celebration involves food, from weddings to funerals, from intimacies shared over coffee and cake to Sunday dinners to Passover and Thanksgiving feasts.

We often have our first contact with the cultures of other lands, whether nearby or across an ocean, through their food. Precisely because the various contributing chefs are rooted in their distinct traditions, some flavors and combinations will be new to North American readers, and occasionally ingredients are called for that may be unfamiliar or even difficult to locate. The texts accompanying each recipe help elucidate and, wherever possible, suggest substitutes for ingredients that are not readily available in North America. A glossary is also included to explain terms that may not be obvious, listing some ingredients.

Because precision is often crucial to the success of recipes of this caliber, a few words regarding measurements and conversions are in order. In Europe, it is customary to use metric units of liquid volume or weight, that is, milliliters or grams. Every household has a kitchen scale and solid ingredients are weighed, rather than measured by volume. Converting milliliters to fluid cups and grams to ounces is straightforward, if not always neat. More problematic are ingredients given in grams that North Americans measure by volume, in tablespoons and cups. Throughout the Eurodélices series, the original metric measurement follows the North American equivalent. The conversions are painstakingly accurate up to 100 ml and 100 g (which necessitates some awkward-looking amounts). Thereafter, they are more neatly, and thus less accurately, rounded off. As with all recipes, measurements are approximate for many ingredients, and a wide variety of factors ranging from temperature and humidity to accuracy of kitchen implements to the way food is sold will affect the amount actually used. If the reader wants to recreate the recipes as given, however, the use of a kitchen scale is strongly recommended.

The unique collection of around 750 recipes contained in Eurodélices aims to excite its readers' curiosity. Classic dishes, which have been enjoyed for generations and thus form the foundations of modern cookery, are liberally presented. But there are also new and surprising pleasures, familiar foods prepared in novel ways, as well as culinary delights composed of ingredients from far away places that we experience for the first time. Allow yourself to be inspired by the European master chefs to try and, perhaps, try again.

Quails with

Preparation time: 1 hour
Cooking time: 10 minutes
Difficulty: ★

Serves 4

20 quails' thighs (or 5 quail, quartered)
10 asparagus stalks
32 mild garlic cloves
24 small potatoes
4 different salad greens
chives

7½ tbsp/100 g flour
1 tbsp ginger
¾ cup/200 ml sunflower oil
sherry vinegar
1 tbsp soy sauce
olive oil
salt and pepper

For the soy sauce:
3 tbsp soy sauce
3 tbsp stock
5 tsp/25 g butter

The hunting season gives the people of Catalonia, in northeastern Spain, many opportunities to try out their skills, for there is no lack of game in the countryside. Quail is constantly turning up in old recipes, and here Fernando Adría adapts an old recipe for new tastes. Farm-raised quail can be obtained all year round. Their flavor is not as strong as that of wild quail, but it goes very well with the other ingredients in this recipe.

The quail has a very delicate flavor and so you must be sure not to overwhelm it with other flavors. You should be careful when removing the thighs from the birds, so as to leave the bone attached to the thigh. This process will take some time, because you should allow 5 thighs per person. As an alternative, you may use 5 quail, quartered.

Our kitchen chef recommends that, contrary to general culinary rules, you can use any kind of meat stock or poultry stock to give the sauce a fine consistency.

The quality of the accompaniments should match that of the birds. Garlic, potatoes and mixed salad greens complement the quail and make for a delicious meal.

1. Remove quails' thighs, leaving the meat on the bone. Prepare the asparagus, using only the tips. Peel and slice the potatoes. Peel the garlic cloves.

2. Dust the quails' thighs with flour. Heat the sunflower oil to 320 °F/160 °C, and fry the thighs until crisp. Drain on paper towels. Broil the asparagus and garlic as close to the heat source as possible. Cook the potatoes over low heat in olive oil and season with salt and pepper. Half a minute before removing them from the heat, add a tbsp of soy sauce.

Soy Sauce

3. To make the sauce, add the stock to the soy sauce. Over low heat, reduce to 4 tbsp and add the butter. Dip the quails' thighs in the sauce. Make a salad dressing with olive oil, vinegar and salt.

4. Arrange 8 garlic cloves around each plate, place the asparagus, cut in half lengthwise, on top, and place a quail's thigh on top of each arrangement. In the center of the dish, pile the cooked potato slices into a pyramid and top with the ginger. Pour some sauce on top of everything. Decorate with whole chives and serve the dressed salad separately.

Roast

Preparation time: 10 minutes
Cooking time: 5 minutes
Difficulty: ★★

Serves 4

4 woodcock
1 onion
2 garlic cloves
3 carrots

9 oz/250 g turnips
9 oz/250 g mushrooms
some butter
oil
salt and pepper

For the sauce:
bones and trimmings of the woodcock
6½ tbsp/100 ml cognac
⅔ cup/150 ml white wine

With its long, thin beak and short legs, the woodcock is one of the most distinctive-looking of game birds. In some countries, the woodcock is a protected bird, so that it can only be eaten during the short hunting season.

First the birds must be prepared as shown in the first illustration: their necks must be twisted so that they can be correctly trussed. Then the woodcock must be cooked until golden brown all over, so that they are nicely crisp. Do not let the oil get too hot, because if they brown too much on one side, it will spoil the uniformly golden-brown effect you are trying to achieve.

Simple root vegetables such as turnips, carrots or onions go well with this dish. And to emphasize even further the gamey taste of the woodcock, you should lightly braise an attractive medley of mushrooms as a garnish.

Other birds that can be prepared in this way are partridge, quail, wood pigeon and squab.

1. Prepare the woodcock; remove the gizzards and reserve. Truss them by pushing the beak through both thighs, so that it comes out at the other side. Season with salt and pepper.

2. Heat the oil in a shallow skillet and brown the woodcock on all sides, then put them in a hot oven for five minutes. Remove from the oven, let cool slightly, and bone the woodcock.

Woodcock

3. Break up the carcasses and put them back in the pan with the gizzards. Add the wine and cognac, reduce the sauce and strain. Heat the woodcock briefly in a skillet with a pat of butter.

4. In a shallow skillet, lightly braise the vegetables in a little water and two pats of butter. Arrange the woodcock on the plates and pour the sauce over them. Serve with the garnish of braised vegetables and mushrooms.

Preparation time: 1 hour
Cooking time: 2½ hours
Difficulty: ★★★

Serves 4

1 free-range chicken (3⅓ lb/1½ kg)
6 ripe tomatoes
2 thick slices of Bayonne ham

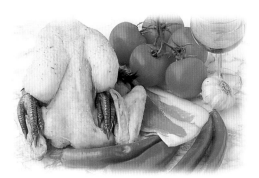

7 oz/200 g mild green chile or green bell
pepper
3 garlic cloves
4½ tbsp/70 ml white Irouléguy (Basque) wine
or other dry white wine
butter
2 tbsp/30 ml water
olive oil

This is a very special, sophisticated version of the famous chicken à la basquaise, in which the golden-skinned and nicely browned bird is served with traditional ingredients: tomatoes, peppers, garlic and Bayonne ham.

A perfect chicken from a Basque farm is the best suited for this dish. But failing that, any good free-range chicken will serve the purpose very nicely, as long as it is plump and tender. The bird must be carefully boned so that it can be stuffed afterwards. This preserves the delicate flavor and allows the aromas of the other ingredients to penetrate the meat. In order to prevent the chicken browning unevenly,

it should be carefully trussed and you should make sure that the flesh is covered all over by skin.

The roulades of chicken are roasted in the oven until golden, so the skin becomes nicely crisp. If the oven is too hot, the meat may dry out. Test to see if it is done by pressing lightly on the flesh with your finger. If you feel a slight resistance, the chicken is cooked.

Firmin Arrambide recommends replacing the chicken with a guinea-fowl if you prefer, and the Bayonne ham with finely sliced prosciutto.

1. Bone the chicken and set aside the heart and liver. Remove and reserve all the bones. The bird should be divided in half. Peel the tomatoes and seed them. Season with salt and pepper, pour olive oil over them and let them cook in a 140 °F/60 °C oven for about 2 hours.

2. Sauté the peppers and ham until brown. Set aside. Peel and slice the garlic, and brown in the pan until golden-brown; do the same with the heart and liver. Distribute the ham, peppers, garlic, heart and liver in the centers of both chicken halves.

à la Basquaise

3. Roll up the chicken halves and truss as for a roast. Season and brown in a braising pan with the crushed bones.

4. Put the chicken roulades into the preheated oven for 12 minutes. Remove them and keep hot. Skim off the fat in the pan, deglaze with the white wine, and reduce with half a glass of water and a walnut-sized piece of butter. Sieve the juices and keep hot. Cut the roulades into thick slices. Arrange on each plate with the cooked tomatoes and pour the juices over them.

Lambs' Brain Salad

Preparation time: 40 minutes
Cooking time: 20 minutes
Difficulty: ☆

Serves 4

6 lambs' brains
1 bunch of spinach
4 Belgian endive
12 sheets of filo pastry
3½ oz/100g mature sheep's cheese, such as Manchego
1 sprig of fresh thyme
balsamic vinegar
salt and pepper

For the court bouillon:
4 cups/1 l water
juice of 1 lemon
1 sprig of fresh thyme
salt and pepper

For the vinaigrette:
1 shallot
mustard
olive oil
balsamic vinegar
juice of 1 lemon
salt and pepper

Brains, like all variety meats, must be absolutely fresh. For this recipe, they should come from a very young milk-fed lamb, which is highly prized for its delicate, juicy flesh, its thin layer of fat, and its crisp skin. Our chef prefers to use Auxuria lamb, which is raised exclusively on its mother's milk in the Basque mountains, and is slaughtered when it is 45 days old. Female lamb from Nîmes or Perpignan is also very good in this recipe.

First remove the skin around the brain and place it in cold water for an hour to remove any remaining blood. Then you can either poach it in a court bouillon or cut it into medium-thick slices and brown them in a little butter. We recommend wrapping the brain in sheets of filo pastry, folded double, and deep-frying it just before serving, so the pastry is pleasantly crisp.

The mature sheep's milk cheese should not have any blue veins, so do not substitute Roquefort. Firmin Arrambide buys his sheep's milk cheese in May and allows it to mature for about 6 months in his own cellar.

Pigs' or calves' brains can be used if no lambs' brains are available.

1. Remove the surrounding skin from the brains and let them soak in cold water. Prepare a court bouillon with water, salt, pepper, lemon juice and thyme. Poach the brains in it for 10 minutes, then remove from the heat.

2. Wash and blanch the spinach. Set aside to cool. Prepare and wash the endive. Prepare a vinaigrette with shallots, mustard, olive oil, vinegar, lemon juice, salt and pepper. Set aside. When the lambs' brains have cooled, cut them in half, sprinkle with thyme and wrap each in two spinach leaves.

with Sheep's Milk Cheese

3. Fold the filo sheets double, and wrap the halved lambs' brains in them. Cut the cheese into thin sticks.

4. Just before serving, fry the lambs' brains until crisp and golden-brown. Dress the salad. Place a little endive on each plate, with the sticks of cheese on top, and arrange beside them three crisp pieces of lamb's brain for each person. Add a dash of balsamic vinegar to each plate.

Saddle of Rabbit

Preparation time:	45 minutes
Cooking time:	40 minutes
Difficulty:	✷✷✷

Serves 4

1 rabbit
pork caul
carrot, onion, and celery mixture
2 cups/500 ml cooking juices from rabbit
(or use rabbit or chicken stock)
¾ cup/200 ml white wine
2 bay leaves

thyme
¾ cup/200 ml olive oil
13 tbsp/200 g duck fat

For the stuffing:
3½ oz/100 g zucchini
3½ oz/100 g mushrooms
salt and pepper

For the garnish:
2 generous lb/1 kg turnips
sage
savory

Rabbit meat is ideally suited to a light summer meal. It is rich in protein, but at the same time low in fat and calories.

The farm rabbits available from the butcher have a less distinctive flavor than the famous *lapins de garenne* (wild rabbits which are raised in a large open-air enclosure and fed on clover). Make sure that the rabbit you use is supplied with the kidneys.

If you would like to prepare the stock yourself, our chef recommends boning the rabbit the day before, and making the stock with the bones. The flesh of farm rabbits can become dry very quickly during cooking. The saddle in particular should be cooked with care, because its flesh should stay pink in the center.

The accompaniments will be particularly tasty if you choose spring vegetables, especially firm, crunchy turnips. Preserve the freshness of the vegetables by braising them on the same day as you cook the rabbit.

Chicken can be prepared in the same way, if you take equal care when browning. If you can't get pork caul, brush the saddles of rabbit with oil and baste them from time to time during cooking.

1. Cut the rabbit into serving pieces. Bone the saddles and stuff them with the chopped kidney, zucchini and mushrooms. Lightly season the saddles of rabbit. Roll up into a cylinder and truss. Wrap with the pork caul.

2. Crush the bones and brown in olive oil with a mixture of diced carrot, onion and celery. Deglaze with ¾ cup/200 ml of white wine, allow to reduce and add 2 cups/500 ml of chicken stock. Add the bay leaves and thyme, simmer for 30 minutes and then strain.

with Savory and Sage

3. Cut the turnips into equal-sized pieces and sprinkle with sugar and salt. Braise lightly in melted butter and chicken stock to cover. Braise over low heat in an uncovered saucepan.

4. Brown the rabbit in duck fat (or olive oil). Add the wine and reduce. Braise with the stock from the rabbit bones, seasoned with sage and savory. Finally braise for 10 minutes more in a 400 °F/200 °C oven. Serve on plates with the braised turnips. Sprinkle with chopped chives. Stir olive oil into the stock until the sauce is creamy, then pour over the rabbit.

Preparation time: 10 minutes
Cooking time: 10 minutes
Difficulty: ★

Serves 4

1 bunch white radishes
basic white sauce

veal stock
horseradish, freshly grated
1 bunch of chives
12 red radishes
1¾ lb/800 g beef tenderloin
10½ oz/300 g bacon slices
butter, peanut oil
salt and pepper

Prized since prehistoric times, beef has formed the basis of the most distinguished dishes throughout the centuries. Fresh beef can be recognized by its strong red color and firm texture. Very pale meat is the sign of a young, immature animal, and very dark color indicates that the meat is from an older animal.

The tournedos is cut from the fillet and should be about ¾ in/2 cm thick and particularly juicy. Cuts of meat "à la tournedos" are cut in the same way but do not come from the tenderloin. The tournedos are quickly cooked in butter and served, according to taste, medium or rare.

The sauce should be kept warm until served. Horseradish and chives are added at the end, after which the sauce should not be stirred again, otherwise the chives may blacken and lose their flavor.

This irresistible tournedos, flavored with horseradish, can be served with turnips instead of white radishes.

1. Peel the white radishes and slice finely, then brown them in butter. They should color slightly on both sides. Add the white sauce and simmer for 4–5 minutes over low heat.

2. Thicken the veal stock to the consistency of a sauce and add the horseradish. Season and then sprinkle the finely chopped chives on top.

with Radishes

3. Cut the red radishes into thin strips and deep-fry in hot peanut oil. Drain on paper towels and set aside.

4. Cut the tenderloin into 4 steaks of equal thickness. Wrap a strip of bacon around each steak. Fry in butter on both sides for 5 minutes and season with salt and pepper. Arrange the radish slices in a circle and place the tournedos in the middle. Garnish with the deep-fried radish and decorate with a border of the sauce.

Lamb Tenderloin

Preparation time:	2 hours
Cooking time:	1½ hours
Difficulty:	★★★

Serves 4

1 rack of lamb, weighing 2½ lb/1.2 kg
10½ oz/300 g spinach
5 oz/140 g pork caul

For the stuffing:
2 tbsp finely chopped fresh herbs (tarragon, chervil, chives)
2 eggs
5 tbsp crème fraîche
salt and pepper

For the garnish:
2 potatoes
4 shallots
1 red bell pepper
1 green bell pepper
4 onions
1 garlic clove
3 cups/200 g finely chopped mushrooms
6½ tbspi/100 g butter

For the sauce:
lamb bones and trimmings
1 bouquet garni
green leaves of 1 leek
tarragon, garlic

There was a time when lamb was eaten primarily at Easter, but nowadays you can enjoy this delicious meat from December to July. You can easily assess the freshness of the meat from its color and brightness. Choose a prime rack of lamb for this dish. After you cook the lamb, it should rest for about 10 minutes so it becomes tender and juicy. This resting period is absolutely necessary to allow the full flavor of the lamb to develop.

There are many ways of using herbs, and they give the lamb a very special flavor. Chopped chervil, chives and tarragon are used to create an herb crust, in which the lamb is snugly wrapped.

The garnish consists of small potato ravioli filled with duxelles, made from finely chopped mushrooms, onions and shallots, which are gently sautéed until the liquid they contain has evaporated. This preparation reminds us of the Marquis d'Uxelles, a gourmet who is no longer well known. His personal chef, the still-famous La Varenne, dedicated this mushroom preparation to him.

To make the ravioli, it is important to use very thin potato slices. The best way to achieve the thinness required to keep them from falling apart is to use a mandoline, or, if you don't have one, a swivel-bladed vegetable peeler.

1. Bone the rack of lamb. Set aside the two tenderloins and prepare a stock with the bones and the other sauce ingredients, except for the tarragon. Prepare the stuffing with the fresh herbs and season it. To make the duxelles, chop the mushrooms and shallots together until very fine. Gently sauté them in butter until all the liquid they give off has evaporated. Set aside.

2. Blanch the spinach and spread it out on a kitchen towel. Sauté the lamb fillets over high heat for 1 minute on each side, then wipe off the fat with paper towels. Cover the fillets with the herb stuffing and wrap first in spinach leaves, then in the pork caul (if you can't find pork caul, brush with olive oil). Set aside to cool.

3. Slice the potatoes very thinly and form them into small ravioli with the duxelles. Sauté the ravioli in clarified butter. Reduce the lamb juices and allow the fresh tarragon to infuse in them. Mix and stir in the butter used to sauté the ravioli.

4. Cook the fillets for 10 minutes in a preheated 355 °F/180 °C oven (basting from time to time if pork caul has not been used). Cut lids off the top of each onion, and hollow out the rest. Braise the bell peppers with the onion scraps. Braise the onion cases and fill with the onion and pepper mixture. After allowing the lamb fillets to rest for 10 minutes in the warm oven, cut into slices and arrange on a serving dish with the vegetables. Decorate it with some of the sauce.

Preparation time: 45 minutes
Cooking time: 35 minutes
Difficulty: ★★★

Serves 4

4 small veal sweetbreads
1 carrot
1 onion
2 garlic cloves
6½ tbsp/100 g butter
2 cups/500 ml veal stock

¾ cup/200 ml oil
6½ tbsp/100 ml sherry vinegar
½ cup/60 g small capers

For the garnish:
8 Belgian endive
1 onion
4½ tbsp/70 g butter
¾ cup/200 ml cream
juice of 1 lemon
sugar
salt and pepper

Capers are the buds of the small, prickly caper bush, which grows around the Mediterranean. In general, capers serve as a garnish, but they are also integral to several recipes, such as tapenade—a sauce that owes its name to the caper (from the Provençal *tapeno*, caper).

The sweetbread is one of the most delicious parts of a calf. Sweetbreads are prized for their firm and juicy texture and delicate flavor, which should not be masked by other ingredients. For this reason we recommend sherry vinegar, whose nutty taste goes very well with the sweetbreads.

Belgian endive used to be a winter vegetable, but there is also a summer variety and it is available all year round. Choose very light-colored heads, with crisp, tightly wrapped leaves.

1. Blanch the sweetbreads in salted water. Refresh them, lay between two wooden boards and weight them down with two heavy food cans or something similar. This makes them easier to cut later. Remove the outer leaves from the endive; take off enough leaves to line four molds, one for each portion. Blanch the leaves in salted water with a little lemon juice, allow them to drain on paper towels.

2. Cut the remaining endive into thin strips. Chop the onion finely and braise lightly in butter. Add the strips of endive and allow the vegetable liquid to evaporate. Add the cream and reduce until there is almost no liquid left. Season with sugar, salt and pepper. Fill the endive-lined molds with this mixture. Fold the leaves over the tops of the molds to seal them.

with Capers

3. Brown the sweetbreads nicely on all sides in hot oil. Add the crushed garlic and the finely chopped carrot and onion. Bake in a 400 °F/200 °C oven, basting frequently. After cooking, keep the sweetbreads warm.

4. Pour off the fat from the pan, deglaze with the vinegar, reduce, add the veal stock and reduce again until a creamy sauce is produced. Whisk in the butter and strain. Finally add the capers. Turn out an endive mold onto each plate, add a sweetbread and pour the sauce on top.

Braised Oxtail with

Preparation time: 1 hour 15 minutes
Cooking time: 3 hours
Difficulty: ★★

Serves 4

4½ lb/2 kg oxtail
3½ oz/100 g salt pork
7 oz/200 g carrots
2 onions
9 oz/250 g celery
1 head of garlic
¼ cup/75 g tomato paste
¾ cup/100 g flour

8 cups/2 l veal or beef stock
4 cups/1 l Burgundy wine
salt and pepper

For the bouquet garni:
1 bay leaf
2 sprigs of thyme
8 sprigs of parsley

For the garnish of spring vegetables
carrots, turnips
pearl onions
new potatoes
peas, beans

Beef is still considered a major delicacy in the British Isles, where Hereford cattle and the Scottish Aberdeen Angus, famous for its protein-rich meat, are only two of the many breeds raised.

For this English oxtail stew you should use the upper, more fleshy parts of the oxtail. The oxtail must be fresh and include firm, red meat. The layer of white fat should only be partially removed, to prevent the meat from drying out. This dish can also be prepared using other cuts of stewing beef.

The garnish should consist of the earliest of spring vegetables, but you can also add chestnuts that have been marinated with the oxtail—their consistency is similar to that of the meat.

Four days are required to make a good oxtail stew, including the day on which the dish is eaten. Marinate it for two days in a robust wine such as a Côtes-du-Rhône, cook it on the third day and simply reheat it on the fourth; this can only improve its flavor.

1. Cut the vegetables (carrots, onions, celery) into large pieces. Bone the oxtail, cut it into large pieces and mix with the vegetables. Add the stock for the marinade, the bouquet garni, the tomato paste, and the garlic. Place in the refrigerator to marinate for at least 48 hours. Drain the oxtail, reserving the vegetables and the marinade, and season and brown on all sides.

2. In a deep pan, braise the vegetables used in the marinade with the salt pork. Add the marinated oxtail. Toast the flour lightly in the oven and stir it carefully into the marinade. Pour it into the pan, bring to a boil, cover and braise in a 350 °F/180 °C oven for about three hours.

Spring Vegetables

3. Prepare the spring vegetables for the garnish (carrots, turnips, small onions and potatoes, peas and beans). Cook each vegetable separately in boiling salted water.

4. After braising, remove the pieces of oxtail from the pan; do not cut them any smaller. Place them in a deep bowl. Add all the vegetables for the garnish. Reduce the Burgundy and add to the braising liquid. Strain and pour over the meat and vegetables. Serve hot.

Medallions of Veal with Lemon

Preparation time: 14 minutes
Cooking time: 25 minutes
Difficulty: ★★

Serves 4

1 veal tenderloin, about 1¾ lb/800 g
1 veal kidney
1 large onion
1 shallot
6½ tbsp/100 ml Madeira
¾ cup/200 ml heavy cream
5¼ oz/150 g shortcrust pastry

salt and pepper
butter
vinegar

For the lemon sauce:
4 tsp/20 g sugar
6½ tbsp/100 ml red wine vinegar
1 lemon
2½ tbsp/40 ml demi-glace (brown veal sauce)
6½ tbsp/100 g butter

Long ago, the sovereignty of what was then the county of Charolles was disputed by the dukes of Burgundy, the kings of France, and the German emperors. Today in the prosperous Lyon region, which lies in the vicinity of the former county, people particularly prize the breed of white cattle that bears the name of this much-contested neighbor.

The quality of Charolais beef is renowned far beyond this area of France, but it is the less well-known Charolais calf that is most prized by Christian Bouvarel. The calf is allowed to stay with its mother and is reared under impeccable hygienic conditions. This guarantees the quality of the meat, which has a very delicate flavor.

For this recipe, take a tenderloin of medium thickness (one that is too thin will dry out in the course of cooking) and a kidney. To ensure that the kidney retains its tenderness, braise it over low heat in its own fat before dicing it and then slightly browning it. As with all variety meats, the kidney must be quite fresh.

The veal is served with a subtle lemon sauce, which combines the acidity of the lemon with the slightly bitter sweetness of caramel. This sauce will bring out the delicate flavor of the meat.

1. To make the lemon sauce, mix the sugar and vinegar in a pan, cook down slightly, then add the juice of half a lemon and the demi-glace, followed by the juice of the other half of the lemon; bring to a boil, then whisk in the butter. Cut the lemon zest into thin slices and set aside.

2. Line 4 tartlet molds with the shortcrust pastry and bake. Cut the onion into thin slices, place in a casserole with butter, braise lightly and season with a dash of vinegar.

3. Remove the sinewy parts from the veal tenderloin. Cut this into 4 steaks and divide each of these into 3 medallions, season with salt and pepper and then brown in butter. Dice the kidney evenly, season and brown in the pan with the finely chopped shallot and deglaze with the Madeira.

4. Add the heavy cream to the kidney and reduce by a quarter, then add a pat of butter. Pile the kidney pieces into the 4 tartlet shells and place 1 in the center of each plate. Arrange the medallions around it, pour the sauce over them and add spoonfuls of the cooked onions between the medallions. Garnish with strips of lemon zest.

Bresse Chicken en

Preparation time: 1 hour 15 minutes
Cooking time: 45 minutes
Difficulty: ★★

Serves 4

4 skinless, boneless chicken breasts or 2
chickens, about 3½ lbs/1.5 kg
6 oz/160 g Gruyère cheese
1 generous lb/500 g leaf spinach
4 slices of cooked ham
7 oz/200 g puff pastry

1 egg for brushing on
salt and pepper

For the cream sauce:
9 oz/250 g fresh morels
6½ tbsp/100 ml white wine
2 cups/500 ml heavy cream
5½ tbsp/80 g butter
3 egg yolks
juice of ½ lemon
7 tbsp/50 g chopped tarragon
salt and pepper

This chicken en croûte was prepared by Paul Bocuse in 1993 on the occasion of an assembly of the "Meilleurs Ouvrieres de France" at his restaurant in Collonges-au-Mont-d'Or, near Lyon. It was in that year that Christian Bouvarel was admitted to this highly selective club. This represented a high point in Bouvarel's career, but not its end, for a distinction such as this brings many obligations with it. Our chef places particular value on this recipe because a typical product of his region, the Bresse chicken, is shown to its best advantage.

Bresse chickens are free-range and corn-fed; they have as much freedom to roam as they need, quite in contrast to those unfortunate battery chickens with which our super-markets are flooded. Other excellent free-range and organic chickens are widely available.

One would not have to make such a fuss about the poultry if the other ingredients were not also of outstanding quality. So seek out a first-class ham and an aromatic cheese. If you prefer a more strongly flavored cheese than Gruyère, Christian Bouvarel recommends Comté from the French Alps. Stuff the chicken breast with the cheese before closing the pastry envelope in order to prevent the cheese from leaking out. The spinach should be very fresh; it can, if necessary, be replaced with curly kale, which goes equally well with chicken, because it does not over-power its flavor.

1. Bone the chicken and remove the breasts, cut part way into them lengthwise, and fill with the grated Gruyère. Season with salt and pepper, then seal.

2. Remove the stalks from the spinach, wash thoroughly in cold water and blanch in boiling salted water. Wrap each chicken breast in spinach, and then in a slice of ham.

croûte with Morels

3. Roll out the puff pastry and cut into 4 pieces. Take each chicken breast and wrap in pastry, forming a turnover. Let rest for 30 minutes in the refrigerator, brush with egg and bake in a 375 °F/190 °C oven for 20–30 minutes.

4. Braise the morels in butter and season with salt and pepper. Deglaze with the wine. Add 1 cup/250 ml heavy cream. Cook for 4–5 minutes; mix the egg yolks with the rest of the cream, the lemon juice and the tarragon. Pour over the morels. Stir very gently to bind the sauce. Reduce without allowing the sauce to boil. When it is nice and creamy, remove from the heat and pour into a sauce boat.

Preparation time: 1 hour
Cooking time: 30 minutes
Difficulty: ☆

Serves 4

1lb 5 oz/600 g T-bone veal chops
(loin and fillet)
¾ cup/200 ml chicken stock
¾ cup/200 ml dry white wine
peanut oil
6½ tbsp/100 g butter
salt and freshly ground pepper

For the sweet and sour onions:
14 oz/400 g pearl onions
1¾ oz/50 g raisins
2 tbsp/15 g sugar
2 tbsp/15 g flour
6½ tbsp/100 ml extra virgin olive oil
6½ tbsp/100 ml vinegar

For the chicken stock
2 chicken carcasses
2 carrots
2 turnips
1 leek
salt and freshly ground pepper

Throughout Lombardy, and above all in Milan, veal cooked in its own fat has been familiar since the Renaissance.

Take care to buy milk-fed veal, because it is particularly delicate. Try to remove as much fat as possible from both the loin and the tenderloin, because the sauce will have a better flavor. The cooking process is divided into two stages, both of which should be watched carefully. First, brown the meat quickly on top of the stove so that it takes on some color, but do not let it acquire a crust. Then braise it in the oven, making sure it stays pink on the inside. Cut the meat into slices and serve it as soon as it comes out of the oven.

You should allow a day for the preparation of the chicken stock, because it is best when cooked very slowly over low heat. If it is refrigerated overnight, it acquires a more delicate and fuller flavor.

The sweet and sour onions were long ago adopted from the cuisine of the Austrian empire, formerly a neighbor of Lombardy. The Milanese enriched the recipe with raisins and it is now a popular side dish.

1. The day before you plan to serve the veal, blanch the chicken carcasses, drain and rinse in cold water. Cover with 2 cups/500 ml of water seasoned with salt and pepper. Bring to a boil and skim off the foam. Add the vegetables and allow to simmer for five hours. Strain and refrigerate. Cut the veal into slices.

2. Brown the chops in 3½ tbsp/50 g of butter and a little oil, so they color nicely without burning. Meanwhile, prepare the sweet and sour onions: prepare a roux with oil, sugar and flour, then add the vinegar. Blanch the onions in boiling salted water and drain. Stir the onions and raisins into the roux and cook for 6 minutes.

à la Milanaise

3. Pour the chicken stock and wine over the veal, bring to boil and braise for 15 minutes in a 350 °F/180 °C oven. Remove the meat and keep warm until you are ready to slice it.

4. Reduce the cooking juices by one third. Remove from the heat and whisk in 3½ tbsp/50 g of butter, cubed. Strain and keep warm. Put a little sauce on a plate and place the sliced meat on top. Serve the onions separately and pass the rest of the sauce in a sauce boat.

Fillet of Beef with

Preparation time: 40 minutes
Cooking time: 15 minutes
Difficulty: ★★

Serves 4

4 filets mignons, about 5¼ oz/150 g each
6 oz/160 g raw duck fois gras
¾ oz/20 g truffles, sliced
7 oz/200 g pork caul

1 small leek, 1 small celery stalk, 1 small
carrot, cut into narrow strips
¾ cup/200 ml vegetable stock
¾ cup/200 ml veal stock
8 oz/240 g fresh narrow tagliatelle
6½ tbsp/100 ml heavy cream
6½ tbsp/100 g butter
grated Parmesan
12 sprigs of chervil
salt and pepper
coarse salt

Beef remains indispensable in gastronomy, and its best cut, the fillet, has been an essential culinary delight since the Middle Ages. For this recipe, our chef uses meat from a Belgian breed of cattle, but you can choose from a number of other high-quality breeds. Try to find well-aged prime beef for this luxurious dish.

The preparation of the steaks, cut into three across the grain, takes a little time. A good appearance can be achieved by wrapping the prepared steaks in aluminum foil, and

leaving them to cool for a good hour. The caul, which is used after this step, is a fine membrane with fatty veins, which is soaked for a few hours in salted water to soften the texture of the caul and thus make preparation easier. If it is unavailable, brush the meat with olive oil before cooking.

For a well-flavored sauce, our chef recommends preparing a good quality, full-flavored veal stock. The steaks should be served very hot.

1. Season the steaks with salt and pepper and sear on both sides in a walnut-sized pat of butter. Let cool. Cut the fois gras into thin slices, season with salt and pepper, and brown quickly in a nonstick pan. Cut the steaks into 3 across the grain.

2. Cover each slice of fillet with fois gras slices and truffles, stack together like a layer cake, wrap in foil and set aside to cool for 1 hour. Cook the tagliatelle in boiling salted water for 3–4 minutes. Reduce the cream with the vegetable mixture. When the noodles are cooked, strain and add to the sauce.

Duck Foie Gras and Truffles

3. Soak the pork caul in salted water for 3–4 hours. When the fillet slices are quite firm, remove from the foil and wrap in the pork caul. Brown the meat on both sides for 4 minutes, then remove the fat from the pan. Add the two kinds of stock, reduce, season to taste and set aside.

4. Cut each steak into two or three pieces, place on a dish and scatter coarse salt on top. Form the tagliatelle into nests with a fork and place next to the fillets; garnish with chervil leaves. Then serve with the hot sauce and grated Parmesan.

Lamb in a Salt

Preparation time: 30 minutes
Cooking time: 20 minutes
Difficulty: ★★

Serves 4

1 saddle of lamb, about 3⅓ lb/1½ kg
7 oz/200 g shelled peas
3 vanilla beans

3½ lb/1½ kg coarse salt
fresh thyme in bloom
lamb stock
4 sheets filo pastry
¾ cup/200 ml heavy cream
3½ tbsp/50 g butter
1 egg
1 tbsp/15 ml olive oil
salt and pepper

In classical times, salt was positively worshiped. This costly seasoning was part of every meal, and Roman soldiers used to receive a handful of salt a day, a custom which was later converted to a cash payment called a salary, from the Latin word for salt. Throughout history, the acquisition, trade, and use of salt have been among the most important of industrial activities. Today, salt still plays a significant role in our kitchens.

Although lamb is obtainable all year round, it is best enjoyed in spring. Our chef tries to use lamb from the salt meadows of Cotentin. These lambs drink water from the salt pools by the coast, and this lends a special flavor to their fine red flesh. The lamb should be boned before cooking, so that it can be browned equally on all sides.

To roast it in a salt crust you will need a large quantity of coarse salt, as the lamb needs to be completely covered with it. This method keeps the meat tender and juicy. You will be surprised by the taste of the sea and the crispness of the lamb.

With this dish we serve filo pastries layered with creamed peas enhanced by a little vanilla; their texture corresponds to the crispness of the meat.

1. Bone the saddle of lamb and tie the 2 tenderloins together. Season with salt and pepper. Brown the meat on all sides. Place it on a layer of coarse salt in a fire-resistant dish. Top with thyme and a chopped vanilla bean and completely cover with coarse salt. Bake for 15 minutes at 390 °F/200 °C.

2. Cook the peas in boiling salted water with a chopped vanilla bean. Purée in a food processor and mix the cream and half the butter with half the purée. Beat the egg and stir it into the other half of the purée.

Crust with Peas

3. Paint each sheet of filo with the egg and pea mixture. Fold each sheet in half twice. With a round pastry cutter, cut out circles, and fry in butter and oil. Deglaze the pan in which the fillets were browned with some lamb stock. Keep warm.

4. Slice the fillets and place on 4 plates with wedges of the pastry circles. Garnish with the fresh thyme, strips of vanilla bean and the sauce.

Shredded Duck Rolls

Preparation time: 45 minutes
Cooking time: 50 minutes
Difficulty: ★★

Serves 4

2 ducks, about 4½ lb/2 kg
4 sheets filo pastry
3 large globe artichoke bottoms
3 carrots
3 turnips

7 oz/200 g haricots verts
6½ tbsp/100 g butter
4 tsp/20 ml vinegar
1 bouquet garni
sugar
egg white
salt and pepper

For the garnish:
chives
cherry tomatoes

This dish was originally conceived using squab, but the chef was disappointed with the result. In this version, he has used duck, a bird that is better suited to the recipe—which now wins him nothing but praise. For a start, duck has a more assertive flavor, which becomes even more pronounced within the pastry roll and disperses its aroma to the whole dish.

The vegetables recommended here are certainly the most delicious way of celebrating the early days of spring. To preserve the color and crispness of the vegetables, blanch them briefly in boiling water and refresh them as soon as possible in cold water. Prepared this way, they will correspond in texture to the filo pastry. The pastry roll will cover even the least presentable ingredients, such as the boned duck thigh; it also keeps the enclosed duck and vegetables nicely warm.

If duck is not available, you could revert to the original version of this dish and use squab.

1. Roast the ducks for 35 minutes at 375 °F/190 °C. Allow to rest, then cut into 12 pieces. Break up the carcass and use it to prepare a stock with a bouquet garni.

2. Wash and prepare the turnips, carrots and artichoke bottoms. Trim the beans and briefly cook each of the vegetables separately in boiling salted water, then refresh in ice cold water.

with Provençal Vegetables

3. Prepare a caramel sauce with sugar and one tablespoon of water. Deglaze with vinegar, then add the duck stock. Reduce, strain and stir in the butter. Season to taste.

4. Shred the duck meat into small pieces. Put ¼ of the shredded duck and blanched vegetables on a sheet of filo pastry, fold up, twisting as for a candy wrapper, and tie each end with a chive. Repeat with the remaining sheets of filo. Brush with the egg-white and bake in the oven for 8 minutes. Arrange attractively on a warmed dish and drizzle with the reduced stock.

Veal Kidney and Potato

Preparation time: 1 hour 30 minutes
Cooking time: 35 minutes
Difficulty: ★★

Serves 4

4 veal kidneys
2 calves' feet
veal stock
shallots
butter
olive oil
thyme
bay leaves
salt and pepper

For the potato purée:
2 lbs/1 scant kg potatoes, preferably Yukon gold or red bliss
6½ tbsp/100 ml milk
6½ tbsp/100g butter
olive oil
salt
bread crumbs

Herbs:
flat-leaf parsley
chervil
coriander

Alain Burnel uses olive oil from Baussane, a small Provençal community surrounded by olive groves containing more than 200,000 trees, which is so famous that many great chefs buy their oil there. But some Baussane olives are destined for a different fate: they are processed into "salonenques," that is, first cracked with a wooden mallet and then stuffed with fennel and orange peel, to be nibbled before dinner.

The olive oil is added to the potato purée at the end of preparation, with the milk, to make it somewhat smoother. Be careful not to add too much oil, so that the purée does not become too liquid.

The original aim of this recipe was to present the somewhat unattractive ingredients in an appealing manner. Without wanting to sing a hymn of praise to that most practical of accessories, aluminum foil, we should mention its virtues in this recipe: it prevents the kidneys from shriveling or hardening and makes it easier to retrieve the blood and juices, which are used to thicken the sauce. And if the kidneys are lightly browned in the pan after cooking, they will also have a good appearance.

1. Boil the potatoes in salted water until tender. Purée them using a sieve or food mill, make the purée smoother by adding milk and butter, and finally beat in some olive oil. Set aside in a bowl.

2. Blanch the calves' feet and cook them in the stock for 4 hours. Let cool and then dice the meat. Brown it in butter, and mix into the potato purée. Remove any fat from the kidneys, remove the sinewy parts, season and wrap in foil.

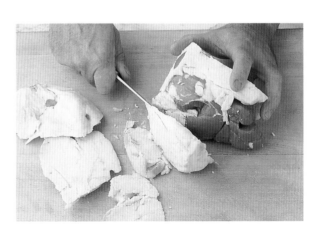

Purée with Calves' Feet

3. Place the kidneys in a roasting pan lightly smeared with olive oil. Braise at 400 °F/205 °C for 10 minutes. Set aside to rest and then carefully unwrap, reserving the blood and juices. Brown the whole kidneys in butter just before serving. Remove the fat from the pan and deglaze with chopped shallots and veal stock. Reduce and strain. Add the chopped herbs, stir in butter and season to taste.

4. Mold the potato purée in 4 individual ramekins. Unmold in the center of each plate, and sprinkle a few bread crumbs on top. Run under the broiler to brown the top, then arrange the sliced kidneys around the potato purée in an overlapping circle and pour the herb sauce, which has been thickened with the blood and juices from the kidneys, on top. Scatter with herbs before serving.

Navarin of Lambs' Sweetbreads

Preparation time: 45 minutes
Cooking time: 1 hour
Difficulty: ★

Serves 4

1 generous lb/500 g lambs' sweetbreads
9 oz/250 g lamb's tongues
1 bouquet garni
boiled potatoes
2 tomatoes
9 oz/250 g button mushrooms

¾ cup/200 ml white veal stock
2 cups/500 ml lamb stock with tomato
¾ cup/200 ml ruby port wine
1 tsp turtle soup seasoning (basil, marjoram, chervil, savory, and fennel)
1 tsp arrowroot
1 lemon
½ tsp dried herbs
1 pinch of cayenne pepper
1 bunch of tarragon
salt and pepper

Jan Buytaert has preserved only the basic principle of this traditional dish. The lambs' tongues and sweetbreads must be absolutely fresh. Everyone knows what a tongue is; but sweetbreads are the thymus gland and pancreas. The thymus is found at the base of the neck of the immature animal, and is part of the immune system. The tongues and sweetbreads must be soaked in cold water for several hours before preparation; they must then be blanched and the veins and membranes should be removed.

The lamb stock should be enriched with ripe tomatoes, so that it acquires a reddish color. Arrowroot is preferable to potato or corn starch as a thickener, because it is less glutinous. If you are not familiar with it, this recipe offers a good opportunity to discover its qualities.

Do not hesitate to eat this dish if reheated even several days later—it can only improve the flavor.

1. Blanch the sweetbreads and tongues. Cool in a bowl of cold water and remove the outer membranes and veins from the sweetbreads. Trim the bones from the base of the tongues. Cook in the white veal stock with the bouquet garni.

2. Skin the tongues and cut each into 4 pieces. Cut the sweetbreads into large pieces. Peel, seed and dice the tomatoes. Brown the mushrooms in butter.

3. Combine the veal and lamb stocks and reduce by two-thirds. Season the resulting sauce with a pinch of salt, a hint of cayenne pepper, the turtle soup seasoning, the port, the dried herbs and the juice of the lemon. Thicken slightly with arrowroot. Strain.

4. Add the browned mushrooms to the sauce, the diced tomato; and the tarragon leaves. Then add the pieces of sweetbread and tongue. Cook over low heat for 10 minutes and serve with boiled potatoes.

Calves' Liver with

Preparation time: 20 minutes
Cooking time: 20 minutes
Difficulty: ★

Serves 4

2 generous lbs/1 kg calves' liver
3½ tbsp/50 g butter
flour

For the ginger and soy sauce:
2 medium/40 g shallots
3 tbsp/50 g fresh ginger root
10 tbsp/150 g butter

2 cups/500 ml veal stock
4 tsp/20 ml soy sauce

For the garnish:
2 generous lbs/1 kg small potatoes
5 tbsp/75 g goose or duck fat
1 garlic clove
1 sprig of thyme
1 bay leaf
chives

For the shallots:
9 oz/250 g shallots
½ cup/125 g butter

The use of soy sauce and ginger in this calves' liver recipe bears witness to Jacques Cagna's interest in Japan. During his frequent stays there he has developed a taste for these important Japanese seasonings and enjoys introducing them into French cuisine.

This is by no means an obvious combination, and the very salty soy sauce must be used with care if it is not to overpower the taste of the meat. Cagna first tried this recipe with eel, with little success; it was only when he tried it with calves' liver, with its more delicate flesh and a less distinctive taste, that he achieved a breakthrough. Use only very fresh liver. Remove the outer skin and the veins

before coating in flour and browning nicely on both sides, so that it becomes slightly crisp.

In this dish, Cagna uses grenaille, a small variety of potato that is grown in western France, especially on the island of Noirmoutier. These potatoes are always planted by hand and carefully checked at harvest time, which ensures consistent quality. They are easy to prepare and are favorites at Jacque Cagna's Paris restaurant, where they are also served with veal cutlets and with snails.

Calves' sweetbreads can be prepared in the same way; if you don't like ginger, you can substitute braised shallots.

1. For the ginger and soy sauce, sweat the chopped shallots and the ginger in butter. Deglaze with the veal stock and soy sauce. Simmer over low heat for 30 minutes, then whisk in the butter.

2. Wash the potatoes. Line a pan with aluminum foil, and add the unpeeled potatoes, the melted goose fat, the garlic clove, the thyme and the bay leaf; cover and cook for 1 hour in a 375 °F/190 °C oven.

Ginger and Soy Sauce

3. If you have bought your liver in 1 piece, skin it and cut into ½ in/1 cm slices. Season and brown in butter in a skillet. Finely chop the shallots and cook slowly in butter until quite soft.

4. Cut each slice of liver into five thin slices, and arrange on a warmed dish, covering with the shallots. Arrange the potatoes around them and add the ginger and soy sauce. Sprinkle with chopped chives.

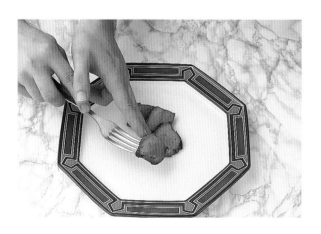

Grouse with Lentils

Preparation time: 1 hour 30 minutes
Cooking time: 1 hour
Difficulty: ★★

Serves 4

4 grouse
1¼ lbs/600 g Puy lentils
2 medium potatoes, about 9 oz/250 g

10 oz/300 g carrots
1 bouquet garni
1¼ cup/300 ml grouse stock, made with the thighs and carcasses of the grouse
6½ tbsp/100 ml orange juice
4 tsp/20 g butter
oil
salt and pepper

The festivities that accompany the start of the grouse-shooting season on the Scottish moors on August 12 can only be compared to the French *palombite*, the hunting fever that breaks out in southwestern France when the wood-pigeons arrive. This fever does not end until 1 November, with the official end of the season. The Scottish grouse lives on the produce of the moors—heather, bilberries, cranberries—which gives its flesh a very special flavor. It is hardly bigger than a partridge, weighing some 10 ½ oz/300 g. The males are usually a little bigger than the females. Traditionally the bird is hung for several days to give its flesh even more flavor. Then it is usually roasted. Chefs have apparently not yet been able to work up any enthusiasm for an alternative method of cooking.

As an ideal accompaniment, Stewart Cameron recommends potato and carrot pancakes, whose consistency and mild taste bring out the flavor of the grouse. And nothing goes so well with this bird as an orange sauce; its slightly acidic flavor highlights the delicate subtleties of the taste of the grouse.

1. If necessary, singe pin feathers off the grouse, and gut them. Remove the breasts, using the remainder of the grouse and a bouquet garni to prepare the stock. Boil the lentils with the bouquet garni for 20 minutes.

2. Peel and grate the potatoes and 7 oz/200 g of carrots. Squeeze out their moisture with a kitchen towel. Season and form into pancakes. Heat a pat of butter in a small pan over medium heat, and brown the pancakes gently on both sides until crisp.

and Orange Sauce

3. Peel the remaining carrots and cut into thin (julienne) strips. Fry in very hot oil. Brown the grouse breasts for a few minutes in an ovenproof pan, then roast in a hot oven until cooked.

4. Deglaze the pan with the grouse stock, reduce and add the orange juice. Strain and stir in the butter, and work in the lentils. Pour the sauce over 4 warmed plates, place a potato and carrot pancake in the center and a grouse breast on top of each.

Medallions of Angus Beef

Preparation time: 45 minutes
Cooking time: 15 minutes
Difficulty: ★★

Serves 4

8 filets mignon, each 1 in/2 cm thick
5¼ oz/150 g cèpes or porcini
5¼ oz/150 g chanterelles
3½ tbsp/50 ml olive oil
salt and pepper

For the sauce:
⅔ cup/150 ml Drambuie
⅔ cup/150 ml beef stock
3½ tbsp/50 g butter
¾ cup/75 g brunoise (finely diced carrots, celery and onions)
thyme
1 bay leaf
½ tsp/1 g black peppercorns

Only a Scottish chef can pay proper homage to the Aberdeen Angus. This breed can be found far beyond the borders of Scotland and ranks with whisky and Mary, Queen of Scots as one of Scotland's finest exports. As its name indicates, this breed originates in the Aberdeen region and has now spread throughout the world, to Argentina and the United States, where the craft of cattle-breeding is well understood. On their home ground, Aberdeen Angus are subject to strict quality control.

After slaughter, each carcass is hung for over a month, which intensifies the natural flavor of the meat. There is no need to prepare a highly flavored accompaniment. Complicated sauces, such as are normally inflicted on beef, become redundant. This treatment also tenderizes the meat and greatly reduces the cooking time.

Here, Stewart Cameron serves Angus beef with braised cèpes and chanterelles, which come from the same soil that nourishes the cattle. This combination is far from accidental. But, of course, you can replace these mushrooms with others of your choice.

1. Trim the tenderloin (if purchased in 1 piece) and cut into medallions about 1 in/2 cm thick. Season to taste.

2. Wash the cèpes and chanterelles and slice thinly.

with Cèpes and Chanterelles

3. Braise the diced vegetables with the bay leaf, thyme and pepper in 5 tsp/25 g of butter over low heat; add the Drambuie and flambé. Add the beef stock, reduce by two-thirds, and strain. Whisk in the remaining butter.

4. Heat the olive oil in a pan, then brown the medallions to the desired doneness. Braise the mushrooms in the same pan. Place a medallion in the center of each of 4 plates, the mushrooms on top, and another medallion on top of them. Pour the butter sauce over before serving.

Poached Breast of Poussin

Preparation time: 1 hour 30 minutes
Cooking time: 50 minutes
Difficulty: ★★

Serves 4

4 poussins
4 cups/1 l chicken stock

¼ cup/60 g barley
4 tarragon leaves
2 medium carrots
12 small zucchini
4 tbsp/60 g butter
6½ tbsp/100 g heavy cream
4 large slices of truffle (for garnish)

Stewart Cameron's staff works like a fine sports team, with team spirit and efficiency. This is not particularly surprising, for their neighbor, who provides them with eggs), is the famous Rugby player Quentin Dunlop.

The combination of chicken and tarragon is a classic alliance, which remains as well-respected as ever. The distinctive aroma of tarragon has an excellent effect on the tender flesh of the poussin. Measure it out carefully, because it would be a crime to overwhelm the taste of this small creature. Choose free-range birds if possible, because their flesh has a better flavor.

The mousse made from poussin thighs and heavy cream will have a better texture if you prepare it over ice. It will

be firmer and thus easier to form into dumplings. The use of barley is a homage to the grain that is so abundantly consumed in Scotland. It is also the basis of Scotch whisky and of Stingo, a barley "wine" similar to beer. Poach the barley in chicken stock to soften it and improve its flavor. Do the same with the finely chopped vegetables, whose delicacy forms a pleasant contrast to the more substantial barley.

This dish is a good example of modern Scottish cuisine, which uses robust flavorings (such as ginger) that are less common in the rest of Europe and often includes rustic grains, such as barley and oats.

1. Separate the poussin wings from the breasts. Cut the meat from the thighs. Poach the barley in 6½ tbsp/100 ml of stock until tender.

2. Purée the thigh meat, with its skin, in a food processor fitted with a steel blade. In a small bowl over ice, beat in the heavy cream and season with salt and pepper.

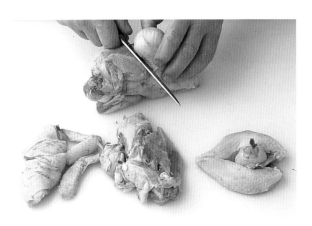

with Barley and Tarragon

3. Peel the carrots and cut into decorative shapes. Cut the zucchini into decorative shapes, then poach the vegetables for 5 minutes in chicken stock, make into small parcels and set aside.

4. Poach the poussin breasts in 3 cups/750 ml of stock over a low heat. Form dumplings out of the chicken mousse and poach, like the poussin. Combine the stocks from poaching the chicken and vegetables in a pan, reduce, then whisk in the butter and the barley. Place the poussin and vegetables on a hot dish and garnish with tarragon leaves. Pour the sauce over the poussin and garnish with slices of truffle.

Braised Rabbit with

Preparation time: 45 minutes
Cooking time: 35 minutes
Difficulty: ★★

Serves 4

2 saddles of rabbit
1 shallot
5 black olives
5 green olives

6½ tbsp/100 ml dry white wine
1 sprig of wild fennel or fennel top
meat stock
4 tbsp/60 g butter
3 tbsp/20 g grated Parmesan
salt

For the *garganelli* noodles:
¾ cup plus 1 tbsp/400g flour
4 eggs

The province of Romagna, now Emilia-Romagna, is the birthplace of the pasta called *garganelli*. They are traditionally served with chicken stock (in earlier times with a meat stew with tomatoes), and in summer, particularly by families with modest means, simply with zucchini.

The preparation of this pasta includes the use of a *pettine*, a wooden board over which parallel threads are stretched, on which the *garganelli* are rolled. This gives them their distinctive ridged appearance. Don't worry if you don't succeed the first time you try to make them; our chef admits that there is a certain knack to it, but assures us that one can quickly acquire the necessary expertise. Once you have got the knack you will make this pasta over and over again.

Here, the *garganelli* are eaten with rabbit stewed with white wine and shallots. For this dish Marco Cavallucci uses the excellent rabbit from Liguria, near the Gulf of Genoa. You should choose young rabbits, with little fat—preferably not frozen rabbit parts. The fennel gives the rabbit a special flavor.

1. Bone the saddles of rabbit; dice the meat from one of them, and roast the other whole for about 20 minutes at 355 °F/180 °C (the inside should remain pink). Chop the shallot and braise in a pan with butter, add the diced rabbit and season with salt.

2. Pit the olives, chop and add to the diced rabbit. Add the wine and reduce until thickened, then add the chopped fennel and cook for 10 minutes. Add a little meat stock if necessary.

Garganelli al Pettine

3. Make a pasta dough with the flour and eggs, form into a ball and let it rest for an hour. Then roll out thinly, cut it into 2 in/5 cm squares, roll these around a thin stick and over the pettine or a ridged board, to form the garganelli. Cook in salted water and drain.

4. Cut the roast saddle of rabbit into thin slices. Add the garganelli with the Parmesan to the braised rabbit. Serve hot, garnishing each portion with a few slices of roast rabbit and sprigs of fennel.

Rosettes of Lamb

Preparation time: 1 hour
Cooking time: 30 minutes
Difficulty: ★★

Serves 4

2 racks of lamb
2 large Yukon gold or red bliss potatoes

4 tbsp/30 g grated Parmesan
½ cup tawny port
1¾ oz/50 g black truffles
1 cup/250 ml meat stock
3½ tbsp/50 g butter
2 leeks
salt and pepper
flour

Lamb, truffles, potatoes and Parmesan are flavorful ingredients, and they combine to make up the powerful character of this dish.

The noble family of *grana* cheeses, rooted deep in the region around Parma, has many branches, one of which is Parmesan, and *parmigiano Reggiano* is well known worldwide. Well over a thousand producers are dedicated to the production and aging of this cheese. To make 2 lbs/1 kg, you need 4 gallons/16 l of milk. Reggiano Parmesan has a northern cousin, *grana padano*, which is less well-known outside Italy, but whose more powerful flavor is in no way inferior. Both should be grated just before serving.

This cheese should be combined with an outstanding piece of lamb and a good variety of potato, in which case you have the makings of a sensational dish. You might also use this opportunity to discover the white truffle of the Romagna, small and irregular in shape, whose flavor has surprising garlic overtones.

1. Bone the lamb, season with salt and roast in a 425 °F/220 °C oven for 15 minutes (or to an internal temperature of 125 °F/50 °C) allowing the flesh in the center to remain pink. Set aside.

2. Peel the potatoes and slice thinly. On a buttered cooking sheet, arrange 4 circles of potato slices to fit your dinner plates, season with salt, dot with butter and sprinkle with grated Parmesan. Bake at 350 °F/180 °C for 10 minutes, or until the potatoes are done.

with Truffles

3. Pour the port into a pan, reduce by about half, and add the sliced truffles and meat stock. Cook for a few minutes, then whisk in small pieces of butter.

4. Cut the leeks diagonally into thin slices. Flour them and deep-fry in hot oil until brown. Cut the lamb into medallions 1 inch/2 cm thick, arrange in the center of the ring of potato slices and pour the sauce on top. Garnish with the deep-fried leek slices.

Medallions of Veal

Preparation time: 45 minutes
Cooking time: 10 minutes
Difficulty: ★★

Serves 4

4 medallions milk-fed veal tenderloin, each
1½ inch/4 cm thick
4 oz/120 g small chanterelles
4 large slices of beef marrow
1 orange
1 lemon
1 tbsp/15 g granulated sugar

1 sprig of marjoram
salt from Guérande (or other sea salt)
crushed black pepper
salt and ground pepper

For the brunoise:
3½ oz/100 g carrots
3½ oz/100 g small green zucchini
1¾ oz/50 g celery
1¾ oz/50 g white onions
⅔ cup sauce from a traditional osso buco
3½ tbsp/50 g butter
extra virgin olive oil

First prepare an osso buco with marjoram, and keep the juices from this dish. Then you can use them to season the tenderloin of milk-fed calf in this recipe.

The small tenderloin, as its name suggests, is one of the tenderest parts of the animal. It is easy to prepare and retains its delicious flavor throughout the cooking process. To preserve the pale color of the flesh, you can sprinkle lemon juice all over it before cooking. It must remain tender, forming a pleasant contrast to the crisp dried peel of the citrus fruits. In this traditional combination, the delicate apricot flavor of the chanterelles underlines that of the veal, whose juices have been strengthened by the slices of marrow. The vegetables, diced small and carefully arran-

ged on the dish, add a further touch of sophistication.

Marjoram is found throughout the Mediterranean area: Italians like to use it in particular to flavor the *piccata*, a small veal cutlet fried in butter. Greeks use it with grilled goat's meat. In Hungary it is often added to the famous goulash. In France it is one of the traditional herbs of Provence.

Instead of the tenderloin, you could also use boned loin chops for this dish, but they sometimes turn out to be too firm.

1. Cut the orange and lemon zest into thin strips, blanch and then put in a pan to simmer over low heat with some water and the sugar. Then strain and place on a plate to dry.

2. Braise the brunoise of vegetables in oil and butter, making sure that the vegetables stay crisp.

with Marjoram

3. Brown the medallions of veal in oil in a pan to give them a good color, then lower the heat and cook until just done. Briefly boil the chanterelles, strain and then brown. Poach the slices of marrow in salted water.

4. Using a ring 4 ½ in/10 cm in diameter, arrange circles of vegetable brunoise in the center of each plate. Place a veal medallion and a slice of marrow on top, and season with some sea salt and crushed pepper. Arrange the chanterelles around them, pour the osso buco juices over them and garnish with some additional vegetables, orange and lemon peel and marjoram leaves.

Tian of Swiss Chard with

Preparation time: 1 hour
Cooking time: 30 minutes
Difficulty: ★★

Serves 4

4 saddles of farmed rabbit
1 lb 12 oz/800 g Swiss chard
7 oz/200 g small chanterelles
1 tomato
1 carrot
1 celery rib

2 shallots
1 garlic clove
1 sprig of rosemary
10 Niçois olives
2 tbsp/15 g pine nuts
3 egg yolks
¾ cup/200 ml cream
¾ cup/200 ml dry white wine
butter
extra virgin olive oil
salt and freshly ground pepper

Swiss chard is used in Provence for the preparation of both savory dishes and desserts, such as chard leaf tarts.

There are several varieties of chard, all of which should be blanched before preparation. In this recipe, the stems, which can be fibrous, must be cooked separately, unless the shoots are very young. Then the vegetables only need to be braised gently in butter.

You will need two very small farmed rabbits, each about a generous 2 lbs/1 kg in weight. Preparation requires a certain degree of care in order to preserve the high protein content of the meat. Remove the fillets from the backbone, and during cooking make sure that the fillets are regularly basted with their own juices. Let them rest briefly after cooking before you cut them into thin strips.

This dish can also be prepared with spinach, which does not need to be blanched before cooking.

1. Remove the silverskin from the rabbit and carve the fillets from the bones. Crush the bones, cut the trimmings and belly flaps into pieces, and brown in oil and butter. Add the carrot, celery, diced shallots, crushed garlic clove, rosemary and the quartered tomato. Brown all these ingredients, deglaze with white wine and water, and simmer to end up with a generous 6½ tbsp/100 ml of rich stock.

2. Remove the leaves from the chard stems, wash, and blanch in boiling salted water. Let cool and squeeze out the liquid. Peel the stems, cut into strips and braise in a pan with butter and water. Reserve 20 chanterelles and braise the rest. Mix the egg yolks and cream. Add the chard, chanterelles and pine nuts, and season.

Wild Rabbit and Chanterelles

3. Now take 4 round tart rings, 5½ in/12 cm across and 1 in/2 cm deep; line carefully with buttered aluminum foil, folding the foil over the rims. Fill with the chard mixture and cook for 10 minutes in a 275 °F/140 °C oven. Then turn out the contents onto the dish and remove the foil.

4. Braise the remaining chanterelles, slice the olives and add. Pan fry the rabbit fillets in olive oil and butter, basting frequently, and set aside to rest on a rack before cutting into slices on the bias. Arrange the slices carefully in a rosette on top of the vegetables, place the chanterelles and olives around them, and drizzle with the rabbit stock.

Quails with Figs

Preparation time:	1 hour
Cooking time:	30 minutes
Difficulty:	✷✷

Serves 4

6 quails
4 dried figs
1¼ lbs/600 g Savoy cabbage leaves
3½ oz/100 g carrots

5¼ oz/150 g onions
1 garlic clove
1¾ oz/50 g celery
1 bouquet garni
½ beef stock cube or 4½ tbsp/60 ml glace de viande
1 cup plus 2 tbsp/260 g butter
2 cups/500 ml red wine
6½ tbsp/100 ml cognac
salt and freshly ground pepper

The fig has many historical associations. Apart from grapes and olives it is the fruit most frequently mentioned in the Bible, and according to legend Romulus and Remus, the founders of Rome, were born under a fig tree. It is well known that the ancient Greeks made extensive use of figs; for one thing, they force-fed their geese with them. The wide distribution of the fig in the Mediterranean area gives it a special role in Mediterranean gastronomy. Although Provence grows excellent fresh figs, our chef uses dried figs in this dish and recommends Turkish figs for their flavor and particular delicacy.

This dish brings out all the advantages of farm-raised quails. They must be partly boned at the beginning of preparation, but reserve the carcasses as these give flavor to the marinade and will later be used to add aroma to the sauce made from the juices.

This recipe can be adapted to many game birds: pigeons, partridges, guinea fowl and pheasant may be prepared in the same way and can be combined with other vegetables, such as mushrooms or black salsify.

1. In the morning, remove the breasts (with wings) and the legs from the quails. Marinate the quails with the carcasses, the carrots, 3 ½ oz/100 g of onions, the diced celery, the garlic clove, the bouquet garni, and some ground pepper in the red wine.

2. Drain the quails, carcasses and vegetables, reserving the wine marinade; brown the bones in 4 tbsp/60 g of butter, then add the vegetables and continue cooking until everything is well colored. Flambé with the cognac and add the stock cube or glace de viande to the wine marinade and the bouquet garni. Cook over low heat until the quantity is reduced to ⅔–¾ cup/150–200 ml. Strain, add ⅓ cup/80 g of butter, and season to taste.

and Savoy Cabbage

3. Remove the stems from the cabbage and boil the cabbage in salted water, leaving it still slightly crisp. Cut the figs into small strips. Place the remaining onions and ½ cup/120 ml of water in a small pan with a cover and cook, covered, until the liquid has been reduced by half. Add the figs, allow to soften and whisk in ⅓ cup/80 g of butter. Add the chopped cabbage.

4. Brown the quails in a nonstick pan in 2½ tbsp/40 g of butter, leaving them still slightly pink. Arrange a pile of cabbage in the center of each plate, place three halved quails around it, and drizzle with the sauce.

Provençal Rib Steak

Preparation time:	*45 minutes*
Cooking time:	*30 minutes*
Difficulty:	★★

Serves 4

1 thick rib steak, about 2.2 lbs/1 kg

For the sauce:
10½ oz/300 g firm tomatoes
2 sprigs of tarragon
2 pinches of chopped garlic
¼ cup/60 ml white wine
¼ cup/60 ml olive oil
1¼ cups/300 ml beef stock
10½ oz/300 g butter

For the garnish:
14 oz/400 g new potatoes
8 small artichokes
8 small spring onions
8 small garlic cloves, peeled
7 oz/200 g small zucchini
4 oz/120 g olives
⅓ cup/80 g butter
2 sprigs fresh of thyme
2 sprigs fresh of rosemary
2 fresh bay leaves

To be added at the end of cooking:
¾ cup/180 ml water
2 tbsp/30 ml olive oil
10 basil leaves, finely chopped
salt and pepper

Beef remains the most popular of meats, and there are many breeds of cattle that produce a high quality of beef. For this recipe, choose a prime rib steak and pan fry it gently, after removing the sinews and excess fat. Some fat, however, should remain, because it is the mixture of fat and lean that provides the flavor. Make a very light beef stock for the sauce with the trimmings, adding an onion, thyme, bay leaf and a little water. Strain the stock before using.

The cooking of the beef must be very even, over low heat. The heat must penetrate right through the meat, without burning the surface. Leave the rib bone intact, as this will intensify the wonderful flavor.

Spring vegetables give the dish a contrasting note of freshness. Braise them in a skillet to preserve all their flavor and crispness. Tiny artichokes are eaten raw in southern Europe; they only need to be warmed up.

1. Trim the rib steak, scraping the meat away from the end of the rib, and removing the small bones. Cut the trimmings into small pieces and prepare a stock with them.

2. Wash the potatoes but do not peel them. Trim the artichokes and cut them into slices; peel the spring onions and the garlic cloves. Blanch the olives twice and cut the zucchini into slices 1 inch/2 cm thick. Cook each vegetable separately in salted water, then braise the vegetables in butter for about 15 minutes in a covered nonstick pan.

with Spring Vegetables

3. Season the braised vegetables with thyme, rosemary and bay leaves. Just before serving, add the water, olive oil and chopped basil. Stir vigorously so that all the vegetables are covered by the sauce and remove from the heat immediately.

4. Season the beef with salt and pepper, pan fry for 15 minutes in oil, turning several times. Keep warm on a plate covered with aluminum foil. Deglaze the pan with white wine and add the meat stock and other sauce ingredients. Bring to boil and stir in 2 tbsp/30 ml of oil. Place the beef and vegetables on a warm plate and pour the sauce over.

Chartreuse

Preparation time: 1 hour
Cooking time: 1 hour
Difficulty: ★★

Serves 4

4 squab, 14 oz/400 g each

For the sauce:
carcasses and skin of the squab
julienne of carrots, onions and celery
2 cups/500 ml white wine

⅔ cup/150 ml veal stock
⅓ cup/80 ml truffle juice
3½ tbsp/50 g butter
oil, salt and pepper

For the garnish:
1 Savoy cabbage
1 carrot
1¾ oz/50 g celery
4 thin slices of bacon, pancetta, or ham
1 shallot
3½ tbsp/50 g butter

Some people maintain that we have the monks of Chartres to thank for this recipe, based on braised cabbage, which goes well with game birds such as partridge or squab; you are entitled to your own opinion on this.

This stuffed cabbage leaf, the so-called "chartreuse," conceals its contents, forming a pleasant surprise for your guests.

The squab should be young, but don't use baby birds, whose flavor is not very well developed; you should choose birds weighing not less than 12–14 oz/350–400 g.

Cabbage is low in calories and very rich in vitamin E. Its medicinal qualities have been known for a long time; the ancient Romans used it as a natural antidepressant and to help counteract the effects of alcohol. Cabbage is highly prized throughout Europe, and particularly in Germany and England, because it is available all year round, although it is best in winter. For this recipe you need Savoy cabbage, which is recognizable by its crinkly edged leaves.

1. Cut the breasts and thighs from the squab carcasses and fold in the wing tips; chop the carcasses and skin into small pieces. Refrigerate the breasts for a short time, before seasoning and then browning them on all sides in a pan for three minutes.

2. Brown the carcasses and skin for 5/10 minutes over high heat in oil and butter with the squab thighs and the julienned sauce vegetables. Drain off the excess fat and deglaze with white wine. Add the veal stock and braise for 30 minutes over low heat. Remove the thighs, and strain the stock. Add the truffle juice and butter just before serving.

# of Squab

3. Remove the outer leaves of the cabbage; blanch the best leaves and let cool. Make a vegetable julienne with carrots, celery, bacon, pancetta or ham, and the rest of the cabbage: blanch the celery, carrot, and ham, braise the shallot in butter, add the pieces of ham and the vegetable julienne, and cook over low heat for 20 minutes.

4. Take the reserved cabbage leaves and line 4½ in/10-cm rings. Fill each with a layer of vegetable julienne, a braised squab thigh and another layer of julienne. Cover with foil and steam for 20 minutes. Put sauce on each serving plate, turn out 1 stuffed cabbage leaf from its ring onto each plate and arrange 1 sliced pigeon breast around it.

Preparation time: 30 minutes
Cooking time: 20 minutes
Difficulty: ★

Serves 4

1 lamb loin roast, about 3½ lb/1½ kg
10½ oz/300 g Yukon gold or red bliss
potatoes
4 slices of fresh duck foie gras
15 tbsp/220 g butter
⅓ cup/80 ml cream
1 truffle

oil
salt and pepper

For the sauce:
lamb bones and trimmings
1 onion
1 carrot
1¾ oz/50 g celery
1 bouquet garni
1 cup/250 ml white wine
⅓ cup/80 ml truffle juice
2 tbsp/30 g butter

Potatoes such as Yukon golds make a very delicate and not too floury purée, which unites all flavors in harmony. This pureé goes perfectly with the sauce that Serge Courville makes to accompany this dish.

The cut of lamb chosen here is the saddle, comprising the 2 loins, directly above the kidneys. Don't forget that the meat becomes more delicate if it is left to rest briefly after cooking; the roasting results in a slight tautening of the fibers, which makes the meat somewhat firmer than is desirable.

Two choice accompaniments complete this dish: the truffle and the foie gras, preferably duck foie gras, which is the richest kind.

1. Bone and trim the lamb. Cut into 4 pieces of equal size, tie each with string to keep its shape, and set aside in a cool place.

2. For the sauce, chop up the trimmings and bones, and brown for 20 minutes over medium-heat with the onion, carrot, celery and bouquet garni. Remove excess fat, deglaze with the white wine and simmer for 40 minutes, adding water if necessary. Strain and reduce until rich and flavorful, then add the truffle juice. Season and whisk in the butter.

Rossini

3. Boil the potatoes, purée them and mix with 13 tbsp/200 g of butter and the cream. Season. Brown the pieces of lamb in a mixture of butter and oil; they should remain pink at the center. Set aside to rest for 5–6 minutes before serving.

4. Sauté the slices of foie gras in a hot pan for 40 seconds on each side. Warm 4 plates, place a piece of lamb and a medallion of foie gras on each plate, and garnish each with a slice of truffle. Pour sauce onto each plate and add a helping of potato purée.

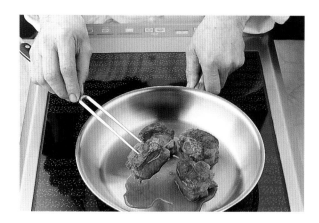

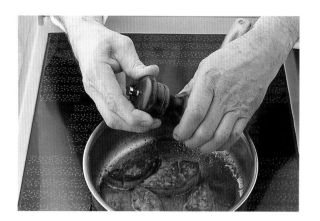

Tournedos of Beef

Preparation time: *1 hour*
Cooking time: *30 minutes*
Difficulty: ★★

Serves 4

4 filet mignon, about 5½ oz/150 g
4 slices of cooked duck foie gras
1 truffle
1 generous lb/500 g white asparagus
1 generous lb/500 g green asparagus
3 tomatoes
4 shallots

1 cup/250 ml sauvignon blanc, preferably from Tursan
1 cup/250 ml thickened veal stock
oil and butter
salt and pepper

For the corn croquettes:
2 cups/500 ml milk
3½ tbsp/25 g flour
2 tbsp/25 g butter
2 egg yolks
9 oz/250 g corn kernels
1 cup/100 g bread crumbs

In the south of the Landes region, between the river Adour and the city of Pau, lies the Chalosse, a region with diverse agriculture, where cattle breeding is predominant. The cattle, whose excellence is guaranteed by a seal of quality, are of the light-colored Aquitaine breed. Before they are slaughtered they are fattened for 4–6 months with corn; their tenderloins can weigh up to 15½ lbs/7 kg. Chalosse beef, preferred by our chef for this dish, is allowed to mature for 3–4 weeks before going to market.

For this dish, the steaks should be about 1 inch/2 cm thick and should be cooked in a hot pan in which a mixture of oil and butter has already been heated. This process caramelizes the steaks and improves their flavor.

Make the sauce for the corn croquettes the day before and let it cool.

The asparagus that accompanies the beef should be cooked for the shortest possible time to preserve its taste and the crispness of the tips.

1. Prepare a very thick Mornay sauce: make a white roux with the butter and flour. Cook gently over low heat for 5–10 minutes. Bring the milk to a boil, then whisk it into the white roux. Simmer for a few minutes over low heat, stirring constantly, then remove from the heat and whisk in 1 egg yolk. Add the corn.

2. Spread the mixture ½ in/1 cm thick on a small greased baking sheet and refrigerate. When cold, cut into croquettes, coat in egg yolk and then bread crumbs, and set aside. Season the steaks with salt, and brown on both sides, in a mixture of hot oil and butter, for 1 minute. Place on a serving dish.

with Spring Vegetables

3. Brown the corn croquettes in butter. Then cook both the white asparagus and green asparagus in salted water, taking care not to overcook it. Peel, seed and dice the tomatoes. Cut the truffle in thin slices. Season the steaks with salt and pan fry until cooked to taste. Place on a serving dish.

4. Remove most of the fat from the pan in which the meat was browned. Add the finely chopped shallots and braise. Add Tursan or other sauvignon blanc wine. Reduce for 5 minutes and then add the veal stock. Bring to a boil, reduce until thickened and then strain. Place a slice of foie gras on each steak, and a thin slice of truffle on top of that. Arrange the asparagus and diced tomato next to the meat and pour the sauce over the steak.

Duck Liver with

Preparation time: 30 minutes
Cooking time: 10 minutes
Difficulty: ★★

Serves 4

1 raw duck foie gras, about 1 generous lb/500 g
7 oz/200 g rhubarb
juice of 1 lemon
juice of 1 orange
pink peppercorns
coriander seeds
nutmeg

French *piment d'Espelette* or Hungarian
paprika
3½ oz/100 g bread for toasting
6½ tbsp/100 g sugar
1 vanilla bean
2½ oz/50 g rhubarb jam
3½ oz/100 g various salad greens
butter
parsley
fleur de sel, black pepper
white pepper
Szechuan pepper

Foie gras is often reserved for holidays, but there is no reason why it should not be enjoyed all year long. A duck's foie gras generally weighs between 14–17½ oz/400–500 g; it should be firm, smooth, round, and uniformly colored.

Rhubarb, whether sweetened or savory, is always eaten cooked. This large plant from the Polygonaceae (dock) family is particularly welcome because it is high in fiber and low in fat, and is thus very healthy to eat, despite the sourness that is often held against it.

Use only stems that are thick, firm and crisp when you buy them. Rhubarb that is overripe, too soft or too fibrous will produce only a bland, tasteless purée. If you are worried that the rhubarb will be too acidic, blanch it first, before continuing with the preparation. Never eat the green leaves; they are poisonous.

The piquant additions of all the various kinds of pepper and pimento must not overwhelm the flavor of the foie gras, so they should be used with discretion.

1. Cut the rhubarb into large pieces and place in a nonreactive pan with the sugar and a vanilla bean, bring to a boil, and simmer for 10 minutes. Then drain the resulting rhubarb compote.

2. Coarsely grind the pink peppercorns and toast in a dry skillet to bring out their full flavor. Add the lemon juice, orange juice, coriander, nutmeg, and paprika.seasonings.

Rhubarb Compote

3. Add the rhubarb compote as well as the grated zest of 1 lemon and rhubarb jam. Cut the bread into small cubes, brown in butter and dry out in the oven, then press through a coarse sieve or chop in a food processor.

4. Cut the foie gras into 1 in/2 cm slices and brown in a nonstick pan. Season with salt and scatter with parsley. Warm 4 plates, place a bouquet of mixed salad greens on one side, and sprinkle a quarter of the bread crumbs on the other. Place the liver on top of the bread crumbs. Add the rhubarb compote and the seasoned sauce before serving.

Squab with Truffle Sauce

Preparation time: 35 minutes
Cooking time: 20 minutes
Difficulty: ★★★

Serves 4

4 squab, about 12 oz/350 g each
10½ oz/300 g potatoes (such as Yukon gold or Charlotte)

9 oz/250 g fresh wild mushrooms
1 shallot
1¼ oz/40 g truffles
3½ tbsp/50 g butter
salt and pepper

In medieval and early modern Europe, pigeon-breeding used to be reserved for the landowning classes: they alone had the right to build dovecotes, in sizes proportionate to the extent of their property. These concentrations of pigeons, incidentally, were very destructive, because the birds ate the crops. This explains the French peasants' demands for the abolition of this feudal right, which appear in the records of complaints for 1789.

Farm-raised pigeons—called squab—are quite different from urban ones; in many cities, there are still complaints about the damage caused by the birds, and campaigns to reduce their numbers. The flesh of specially bred pigeons is delicate and well-flavored. Choose birds that weigh 10–12 oz/300–350 g, and cook them gently in a pre-heated oven. Before they are eaten they should rest briefly, so that the flesh will become even more tender.

Presented in a potato "millefeuille," the tender wild mushrooms form a pleasant contrast to the crisp potatoes. Be careful not to garnish the millefeuilles too liberally with the finely chopped mushrooms, so that potatoes and mushrooms are balanced in quantity.

1. Remove the breasts and legs from the squab and refrigerate until needed. Prepare a well-seasoned stock with the carcasses and set aside. Finely dice the mushrooms and sauté over medium heat in butter until tender; season with salt and pepper to taste.

2. Roast the squab parts with the quartered shallot in a 400 °F/205 °C oven. Deglaze the pan with the pigeon stock, reduce, then whisk in butter and a purée of fresh truffles.

and Potato Millefeuille

3. Thinly slice the potatoes in equal-sized slices, line 12 buttered tart pans with a single layer of sliced potatoes and bake for 20 minutes.

4. Layer the cooked potato slices and wild mushrooms. Serve on warm plates with the squab and sauce.

Stuffed Lamb in a

Preparation time: 20 minutes
Cooking time: 20 minutes
Difficulty: ★★

Serves 4

2 pieces lamb loin roast, about 2.2 lb/1 kg each

10½ oz/300 g foie gras
1¾ oz/50 g truffles
4 russet or other starchy potatoes
16 green asparagus spears
peanut oil
salt and pepper

Jean Crotet uses lamb from Sisteron or the Limousin, a region distinguished for the quality of its pasture land and its small family farms. This meat is particularly tender, rich in flavor and very low in fat.

You should choose only A-grade foie gras, which should maintain its firmness during cooking. As an alternative to truffles, you could substitute dried morels.

Do not wash the shredded potatoes shred, or they will lose their starch, which holds together the mantle of potatoes during cooking.

Our chef recommends asparagus with this dish, to emphasize its springlike character.

1. Bone the lamb, keeping the bones and skin for the stock. Butterfly and season the meat. Trim the asparagus and cook in salted water. Refresh, drain and cut into 3½ in/8 cm lengths, then set aside.

2. Slice half the truffles, keeping the rest for the sauce. Line each piece of lamb with the sliced truffles, and put a thumb-sized piece of foie gras in the middle and fold the meat over the stuffing. Peel the potatoes and shred them with a grater or cut into fine julienne. Season with salt and pepper.

Potato Crust with Truffles

3. Wrap the lamb in the potato julienne. Finely chop the rest of the truffles and add the sauce previously prepared with the bones and trimmings. Strain the sauce before using.

4. Brown the lamb in oil on both sides for a total of about 12 minutes, then finish cooking in the oven at 320 °F/160 °C for 4–5 minutes. Cut each piece in half and place on warmed plates. Garnish with warm asparagus spears and the truffle sauce.

Saddle of Hare Rossini

Preparation time: 40 minutes
Cooking time: 1 hour
Difficulty: ★★

Serves 4

4 saddles of hare
7 oz/200 g raw duck foie gras
½ red cabbage
2 apples

5 large onions
1 carrot
2 garlic cloves
1 sprig of thyme
3 cups/750 ml white wine
6½ tbsp/100 ml red wine
6½ tbsp/100 ml mild brandy
⅔ cup/150 ml vinegar
10 tbsp/150 g butter
salt and black pepper

If whole animals are available, choose a hare weighing about 7–8 lb/3½ kg, from which you can cut a fine fillet. The skin should be taut and the limbs firm. Remove any shotgun pellets that remain in the animal, and any parts of the flesh that may have been damaged by them.

Our chef advises against marinating the hare, which is traditional, because he believes that this deprives the meat of most of its flavor. Be careful just to brown the hare fillet, not to cook it through, so that it will be pink inside when served.

The braised red cabbage and compote of onions and apples make an original addition. If you like, you can enrich these accompaniments further with raisins, marinated in boiling white wine and served separately.

In the winter you can also add fresh chestnuts to this dish. Chop these finely and sauté in duck fat with onions and a little diced celery, which will produce a thick sauce.

1. Remove the loins from the saddles of hare and refrigerate until needed. Chop the bones and brown in oil, add half the onions, the carrot, garlic and thyme, white wine, some water, and some of the brandy, and simmer for at least 3 hours. Butterfly the fillets, place a portion of duck foie gras in the center and close up again. Then cut into 1½ inch/1.5 cm segements and tie with string.

2. Quarter, wash and finely chop the red cabbage. Cut 2 onions into thin strips and the apples into ½ in/1 cm dice. Brown the onions in ⅓ cup/80 g of butter, add the apples and red cabbage. Cook for 10–15 minutes, stirring constantly. Add the red wine and 1–2 tbsp/20–30 ml vinegar. Cover the pan and continue to cook for 1 hour. Season.

3. Heat the oil in a pan, season the hare with salt and pepper, brown nicely on all sides, then remove and set aside.

4. Pour off the fat, deglaze with the remaining brandy and vinegar, reduce, add the hare stock, reduce again and strain. At the last moment, whisk in the rest of the butter. Place a large helping of red cabbage in the center of each plate, surround with slices of the stuffed hare and pour sauce on top.

Preparation time: 45 minutes
Cooking time: 15 minutes
Difficulty: ★★

Serves 4

3½ lb/1½ kg loin of veal, cut into ¾ in/1.5 cm
slices
4 tomatoes
2 carrots
3 fennel
8 mild onions
1 celery rib
flat-leaf parsley
butter

olive oil
sugar
thyme
garlic
salt and pepper

For the veal stock:
veal trimmings and bones
1 tomato
2 onions
1 bouquet garni
4 cups/1 l white stock
1 lemon
1 orange
butter

Very tender milk-fed veal is delivered to Michel Del Burgo from local breeders (from the Carcassonne and Limoux regions), whose quality he respects. Everything that comes from the Aude calf is good: loin, fillet, knuckle, the offal—everything.

Here our chef presents a personal variation on the "osso buco" theme, a classic Italian recipe for veal shank. The originality consists in preparing a veal cutlet in the same way. Thus it is cut from the loin and carefully boned—preferably by your butcher. Make sure that some fat is retained around the meat, which will form a crisp and tasty crust after cooking. Ask your butcher for

the bones, to use when making the stock.

The cutlet is first browned in a skillet, with a suitable garnish of small vegetables to give flavor to the oil and butter. When it is well browned, the cooking is completed in the oven at low heat, after the aromatic garnish has been prepared. The meat must be frequently basted during cooking, so that it does not dry out.

The fennel should be quartered carefully so it does not fall apart. Michel Del Burgo suggests artichokes as a possible alternative to the fennel, and any other tender cut of veal instead of the cutlet.

1. Peel and quarter the tomatoes. Remove the seeds and place the quarters on a baking sheet lined with lightly oiled waxed paper, then sprinkle with sugar, salt and pepper, brush with oil and sprinkle with thyme. Place a slice of garlic on each piece of tomato. Let the tomatoes dry out for 2½ hours in the oven at 210 °F/100 °C.

2. Prepare the veal cutlets: brown them in a pan in some butter and olive oil, together with a garnish of chopped onions, carrots and garlic. Then transfer to the oven and cook for 15 minutes at 320–340 °F/160–170 °C. Prepare a fine dice of lemon and orange zest, and set aside.

"Osso Buco"

HÔTEL DE LA CITÉ
★★★★

3. For the veal stock, brown the trimmings and bones and add the fresh tomato, onions and bouquet garni. Skim the fat from the pan and add some water. Reduce until it is thickened, then add the white stock. Simmer for 3 hours, and strain. Finally, add the butter and, at the last moment, the diced lemon and orange zest.

4. Prepare the rest of the onions and the fennel pieces, add the chopped celery, and braise everything in a pan, then add the dried tomatoes and finely chopped parsley. Cut the cutlets into slices and arrange attractively on each plate with the braised vegetables.

Preparation time: 20 minutes
Cooking time: 20 minutes
Difficulty: ☆

Serves 4

4 duck breasts, preferably from Muscovy duck

4 apples
1 tbsp/10 g coriander seeds
1 cup/250 ml duck stock
1 bunch of watercress
a little butter
salt and pepper

Here the duck is seasoned with coriander, a combination used by the Roman Apicius in his famous cook book. This aromatic Asian seasoning finds an ideal partner in duck, which can absorb the strong flavor without sacrificing any of its own.

The Challans duck used by our chef is a remarkable bird. In the Vendée, near Nantes, they breed small ducks, which are distinguished by a red seal of quality. These are wild breeds, which are reared in the open air on the rich grass of the region with a carefully measured daily allotment of corn. The bird is slaughtered by strangulation at 77 days old (for a female) or 84 days (for a male). The flesh is tender and full of flavor. Under the duck's wings are the small fillets whose shape and character, when removed with the skin intact, are particularly suitable for this dish. You can also use the flesh of a medium-sized duck cut into thin, long strips.

Joseph Delphin chooses Melrose apples - a variety that has a thin skin, is very aromatic and goes remarkably well with the duck fillets.

1.Remove the breasts from the ducks and trim away excess skin and fat. Score the skin so that the fat can escape during cooking.

2. Place the whole breasts, skin downwards, in a buttered pan, season with salt and and cook over medium heat for 10–12 minutes, then place on aluminum foil and set aside to rest for about 10 minutes.

Coriander

3. Peel and core the apples and cut each into six pieces. Brown on both sides in butter until slightly colored.

4. Pour the fat from the pan, add the crushed coriander seeds, and the duck stock, and reduce by one third, then whisk in the butter. Slice the duck and arrange with the apples in a fan shape on each plate. Pour the sauce on top and garnish with watercress. Serve hot.

Preparation time: *1 hour*
Cooking time: *1 hour*
Difficulty: ★★

Serves 4

2 saddles of rabbit, with their kidneys, about 2 lb/900 g
3 oz/80 g carrots
turnips
1½ oz/40 g dried tomatoes
1½ oz/40 g tomatoes
¾ oz/20 g lavender
2½ tbsp/40 ml red wine

8 oz/240 g pasta, such as fusilli
salt and pepper

For the rabbit stock:
bones from the saddles of rabbits
1 onion
shallots
1 carrot
1 leek
1 sprig of lavender
lavender oil
garlic
thyme and bay leaf

Philippe Dorange is from Mougin; this means not only that he appreciates lavender, which is characteristic of the whole of Provence, but also that he has a great admiration for his former teacher Roger Vergé. It is not surprising that he has developed his own recipes that are given subtlety by the use of lavender, because this aromatic plant has many culinary qualities.

Instead of the usual rabbit thighs, which he prepares for his friends with garlic and potatoes sautéed in butter, our chef here uses the saddle of the rabbit, with an exquisite

sauce based on lavender and red wine. The red wine should ideally come from Provence or Corsica.

Take care to cook the rabbit very gently and slowly and to serve it pink. The rest of the animal can be used to make soup or sautéed rabbit with mustard, olive oil and rosemary.

It is appropriate to serve pasta with this dish, as Provence and Italy are neighbors and they have enjoyed continual gastronomic and cultural exchanges.

1. Bone the saddles of rabbit and keep the bones to prepare the sauce; reserve the kidneys for the stuffing.

2. Cut the carrots and turnips into strips of 1½ x ¼ in/3 x 0.5 cm. Cook separately in salted water, then let cool.

Rabbit with Lavender

3. Season the rabbit and stuff it by placing the strips of vegetables at the sides and the dried tomatoes, lavender and kidneys in the middle. Roll up the stuffed meat, secure with string and refrigerate until 30 minutes before cooking.

4. Brown the bones in lavender oil with the ingredients given for the stock, then pour off the fat from the pan. Add the tomato peels and red wine. Simmer for about 1 hour and strain. Roast the rabbit in a 350 °F/180 °C oven for 8 –10 minutes and cut into medallions. Meanwhile, boil the pasta. Mound the sauced pasta in the middle of each plate and surround with rabbit medallions and more sauce.

Saddle of Lamb

Preparation time: 1 hour
Cooking time: 45 minutes
Difficulty: ★★★

Serves 4

2½ lb/1 kg loin roasts of lamb
6 sheets/120 g filo pastry
3½ oz/100 g button mushrooms
5 oz/140 g chanterelles
9 tbsp/140 g butter
1 cup/240 ml olive oil
8 basil leaves
1½ oz/40 g cinnamon
⅓ oz/10 g nutmeg
chives

⅓ oz/10 g ground cloves
1½ oz/40 g poppy seeds
white pepper
salt and pepper

For the lamb stock:
lamb bones from the loin roast
1 onion
carrots
shallots
garlic
onions
thyme and bay leaves
2½ tbsp/40 ml sherry vinegar
6½ tbsp/100 ml port

There are some chefs who from time to time like to give their guests a little surprise, as in this recipe, in which the lamb, stuffed with mushrooms, is hidden within a crisp pastry covering.

For this recipe our chef prefers the delicate milk-fed lamb of Pauillac, which comes from a region already blessed with famous wines: Château-Lafite and Mouton-Rothschild.

The art of this recipe lies in the choice and quantity of the herbs and spices: one should be able to taste them without their overwhelming the flavor of the lamb. The poppy seeds in which you roll the pastry will stick to it and enclose it with a dark, crisp layer full of flavor.

Our chef tells us that he has also prepared fish (monkfish or salmon) in the same way, using well-seasoned button mushrooms instead of chanterelles.

1. Bone and trim the lamb, reserving the bones to prepare the stock from them. Dice the chanterelles if large.

2. Braise the button mushrooms in butter and season them. Using a sharpening steel or thin-bladed knife, make a hole through the center of each boneless loin and stuff with the mushrooms. Brown the lamb in the olive oil, cook until nearly done, and season with the cinnamon, pepper, nutmeg and cloves. Set aside.

in Spiced Pastry

3. For the stock, brown the bones and trimmings with the aromatic ingredients. Skim off the fat, add the sherry vinegar and port, and simmer for 1 hour. Strain and keep warm. Brown the chanterelles in butter.

4. Brush the pastry with melted butter, using three layers, one on top of the other. Wrap the lamb with the basil leaves in the pastry and put in a 400 °F/200 °C oven for 5 minutes to brown the pastry. Then roll in the poppy seeds (if necessary, brush the pastry with honey first) and cut into thick slices. Place slices of lamb with a little bouquet of chanterelles on each plate, and garnish with chives.

Calf's Sweetbreads with Curry

Preparation time: 40 minutes
Cooking time: 10 minutes
Difficulty: ★★

Serves 4

9–10½ oz/250–300 g calf's sweetbreads
2 cups/500 ml chicken stock
7 oz/200 g fresh noodles
2 zucchini
2 tomatoes
a little chervil

flour
butter
olive oil

For the curry sauce:
2 tbsp curry powder
2 onions
1 tomato
1 apple
1 banana
2 cups/500 ml heavy cream
salt and pepper

The thymus gland, which is situated at the base of the neck in front of the windpipe, protects young animals from certain infectious diseases and disappears in adulthood. These glands are found in lambs and calves, among other animals, and are known as sweetbreads. Many gourmets find them to be a great delicacy.

Calf's sweetbreads can be used in all sorts of recipes: they can be braised, grilled or roasted. Here Claude Dupont has chosen to brown them in a skillet with butter.

The sweetbreads must first be cleaned of all contamination and residual blood by washing them in cold water. A further thorough cleaning may be necessary after that. The careful removal of the very fine skin should be approached with concentration. Not a trace of it should remain.

The somewhat unorthodox curry sauce demands some attention; adjust the quantities of curry powder to taste. Cut the zucchini into strips of the same width as the pasta, to maintain a balance when they are combined.

1. Thoroughly wash the sweetbreads, blanch, remove the outer membrane, press out excess moisture with paper towels. Braise in the chicken stock, cut each sweetbread on the diagonal into 4 cutlets and dry on paper towels. Reserve the chicken stock.

2. Season each cutlet and lightly dredge in flour; brown in butter until crisp. Cook the pasta and keep warm.

Sauce and Fresh Noodles

3. Julienne the zucchini finely. Heat some olive oil in a pan and quickly sauté the zucchini without allowing them to brown. Add the pasta and season the mixture.

4. For the sauce, braise the chopped onions, quartered apple, tomato, and 2 slices of the banana with 2 tbsp of curry powder. Add the chicken stock, reduce, add the cream, reduce again, adjust the seasoning and strain through a fine sieve. Place a mound of pasta on each plate, make a hollow in it, place two cutlets in the hollow, and add the curry sauce. Garnish with chervil and tomato quarters.

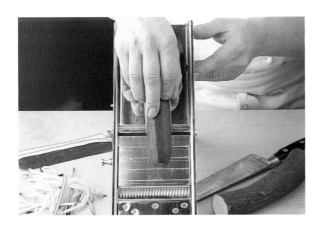

Chicken Legs

Preparation time: 45 minutes
Cooking time: 25 minutes
Difficulty: ★

Serves 4

2 chickens, about 2 generous lb/1 kg each (or use capon, turkey, guinea fowl or duck)
14 oz/400 g hop shoots

juice of 1 lemon
2 shallots
parsley, chervil
6½ tbsp/100 g butter
6½ tbsp/100 ml Scotch whisky
¾ cup/200 ml white wine
¾ cup/200 ml chicken stock
2 cups/500 ml heavy cream
salt and pepper

Which kind of poultry to use for this recipe is left to your discretion: chicken, capon, turkey, guinea fowl or duck are all equally suitable. The Belgians are proud of their spectacular presentations of poultry, as in the famous "Coucou de Malines" and "waterzooi," which are actually much more lavish recipes than this one.

The preparation of the chicken legs is not very difficult, but the skin must be carefully cut so as to insert the bone as shown. The rest is easy.

The young shoots of the hop plant are very popular in Belgium and can be found on the menus of many restaurants there. Their season is very brief—from mid-March to the end of April. This climbing plant is grown for brewing beer, and can reach a height of 16 feet/5 m. Medicinal properties were attributed to hops in the 15th century, and in the 16th century it was believed to be an aphrodisiac. Today there is a great interest in Europe in this Belgian speciality, which many compare with asparagus. Before sautéing them in butter, the hops should be briefly blanched.

1. Cut each bird into four parts – two breasts and wings and two legs. Bone each piece so that only the meat, the skin and one bone (the wing and drumstick bones) remain.

2. Wrap the meat in its own skin, cutting a little hole in the skin so as to insert the bone in order to close up the pockets.

with Hop Shoots

3. Brown the chicken pockets with the shallots and parsley. Lower the heat and cook, covered, for 5 minutes. Deglaze with whisky and reduce. Add the white wine, reduce again, then add the chicken stock and bring to a boil. Remove the chicken pockets and keep warm. Reduce the remaining liquid and add the cream.

4. Reduce further, until a creamy consistency has been achieved, and season. Add the butter and strain through a fine sieve. Blanch the hop shoots with the lemon juice and then cook gently in butter. Place a quarter of them on each plate with a chicken pocket beside them and spread sauce all around. Garnish with chervil.

Chartreuse of Poussin

Preparation time: 1 hour
Cooking time: 20 minutes
Difficulty: ★★

Serves 4

For the chartreuse:
2 poussins
4 slices of raw goose foie gras
7 oz/200 g veal
4 slices of black truffle
4 small carrots, about 3½ oz/100 g
2 kohlrabi, about 14 oz/400 g
4 basil leaves
2 Savoy cabbage leaves

6½ tbsp/100 ml cream
butter
truffle oil
Madeira
cognac
apple pie spice

For the cèpes:
1⅓ pound/600 g small fresh cèpes or porcini
1 tbsp parsley and chervil, chopped
1 tbsp/15 ml vinegar
¼ cup/60 ml red wine
¼ cup/60 ml veal stock
8 tsp/40 g butter
salt and pepper

This chartreuse usually transports Lothar Eiermann's guests into a state of gratitude close to ecstasy. It is not often that poussin, foie gras and cèpes are combined in the same dish, and even less often does one get the chance of preparing such a sophisticated dish oneself.

It is important to choose very fresh, fairly large poussins, and be sure to keep the hearts and livers, which will be delicious additions to the dish.

You may vary the flavor of the stuffing with cognac,

Madeira or port, all excellent for this purpose.

Is the dish called "chartreuse" really the invention of the Carthusians—the monks of Chartres—who used it to preserve the meat they were not allowed to eat during periods of fasting? We do not know.

This chartreuse can be prepared a few days ahead and kept in the refrigerator, which will make it easier to unmold. And be careful when unmolding, because the vegetables can fall apart.

1. Cut up the poussins and skin the breasts. Bone the thighs and marinate in cognac and Madeira. Brown the poussin livers and hearts. Dice, season, add to the veal, and chill well. Briefly brown the foie gras. Flatten the breast pieces, flavor them with truffle oil and place on each a slice of foie gras with a basil leaf and a slice of truffle. Close up like a pocket and chill.

2. In a food processor, make a stuffing with the marinated thigh meat and the veal. Strain and add the apple pie spice, cognac and cream. Wash the carrots and kohlrabi and cut into strips, reserving the trimmings. Blanch, refresh in cold water and dab them dry. Blanch the Savoy cabbage and cut out 8 circles, 2½ in/5 cm in diameter.

with Cèpes

3. Then take 4 small soufflé dishes, butter them and line their sides with alternating strips of carrot and kohlrabi. Place a savoy cabbage leaf and some stuffing in the bottom of each dish. Press the filling down with a spoon, then put a poussin breast into each dish, add some more stuffing and top with a piece of Savoy cabbage. Bake in a 300 °F/150 °C oven in a bain-marie for about 25 minutes.

4. Clean the cèpes, cut in thin slices and cook in a hot pan with the butter and herbs. Keep warm. In the same pan, brown the poussin bones and vegetable trimmings, deglaze with the red wine and veal stock, reduce, strain, and add the vinegar. Put some of the sauce on each plate, unmold 1 chartreuse and garnish with slices of cèpe, truffles and chervil.

Lacquered Leg of Suckling

Preparation time: 20 minutes
Cooking time: 1 hour 30 minutes
Difficulty: ★ ★

Serves 4

1 leg of suckling pig with rind, about 1 kg
¾ cup plus 1 tbsp/200 g sugar
1 tbsp/10 g each lemon thyme, marjoram, rosemary
1 tbsp/22 g honey
1¼ cup/300 ml freshly squeezed orange juice
2¾ oz/80 g shallots, chopped
1 tsp black pepper, ground
white pepper, ground
salt

For the sauerkraut:
14 oz/400 g raw sauerkraut
1 oz/30 g smoked bacon, in 2 pieces
1 potato
3½ oz/100 g onions
½ apple
¾ cup/200 ml white wine
3½ tbsp/50 ml apple cider
6½ tbsp/100 ml stock
1 tbsp peppercorns
1 clove
1 bay leaf
1 juniper berry
5 white peppercorns
salt, sugar and freshly ground white pepper

At Lothar Eiermann's restaurant, the white wine used for this dish is Verrenberger Riesling, one of the best produced in Baden-Württemberg, from the nearby estates of Prince von Hohenlohe. You will probably find it more practical to use a more modest Riesling for the preparation of the suckling pig, but if you can, end the meal with a glass of something closer to "the nectar of Verrenberg."

The first layer of glaze is applied 30 minutes after the start of cooking—on no account earlier. The further layers are applied at regular intervals. Keep basting the meat with its own fat as well, so it does not dry out.

The most important ingredient for the glaze is the honey. Use a flavorful variety and do so sparingly, as its strong flavor might otherwise upset the balance of this dish. Prepare the sauerkraut according to the rules: use goose fat and flavor it with juniper and beer or white wine—or, if you like, with champagne.

1. Score the rind of the pork and brown on all sides in a very hot pan. Roast in a 355 °F/180 °C oven for 30 minutes, skin side down.

2. For the glaze, reduce the orange juice, sugar, honey, shallots and seasoning to a syrup. Remove the meat from the oven and let cool. Glaze with the syrup and return to the oven. Reduce the temperature to 325 °F/160 °C and roast for 1 hour more, basting with the glaze 2 or 3 times during cooking.

Pig with Sauerkraut

3. Rinse the sauerkraut in cold water and squeeze it dry. Place the herbs and spices in a sachet. Braise the onions and smoked bacon, but do not allow to brown. Add the sliced apple, wine, apple cider and stock. Add the sauerkraut, herbs and spice sachet, and cook for 1½ hours.

4. Grate the potato finely. Remove the bacon and the sachet from the pan and add the potato. Adjust the seasoning. Carve the meat and serve with the sauerkraut.

Preparation time: 25 minutes
Cooking time: 45 minutes
Difficulty: ☆

Serves 4

2 small Muscovy ducklings
2 fresh figs
2 lemons
2 potatoes
olive oil
13 tbsp/200 g butter
2 sprigs of tarragon

salt and pepper

For the duck stock:
the duckling carcasses
3½ tbsp/50 ml dry white wine
3½ tbsp/50 ml cognac
¾ cup/200 ml veal stock

For the caramel:
½ cup plus 2 tbsp/150 g sugar
3½ tbsp/50 ml red wine vinegar
1 tbsp/22 g honey

Duck meat is tender and tasty, and offers a whole range of different flavors. Jean Fleury favors the Challans duck, which is subject to strict quality controls. The birds are fed grain and each has 8 square feet/2.5 square meters of space. They are slaughtered at 11 weeks, when their flesh has reached a certain maturity. A small duck, such as a muscovy duck, may be substituted.

Duck is suitable for a number of delicious dishes. Black olives go well with it, as do mint, bitter oranges, black currants, cherries, and sauces using port or other richly flavored wines. For this dish, our chef, following tradition, recommends fresh figs, dry white wine and good cognac, to which a savory veal stock is added.

The fig, so often mentioned in the Bible, has maintained its popularity to the present day. Jean Fleury also likes to use figs with guinea fowl.

The preparation of the potatoes is not difficult. The paper-thin slices of potato become almost transparent when sautéed, so that the tarragon leaves will show through. Be careful with the quantities of vinegar and honey, which can dominate the flavor of the dish if too much of either is used.

1. Prepare the ducks for roasting and roast in a 400 °F/205 °C oven for 25–30 minutes; the flesh should remain pink. Remove the breast and legs, and roast the legs until cooked through. For the stock, break up the carcasses and braise, then add the white wine, cognac and finally the veal stock. Cook for about 15 minutes, then strain.

2. Meanwhile, prepare a light-colored caramel with the sugar. Add the red wine vinegar and honey and bring to a boil. Mix with the duck stock, bring back to a boil, simmer briefly and strain. Skim the fat from the surface, add the zest of the lemon and the butter, and season.

Lemon and Honey Sauce

3. Wash and peel the potatoes. Cut them into very thin slices with a mandoline and place a few tarragon leaves on half of the slices. Cover with the remaining potato slices. Roast the figs in the oven with some butter.

4. Brown the potato slices in a nonstick pan with some butter. On each plate place a duck leg, some slices of duck breast, and 4–5 potato slices. Pour over the lemon-and-honey sauce and garnish with a julienne of blanched lemon zest.

Stuffed Pig Tails

Preparation time: 30 minutes
Cooking time: 2 hours
Difficulty: ★★★

Serves 4

8 pigs' tails, lightly salted
2.2 lb/1 kg white beans and string beans, cut, salted and preserved in clay pots (see description below)

7 oz/200 g lean pork
3½ oz/100 g veal
2½ oz/70 g foie gras
6½ tbsp/100 g butter
6½ tbsp/100 ml heavy cream
1 tbsp/15 ml white wine
1 tbsp shallots
nutmeg
salt and pepper
white stock

These preserved beans—a reminder of the days when the Netherlands were governed by Spain—are prepared in the autumn and eaten throughout the winter. After being washed and cut, the beans are layered in a clay pot so that the firmest ones are at the bottom. Then they are covered with salt up to the rim of the pot, before being pressed under a weighted plate. To prepare for eating, they must be rinsed several times and then boiled for 15 minutes.

Before you start to prepare the salted pigs' tails, they must be soaked for 24 hours to get rid of the salt, and then conscientiously cleaned. They should be cooked in barely simmering water and finally refreshed in cold water, which will make them easier to bone. If you do not intend to eat them right away, you can keep the boned tails in the refrigerator for some time.

In any case, the success of this dish depends on the stuffing. Choose only the best quality ingredients. To poach the pigs' tails we recommend wrapping each piece in aluminum foil, then in cheesecloth.

1. Soak the tails for 24 hours. Simmer for 1½–2 hours, drain and allow to cool in cold water until luke-warm. Prepare the stuffing: chop finely the meat of 4 of the pigs' tails, braise the shallots and add the white wine. Add all other ingredients except the beans and butter to the meat, mix carefully and season.

2. Bone the remaining tails: cut open lengthwise, remove the bones and stuff with the prepared filling.

with Preserved Beans

3. Put the tails back together in pairs, the thick end of one with the thin end of the other; wrap in foil, roll up like a sausage and fasten. Rinse the cut beans 2–3 times under running water and soak. Cook in boiling water for about 15 minutes, then prepare both kinds of beans as usual.

4. Poach the stuffed tails in white stock for about 30 minutes. They can then be browned in a pan. Mix the two kinds of beans and add butter. Place on 4 warm plates. Cut the stuffed tails in slices and place them on the plates near the beans. Use the thickened veal stock as a sauce.

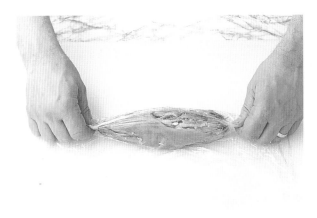

Roast Fillet of Lamb

Preparation time: 2 hours
Cooking time: 2 hours
Difficulty: ★★

Serves 4

2 lb/900 g loin of lamb
10½ oz/300 g lamb shoulder

For the moussaka:
14 oz/400 g eggplant
5½ oz/150 g onions
3½ oz/100 g tomatoes
1 sprig of thyme
1 garlic clove

For the braised zucchini:
4 small zucchini
4 small onions

6 cherry tomatoes
1 pinch of thyme
olive oil

For the lamb shoulder and sauce:
fine dice of carrots, onions and celery
1 tomato
2 garlic cloves
1 bouquet garni
2 cups/500 ml lamb stock
1 cup/250 ml olive oil
salt and ground pepper

For the mantle of herbs:
3½ oz/100 g fresh bread crumbs
4 tbsp/25 g rosemary, savory, sage, thyme, marjoram
2 egg whites
salt and pepper

Lamb has the best flavor in spring, but it can be eaten all year long. Lamb is appreciated not only in Europe and the United States, but is used in Asian and African dishes.

Our chef is particularly fond of lamb from the Gironde, which is slaughtered at less than 65 days old and whose white flesh has a very strong flavor. You can use any good quality young lamb for this dish, but it pays to seach out the best. Choose the ribs, because the flesh nearest to the bone always has the most flavor.

The moussaka can be prepared in advance, and this intensifies its flavor. It can also be eaten cold, or reheated.

The preparation of the mantle of herbs requires a little patience. While the British like mint with lamb, our chef prefers herbs from the South for this dish: rosemary and thyme or savory. Sage and marjoram, too, underline the taste of this meat. The mantle of herbs should be prepared in a cool place to give it the best consistency.

This spring dish should be served very hot.

1. Cut the shoulder into 1¾ oz/50 g pieces, dab off the moisture, and brown them; add the diced vegetables and braise. Deglaze with lamb stock; add the garlic, tomatoes and bouquet garni, and season with salt and pepper. Simmer for 90 minutes over low heat. Strain, skim off fat, and reduce until the sauce becomes creamy. Keep warm in a bain-marie. Coarsely chop the cooked lamb.

2. For the moussaka, cut half the eggplant, unpeeled, into thin strips, brown, then roast in a 250 °F/120 °C oven for 15 minutes. Dice remaining eggplant, chop the onions and braise with the chopped garlic and the crushed tomatoes. Line 4 small molds with the eggplant strips, and fill with the vegetables and chopped lamb. Cut the tips of the eggplant strips to a point, and fold them into the center to cover the stuffing.

3. Boil the zucchini in salted water and let cool. Cut into a fan shape. Cut the cherry tomatoes into fan shapes. Place the zucchini fans between the "slats" of the fan slices of cherry tomato, and place slices of onion on top; season with salt and pepper. Sprinkle with thyme. Drizzle with olive oil and roast for 10 minutes in a 350 °F/150 °C oven.

4. Bone the loin, remove the sinews, season with salt and pepper and brush with fat. For the mantle of herbs: sieve the bread crumbs, add the freshly chopped herbs, mix, season with salt and pepper. Roll the fillets in the mixture, brush with egg and sauté gently in butter for 4–5 minutes without allowing the crust to brown; the lamb should remain pink. Serve with moussaka, zucchini and sauce.

Preparation time: 1 hour
Cooking time: 20 minutes
Difficulty: ★★★

Serves 4

1 generous lb/500 g veal tenderloin
1 young cabbage
1 bunch young carrots
1 bunch scallions
1 bunch turnips

3½ oz/100 g green beans
9 oz/250 g green asparagus
1¼ cup/300 g butter
¾ cup/200 ml white chicken stock
1 bunch chives
salt and pepper

For the vegetable sauce:
brown truffle sauce
red, green and yellow bell peppers

The meat of the calf has been appreciated at least since antiquity. When Moses received the Ten Commandments on Mount Sinai, the Hebrews constructed a golden calf. A fatted calf was slaughtered to celebrate the return of the prodigal son.

All parts of the calf can be eaten: the glands, the offal and, of course, the meat itself all provide the ingredients for innumerable dishes for the gourmet. Different cuts of veal appear in braised veal shanks, in ragouts and fricassees. It is eaten with particular relish in France, which maintains its position as the greatest producer of veal in Europe.

After some difficult years, the breeders succeeded in regaining the confidence of the French consumer, and now more than 8 lb/4 kg of veal is consumed per person per year in France.

For this dish of veal tenderloin *à la ficelle* (tied with string and poached), which is based on an old household recipe, our chef recommends veal from the Limousin, which is now protected by a seal of quality, from calves reared only on milk. Its flesh is a shining pale pink, very firm and with white fat.

1. Remove the sinews and fat from the veal, season and tie up. Blanch the cabbage leaves, pat dry and place on aluminum foil.

2. Cut the vegetables (carrots, scallions, turnips, asparagus, and green beans) into small pieces and blanch in boiling salted water. Place in rows on each cabbage leaf. Mix the chives with the melted butter and pour over the vegetables. Fold up the foil and roll into a roulade.

Chartreuse of Vegetables

3. Poach the veal tenderloin for about 8 minutes in the chicken stock, then remove and keep cool.

4. Reduce the stock by half, then add butter. Add the brown vegetable sauce (the peppers mixed with the truffle sauce). Season to taste, cut the tenderloins into slices, place on the plates and pour the sauce over. Reheat the chartreuses by steaming, then place one on each plate.

Preparation time: 50 minutes
Cooking time: 30 minutes
Difficulty: ✩

Serves 4

2 pork tenderloins, about 28 oz/800 g
2 tbsp/30 g butter
1 medium onion, chopped
stock
4 cardamom seeds 2 cloves
1 pinch of curry powder
1 pinch of caraway seed
2 pinches of paprika
1 pinch of cinnamon
1½ cups/200 g couscous

1 tbsp/15 ml tomato paste
10 small mint leaves
6½ tbsp/100 ml cream
3½ tbsp/50 ml olive oil

For the preserved fruit:
juice of 1 lemon and 1 lime
2 dried figs
3 dried apricots
2 prunes
10 roasted peanuts
5 roasted almonds

Coconut and curry sauce: (see basic
recipes for ingredients)

Philippe Groult created this dish on a business trip to Tunisia, where he discovered a veritable garden of Eden, and was inspired by the many unfamiliar spices he found there.

When choosing the couscous, the size of the grains is irrelevant; what is important is its quality and its preparation in olive oil.

The peanuts, almonds and, if you like, chickpeas and pine nuts are fried in the pan. In summer you can also use fresh almonds. Similarly, the dried fruit can be replaced with fresh fruit in summer. For soaking the fruits, the lemon and lime juices play important roles. The lemon counteracts any excessive sweetness in the fruit and the lime enriches it with a subtle note.

The medallion is cut from the top of the tenderloin and is roasted to remain pink in the center. In this recipe, the pork and vegetables form a well-balanced relationship.

1. Soak the figs, apricots, prunes, peanuts and almonds for 10 minutes in the juice of 1 lemon and 1 lime.

2. Briefly toast the couscous in a pan with olive oil, then add the stock with tomato paste. Boil the cream with the crushed spices and add to the couscous with two thirds of the soaked fruits. Remove from the heat and set aside to plump.

Coconut-Curry Sauce

3. Trim the pork and season with salt and pepper; braise it with a chopped onion in a little butter and 2 tsp oil, leaving the meat just barely pink inside, and keep warm on a plate. Add 2 tbsp/30 ml of water to the meat juices and set aside. Cut the pork into 12 medallions.

4. For the coconut and curry sauce: braise the onion, apple and banana in olive oil, add curry powder, coconut milk and chicken stock, bring to a boil, and simmer for 3 minutes. Purée, strain and add the butter. On each plate, place 3 tbsp of couscous in 3 piles, place a medallion of pork on top of each, pour the roasting juices on top and the curry sauce around, and garnish with a piece of coconut and a mint leaf.

Preparation time: 2 hours
Cooking time: 45 minutes
Difficulty: ★★

Serves 4

2 wood pigeons or squab
4 quails
1 mallard or other wild duck
9 oz/250 g duck liver
5 chestnuts
1 shallot
1 garlic clove
2 onions
1 sprig of thyme
5 juniper berries

¾ cup/200 ml red wine
cognac
4 mushrooms
3 large potatoes
juice and zest of 1 orange
10 tbsp/150 g unsalted butter
3½ oz/100 g dandelions
1¾ oz/50 g mâche
1 endive
1 radicchio
chives
1 tbsp/15 ml honey
1 tbsp/10 g Szechuan peppercorns
10 coriander seeds
4 tsp/20 ml vinaigrette dressing

These brochettes were the foundation of Philippe Groult's fame. The varying types of meat and flavor of the three game birds selected may discourage the inexperienced cook. But the problems are easily overcome and you will impress all of your friends if you master this dish.

The duck should be small, tender and juicy. The wood pigeon is widely distributed throughout Europe but you should be able to obtain a domestic squab easily, like the quails. In any case, choose large, firm quails, which have a strong flavor. If wild, all birds should be carefully examined for gun shot, which must be removed. Marinating is unnecessary and would adversely alter the flavor of the duck, squab and quail.

A good accompaniment to game dishes are grilled cèpes and fresh chestnuts, which can be made pleasantly crunchy by slicing them thinly while raw and then browning.

You can change the composition of the brochettes according to your fancy: venison or wild boar can be substituted for the game birds suggested by our chef, if the appropriate preparation and cooking times for each type of meat are taken into account.

1. Prepare the birds; remove the breast and thighs from the pigeons and duck. Rub some of the duck liver through a sieve and set aside. Bone the quails without cutting in half, and fill with a stuffing made from the liver, herbs, juniper berries, and some cognac. Season the breasts with salt, pepper and crushed coriander seeds.

2. Crush the carcasses. In a pan, braise the shallot, garlic, and onions. Add the bones and brown for 2 minutes, then flambé with some cognac. Reduce the red wine by half and add to the pan with the thyme, then simmer for 15 minutes and strain.

Game Birds

3. Cut the rest of the duck liver into four pieces, cook for 8 minutes and add the quails, the pigeon and duck breasts, and the mushrooms. Cook these lightly (they should not be too well done). Bone the pigeon and duck thighs and brown until crisp. Mix the salad greens and add the vinaigrette. Brown the sliced potatoes. Peel the chestnuts and slice them thinly.

4. Spear the duck, mushrooms, quails, liver, and pigeon on a skewer and keep warm. Complete the preparation of the sauce: add first the orange juice, then the cooking juices. Add the liver and the pepper and crushed coriander seeds. Caramelize the orange zest with the honey and add to the duck.

Duckling with Orange

Preparation time: 1 hour
Cooking time: 45 minutes
Difficulty: ★

Serves 4

2 small ducklings, about 3¼ lb/1½ kg each
9 oz/250 g coriander seeds
⅔ cup/150 ml honey
juice and zest of 4 oranges
1 large onion
1 carrot
½ cup/120 g unsalted butter
3½ tbsp/50 ml wine vinegar

1 bay leaf
¾ oz/20 g chives
1 tbsp/10 g tarragon
salt and pepper

For the garnish:
16 potatoes
3½ oz/100 g mushrooms, quartered
7 oz/200 g smoked bacon, diced
16 onions
⅔ cup/150 ml peanut oil
2 tbsp/30 g butter
1 pinch of sugar
salt

The leaner and more tender flesh of a duckling is often preferred to that of a mature duck. In any case, avoid birds with a soft carcass, and make sure the duck has a golden-yellow skin.

As a native of Normandy, Philippe Groult likes to use ducks from Rouen, particularly the Duclair breed, whose reddish flesh is very delicate. But other small ducks can be equally good.

Groult thinks that coriander, which has for centuries been credited with healing and calming powers, is the most suitable seasoning for duck. It is said that Amphycles, a gastronomic expert of ancient times, knew this umbelliferous plant and used it to preserve meat. Your guests will like the coriander seeds, which will have swollen up by absorbing the juices from the duck, as well as being coated with the honey.

This dish, which is both simple and out of the ordinary, is in accordance with the culinary principles of Philippe Groult, whose motto is: "I want to refine without exaggeration, to harmonize without disguising, to surprise without provoking."

1. Prepare the ducklings; season with salt and truss for roasting. Mix 2 tsp/15 g of honey with melted butter, and brush all over the ducks. Roast for 25 minutes in a 355 °F/180 °C oven.

2. Deglaze the roasting pan, add the remaining honey and the crushed coriander, and caramelize the orange zest.

and Coriander Sauce

3. For the garnish: blanch the peeled potatoes, garnish with the quartered mushrooms, add the fried bacon dice, and season. Braise the onions in peanut oil, then add a little butter and a pinch of sugar and of salt.

4. Brush the ducks with the caramelized mixture and roast for a further 10 minutes. Take them out of the oven and keep warm. Skim the fat from the roasting juices and reduce until no moisture remains, deglaze with the wine vinegar and orange juice, and strain. Serve the ducks with the garnish. Scatter on top finely chopped chives and tarragon. Serve the sauce separately.

Mallard with Figs

Preparation time: 1 hour 30 minutes
Cooking time: 1 hour 30 minutes
Difficulty: ★★

Serves 4

2 mallard or other wild ducks
7 tbsp/150 g honey
2 garlic cloves
4 tbsp/30 g Szechuan pepper
4 tbsp/30 g coriander
1 tbsp/10 g caraway seed
4 cardamom seeds
1 tbsp/15 ml soy sauce

2 tbsp/30 ml sherry
salt

For the red cabbage with figs:
1 red cabbage
8 dried figs
2 large onions
1 fresh ginger root
⅔ cup/150 ml red wine
½ cup/120 ml port
6½ tbsp/100 ml olive oil
2 tbsp/30 ml vinegar
1 pinch of sugar
salt

The imaginations of Europe's best chefs have in recent years been stimulated by the flavors of Asian spices and their potential for combination. Here, the mallard, the most widely distributed breed of wild duck in Europe, is enhanced in a wondrous manner by these spices. If you are unable to obtain a true mallard, you can use other varieties of wild duck.

Red cabbage tastes best in the autumn and winter. A medium-sized head of red cabbage is just right for this recipe. Remove the largest leaves and the stalk, before chopping the cabbage finely and marinating. It should marinate overnight, which will make the cabbage more digestible. Don't use too much sherry: it has a powerful taste which should not be allowed to dominate the flavor of the cabbage. Measure out the Szechwan pepper with care as well.

This recipe is a variation on the Alsatian tradition of serving roast goose at Christmas with red cabbage or sauerkraut. The Auberge de l'Ill, which was established 100 years ago, successfully practices the fine art of variation, and this dish would be a suitable one for a festive occasion.

1. The day before, marinate the cabbage: cut out the stalk, quarter the cabbage and cut in thin strips, season with salt, sugar and vinegar, and let stand overnight.

2. The next day, braise the finely chopped onions in the olive oil. Then add the marinated red cabbage and the diced figs. Add the red wine, port and 3 slices of ginger. Braise gently in a 300 °F/150 °C for 1 to 1½ hours. Season to taste.

and Red Cabbage

3. In a clean coffee grinder, grind the Szechwan pepper, coriander, caraway and cardamom very finely. Mix the spices with the honey, soy sauce, sherry and garlic. Season the mallards inside and out with salt.

4. Prepare and truss the ducks and paint them with the spiced honey. Roast them in a 425 °F/220 °C oven for 20 minutes, then set aside to rest for about 15 minutes. Before serving, give them another coating of spiced honey, and reheat in the oven. Serve with the braised red cabbage.

Squab and Foie Gras

Preparation time: 1 hour 30 minutes
Cooking time: 35 minutes
Difficulty: ★★★

Serves 4

4 squab, about 1 generous lb/500 g each
8 slices raw foie gras
8 slices truffle
16 spinach leaves
2½ lb/1.2 kg puff pastry (see basic recipe)
8 Belgian endive
8 carrots

1 egg yolk
clarified butter
salt and pepper

For the stuffing:
7 oz/200 g lean pork
5¼ oz/150 g fatty pork
3½ oz/100 g pork fat
1¾ oz/50 g ham
1 small truffle, chopped
6½ tbsp/100 ml truffle juice
2 cups/500 ml port
salt and pepper

The truffle was once the subject of a superstition: the places where truffles grew were supposed to be avoided at night, as unholy powers were attributed to them, unless one took care to make the sign of the cross on each occasion. Later the fine flavor of this noble fungus was acknowledged and it became known as the "black diamond." A truffle takes several years to reach maturity. The black truffle is the ideal accompaniment for game birds: in this recipe it adds refinement to a squab in a puff pastry crust.

As the preparation of the stuffing is quite a lengthy process,

it is best to make it the day before, which also gives it a finer flavor. If making your own puff pastry intimidates you, by all means substitute frozen all-butter pastry.

Glazing the carrots is not difficult: after cutting them into attractive shapes, give them 10 minutes in a hot pan with a little water, some butter and a pinch of sugar. They should stay crisp, which will also give them a better appearance.

1. Remove the breasts from the squab, and skin them. Bone the thighs, leaving a small length of drumstick intact. Heat clarified butter in a hot pan, and brown the seasoned squab breasts and slices of foie gras.

2. Place 1 slice of truffle on each squab breast and top with a slice of foie gras. Let rest for 30 minutes. Prepare a stuffing from the ingredients listed. Blanch and refresh the spinach leaves. Spread the spinach leaves and the boned squab thighs with stuffing, and wrap the squab breasts and foie gras in the spinach leaves. Brown the stuffed squab thighs for 10 minutes.

Tourte with Truffles

3. Roll out the pastry. With a pastry cutter, cut out one small and one somewhat larger circle from the pastry. Paint the edges with egg yolk. Place the spinach-wrapped squab on the smaller circle, them cover with the larger. Wash the endive and slice diagonally. Braise the endive and glaze the carrots.

4. Close up the pastry edges with a fork, then paint with egg yolk. Set aside to rest for 15 minutes, then bake in a 425 °F/225 °C oven for 10–15 minutes. Let rest for 1 minute and then cut in half. Serve hot with the endive and carrots.

Sautéed Chicken with

Preparation time: 1 hour
Cooking time: 30 minutes
Difficulty: ★★

Serves 4

4 small poussins
2 carrots
2 turnips
2 black salsify

2 celery ribs
9 garlic cloves
8 cloves
24 walnuts
8 cups/2 l duck fat
1¼ cup/300 ml chicken stock
2 cups/500 ml milk
1 cup/250 ml cream
5 tsp/25 ml caraway liqueur (kümmel)
salt and pepper

Although Paul Heathcote is British, he was so impressed by French poultry from the Landes or Bresse that he persuaded his local breeders to adopt their methods: free-range rearing of the birds as well as feeding them on grain and dairy products. Paul Heathcote is happy with the resulting dense breasts, which are very tender after cooking.

Poussins must be cooked carefully because their flesh is very tender,. and as their flavor is not very powerful, you can serve them with a piquant sauce, like the walnut sauce of this dish.

The turnips should be as young as possible, as they will then be more tender and mild-tasting. Turnips have long been regarded as an everyday vegetable, fit only for the stock pot. However, they certainly come into their own in more elegant dishes. Alternatively they can be replaced by parsnips, a vegetable that remains popular in Great Britain and the United States, although the French have nearly forgotten its existence.

This recipe may perhaps induce you to discover the taste of kümmel, a liqueur based on caraway.

1. Cut the poussins into serving pieces. Peel the carrots, turnips, and salsify. Cut into strips, braise lightly and then brown for about 15 minutes with the cloves in the duck fat. Sauté the poussins on all sides for 7 minutes, remove the breasts and continue cooking the legs and thighs for a further 15 minutes; keep warm.

2. Dice the celery and boil in the milk for 20 minutes. Simmer two-thirds of the cream until it thickens. Drain the celery and purée in a blender; add all the cream and season to taste.

Celery and Walnuts

3. For the walnut sauce, blanch and peel the walnuts, add to the chicken stock and cook gently until the sauce is reduced by half. Braise the garlic cloves in butter until golden brown, add the vegetables and season to taste.

4. Spoon some celery purée onto the center of each plate, place thinly sliced chicken breast on top, and arrange the thighs and vegetables around. Pour the walnut sauce over the poussin and add a few drops of kümmel.

Preparation time: 1 hour 40 minutes
Cooking time: 1 hour 30 minutes
Difficulty: ★★★

Serves 4

2 pheasants
8 Savoy cabbage leaves
⅔ cup/200 g lentils
4 black salsify
8 shallots
1 lemon
parsley
¾ cup/200 ml duck fat
3½ tbsp/50 g butter
salt and pepper

For the Hochepot potatoes:
1 generous lb/500 g potatoes
1 carrot, sliced
½ onion, sliced

1 sprig of rosemary
10 tbsp/150 g melted butter

For the port wine sauce:
the pheasant carcasses
2 celery ribs
1 carrot
1 onion
1 garlic clove
1 bay leaf
1 sprig of thyme
6 peppercorns
¾ cup/200 ml port
¾ cup/200 ml veal stock
2 cups/500 ml white chicken stock
3½ tbsp/50 g butter
salt and pepper

Hochepot is originally a Flemish recipe; here Paul Heathcote introduces a variation using pheasant. Choose a hen pheasant, which has a more refined flavor than the male and does not have to be hung for as long, only a couple of days. If you are unable to obtain a hen pheasant, you could substitute another tender game bird, such as young partridges, grouse, or squabs.

The potato dish suggested here as an accompaniment is prepared in a traditional way. Use a "Pommes Anna" dish, a heavy, deep, straight-sided dish with a lid.

Experts are unable to agree over the origin of the word "hochepot." Some believe that it comes from the verb *hocher*, to shake, and reflects a need to shake the container, but this is not done in any of the recipes in which this term is used. We might conclude that the original dish, whose recipe has apparently been lost, was perhaps a kind of beef stew, which was cooked without water and could not be prepared without an energetic intervention on the part of the cook. On the other hand, it could just be a corruption of "hot pot," which brings us back to Paul Heathcote's Lancashire.

1. Prepare the pheasants if necessary. Remove the breasts and brown on both sides for 7–8 minutes until golden brown. Peel the shallots and braise in duck fat, season and set aside. Wash and blanch the Savoy cabbage leaves.

2. Peel and quarter the salsify and brown in butter until golden brown. Season with salt, pepper, lemon juice, and chopped parsley. Cook the lentils.

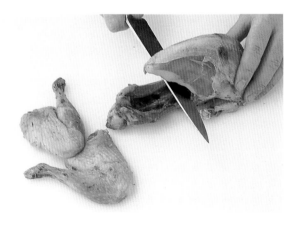

Hochepot Potatoes

3. Season the ingredients for the hochepot, line a buttered Pommes Anna mold or cake pan with a thick layer of potato slices, then fill it with the rest of the potatoes, the carrots, and the onions. Bake for 1 hour in the oven until it is cooked through and nicely colored on top.

4. For the sauce, brown the pheasant bones and the vegetables with the seasoning, deglaze with the port and reduce by half. Add the chicken stock, reduce by half again, finally adding the veal stock, deglaze for a few minutes, and strain. Bring to a boil, skim off the fat and impurities and reduce until it has the consistency of a sauce. Serve on warm plates.

Fillet of Beef with Braised

Preparation time: 1 hour 40 minutes
Cooking time: 3 hours 30 minutes
Difficulty: ★★★

Serves 4

6 beef tenderloin steaks, about 5½ oz/150 g
1 oxtail
1 Savoy cabbage
1 lb/450 g carrots
1 kohlrabi
7 oz/200 g leeks
oil

2 tsp/15 g arrowroot
1 bunch flat-leaf parsley
14 tbsp/100 g thyme
8 cups/2 l beef stock
2 cups/500 ml red wine
2 cups/500 ml beer, preferably Guinness stout
½ cup/125 ml red wine vinegar

For the potato purée:
2 lb/900 g potatoes
3½ tbsp/50 g butter
6½ tbsp/100 ml whipped cream

Paul Heathcote is partial to beef from both England and France, especially the Angus from the north of Scotland and the Charolais from France. For this recipe, you should choose high-quality beef that is full of flavor, juicy, rich in protein and very tender. The steaks should be cooked over medium heat and not for too long, so that the meat remains juicy.

The oxtail gives flavor to the sauce, and you should use the thickest part of the tail, which will provide more flavor. It

should be cooked until the meat is falling off the bone.

The vegetables are cut into large dice and browned only briefly, so that they do not get too soft. The choice of beer for the sauce depends on your taste, but our chef recommends Guinness, the famous stout of which the Irish are so rightly proud: daily consumption world-wide is said to exceed 8 million glasses. If you prefer some other beer, many others can be used in this dish.

1. Remove fat and sinews from the oxtail. Cut the carrots, leek and kohlrabi into large dice and the Savoy cabbage into small pieces, and cook. Reserve the vegetable trimmings.

2. Brown the oxtail pieces in oil for about 5 minutes, add the vegetable trimmings and deglaze with the vinegar and red wine.

Oxtail and Beer Sauce

3. Add beer, beef stock and seasoning, and braise in the oven until well cooked (about 3 hours). Remove the oxtail, skim off the fat, thicken the sauce with the arrowroot, and strain. Season the fillets of beef, sauté until done to your liking, and set aside to rest.

4. Boil the potatoes in their skins, then peel while they are still hot, and purée. Add the cream, beat with a whisk, then beat in the butter in small dice. Season to taste. Before serving, slice the steaks, and place on warmed plates with a piece of oxtail. Garnish with the vegetables, cabbage and a mound of potato purée. Pour the sauce around and serve hot.

Ptarmigan (or Grouse)

Preparation time: 50 minutes
Cooking time: 30 minutes
Difficulty: ★★

Serves 4

4 young ptarmigan or grouse
1 cup/250 g "Russian peas" (see comments below) or green lentils
4 Belgian endive
2 heads of garlic, divided into cloves
6½ tbsp/100 ml truffle juice
butter
juice of 1 lemon

parsley
salt and pepper

For the sauce:
carcasses and thighs of the ptarmigan
onions, carrots and celery, diced
1 garlic clove
2 cups/500 ml robust red wine
6½ tbsp/100 ml cream
6½ tbsp/100 g butter
juniper berries
lemon
salt and pepper

Hunting is permitted in Norway throughout the entire Arctic winter, providing a first-class opportunity to wander through the vast forests and get to know their wild life. Most interesting is the ptarmigan, with its feathered feet. It changes its plumage three times a year. While it is brownish in the summer, in winter it is as white as snow and thus well camouflaged in its natural surroundings. Ptarmigans live on buds and small fruits, which they find under the snow.

Choose young birds, which are more delicate and fine-flavored. As with all game birds, the meat must be carefully examined for gun shot before preparation. Like its distant relative, the wood-pigeon, the ptarmigan can become bitter if cooked too long, so you should limit the cooking time to 30 minutes.

Apart from the birds, this dish includes "Russian peas". These are roasted split peas that have a powerful flavor. They should be soaked in cold water the day before. During cooking, you should add plenty of butter. Their flavor can be enhanced even further by adding some truffle juice.

If you cannot get Russian peas, you can substitute lentils; other good accompaniments would be morels, or a fricassee of snails.

1. The day before, soak the Russian peas in water. Then gut and singe the birds. Remove the thighs. Brown for 10 minutes in plenty of butter with unpeeled garlic, until the skin is golden.

2. Prepare a sauce with the bones and the thighs, the diced vegetables, the juniper berries and lemon juice. Deglaze with the red wine, reduce and strain, then stir in butter and cream. Braise the endive with a little butter and lemon juice, in a covered pan; to finish, let them brown slightly so that they acquire a hint of color.

with Russian Peas

3. Cook the Russian peas in water and finally add butter, truffle juice and a little chopped parsley.

4. Carve the breasts of the birds into thin slices, and arrange on each plate with the braised endive. Distribute the Russian peas over the meat and pour some sauce on top.

Pickled Goose

Preparation time: 1 hour
Cooking time: 1 hour 20 minutes
Difficulty: ★★

Serves 4

1 goose, 8–9 lb/4 kg
10½ oz/300 g raw foie gras
16 turnips
16 carrots
1 rutabaga

1 onion
2 apples (such as Golden Delicious)
1¾ oz/50 g dried figs
⅔ cup/200 g green lentils
cloves, cardamom, nutmeg, aniseed, coriander
8 cups/2 l chicken stock
6½ tbsp/100 g butter
truffle juice (optional)
⅔ cup/200 g coarse salt
salt and pepper

Because of the severe climate and long winter, the nearer one gets to the Arctic Circle, the more important it becomes to make sure that foodstuffs can be preserved, because it is very difficult to obtain fresh food. For this reason, Norwegians preserve both fish and meat in coarse, iodine-rich sea salt.

The goose, with its thick layer of fat, is well suited to this treatment. But you should realize that salt makes the flesh firmer, and the meat must be rinsed several times after removing it from the brine. Then it should be coo-

ked over low heat in well seasoned stock. Eyvind Hellstrom recommends a traditional Norwegian accompaniment based on rutabagas and young turnips, cut into large pieces. Season this with spices such as cardamom and ground nutmeg. If you wish to give a southern accent to this Nordic dish, you can add thyme, rosemary or parsley.

In the spring you can change the accompaniment to fresh, crisp vegetables, cut small, such as carrots, new potatoes, and green beans.

1. Remove the liver from the goose. Place the goose in the coarse salt and leave it 24 hours. Next day, rinse several times in water. Remove the breasts carefully; cut them open and stuff with a mixture of foie gras, apples, diced dried figs, and the seasoning.

2. Wrap the roulade in cheesecloth and tie securely. Cut the vegetables into attractive shapes and rinse the lentils several times.

Breast with Lentils

3. Poach the roulade for about 1 hour in chicken stock, adding the lentils for the last 20 minutes. Cook the vegetables separately in boiling salted water.

4. Finally brown the roulade in a pan, skin side down. Slice it and place the slices on a bed of the lentils. Arrange the vegetables around the lentils and pour some melted butter, or truffle juice, over them.

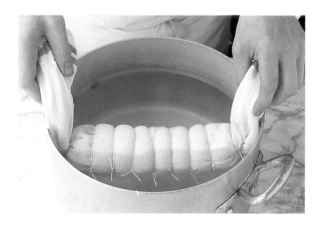

Karasjok Reindeer

Preparation time: 50 minutes
Cooking time: 1 hour
Difficulty: ✷✷

Serves 4

1 saddle of young reindeer, about 3⅓ lb/1½ kg
1 generous lb/500 g morels
4 potatoes
2 pears
2 tbsp/30 g goose fat
¾ cup/200 ml heavy cream
thyme
20 juniper berries
1 tbsp/30 g ground pepper

salt and pepper

For the sauce:
bones and trimmings from the reindeer
1 carrot
¼ celery rib
3 garlic cloves
1 onion
4 cups/1 l robust red wine
¾ cup/200 ml port
13 tbsp/200 g butter
10 ground coffee beans
thyme
gin

On the border between Norway and Finland lies the Karasjok region, a very large, icy area, which is partly inhabited by the Sami people and is particularly well suited for the rearing and hunting of reindeer. In these endless plains, neither time nor space seems to matter. Reindeer meat has a very strong flavor; particularly prized are the two-year-old reindeer calves.

The meat should remain pink after its brief cooking. The juniper berries form a kind of crust; there is great enthusiasm for this aromatic berry in northern Europe, where it is used to season sauerkraut and game. In Belgium the liqueur genever is made from it, and the town of Hasselt in the province of Limburg has even dedicated a museum to it.

The indispensable accompaniment to this dish is mushrooms: a fricassee of morels, which should first be cleaned with great care. In addition, our chef recommends the unusual combination of potatoes and pears, which will certainly surprise your guests; after cooking, these two ingredients can no longer be distinguished from one another.

The originality of this recipe lies in the sauce, which is made with coffee.

1. Cut the fillets from the saddle of reindeer and cut into 4 pieces of equal size. Season with juniper berries, thyme, salt and pepper. Wash the morels, brown them just before serving, and add a little heavy cream.

2. Prepare a sauce with the bones and trimmings, vegetables and seasonings. Add the red wine and port, reduce and infuse with the ground coffee beans. Strain, and whisk in butter just before serving.

with Juniper Berries

3. Peel and slice the potatoes and pears. Fry in goose fat. Drain on paper towels and then form into the shape of 4 pears with alternating slices of pear and potato. Bake for a few minutes in a 375 °F/190 °C oven and then keep warm.

4. Pan-fry the reindeer fillets for about 10 minutes, or until medium rare, then cut across the grain into thin slices. Lay the slices in the middle of 4 plates, place beside them a baked "pear," add the morels to the arrangement and pour the sauce around.

Roulade of Beef with Raisins,

Preparation time: 30 minutes
Cooking time: 5 minutes
Difficulty: ★★

Serves 4

3⅓ lb/1.2 kg sirloin steak
4 tbsp/30 g raisins
4 tbsp/30 g pine nuts
parsley
garlic

For the tomato sauce:
6 tomatoes
1 garlic clove
2 cups/500 ml olive oil

For the garnish:
3 tbsp/20 g raisins
3 tbsp/20 g pine nuts
some young chicory leaves
1¼ cup/300 ml oil
garlic

Alfonso Iaccarino's restaurant is called Don Alfonso in memory of his grandfather, to whom this recipe is also dedicated.

Up to the beginning of the 20th century in southern Italy, meat was eaten only on Sundays, because the dry climate precluded the development of pasture land, and the region was thus not suited for the rearing of cattle. Meat was simply grilled or fried and served with raisins and pine nuts. In the evening the meat juices served as a sauce for pasta.

Today, it is easy to obtain meat of excellent quality, and this method of preparation has been greatly refined. Use sirloin steak for preference; it is tender and juicy and will be even more tasty if you beat it flat.

Our chef likes to use very bright red tomatoes, which form the most important part of the accompaniment for this dish. They are puréed and seasoned with garlic. Braise the raisins with chicory leaves, whose bitter flavor forms a subtle contrast to the sweetness of the raisins.

1. Pound the slices of sirloin flat on a sheet of plastic wrap. Toast the pine nuts over moderate heat.

2. Lay on each piece of meat a few pine nuts and raisins, and some chopped garlic and parsley. Form a roulade and fasten with a skewer. For the tomato sauce, braise the garlic in olive oil. Remove the garlic, and add the peeled, seeded and diced tomatoes. Cook for a good 5–10 minutes.

Pine Nuts and Tomato Sauce

3. Brown the roulades on all sides in olive oil in a nonstick pan. When it is half cooked, add the tomato sauce. Simmer for 5 minutes.

4. Blanch the chicory leaves and brown over high heat with the pine nuts, raisins and garlic. Pour the sauce onto each of 4 plates, add the pine nuts, chicory leaves and raisins, and finally the meat, cut in half diagonally

Veal "Teriyaki"

Preparation time: 45 minutes
Cooking time: 15 minutes
Difficulty: ★

Serves 4

1 loin of veal
4 Belgian endive
1 small truffle
½ cup/60 g glutinous or sticky rice
¼ cup/60 ml Chinese oyster sauce
salt and pepper

For the marinade:
1 chile, chopped
2 tbsp/30 ml soy sauce

1 tsp chopped fresh coriander
1 garlic clove
3½ tbsp/50 ml olive oil
parsley

For the teriyaki sauce:
2 tbsp/30 ml soy sauce
1 tbsp/15 ml sesame oil
1 tbsp/15 ml stock
1 tomato

For the brunoise:
1 red pepper
1 zucchini
2 tbsp chives

When it is said that travel broadens the mind, it should be added that the palate also benefits, because without a doubt the flavors and traditional cooking techniques of other cultures expand and refine our eating habits and our taste. This is true, for example, of teriyaki, which is based on soy sauce. It is very popular in Japan and today enriches our Western cuisine.

The meat will gain in flavor if it is marinated overnight. It should be refrigerated until 30 minutes before preparation. You can make your meat even spicier with chile, but remove the seeds first and use it with discretion, because it is very pungent and may not suit all tastes.

It is important to use sticky rice for the truffled rice balls. The adjective "sticky" is not intended to be derogatory: it refers to an Asian round-grained rice that tends to stick together when cooked. You can form small balls with it that are so firm that they can be deep-fried without falling apart.

Instead of veal, you can also use thin slices of chicken breast for this dish.

1. Cut the veal into 4 equal steaks. Chop the truffle, mix with boiled rice and form 8 small balls. Prepare the brunoise with the chives, red pepper and zucchini.

2. Paint each steak with oyster sauce. Scatter with coriander, chile, garlic, soy sauce and finely chopped parsley. Then marinate for at least 2 hours.

and Rice Balls

3. Peel, seed and dice the tomato, place in a bowl and mix with a vinaigrette. Brush some oil on the steaks and broil until done to taste.

4. Deep-fry the rice balls in 360 °F/185 °C oil. Cut the meat into thin slices, then arrange in a fan shape on each plate and garnish with endive. Pour the oyster sauce over the endive and cover the edges of the meat with the teriyaki sauce.

Guinea Fowl

Preparation time: 1 hour
Cooking time: 20 minutes
Difficulty: ★★★

Serves 4

1 guinea fowl

For the liver ravioli:
¾ cup/100 g flour
3½ tbsp/50 ml water
liver of the guinea fowl
1 tsp/5 ml Chinese black bean sauce
chopped parsley
salt

For the guinea fowl and noodle nests:
guinea fowl thigh meat

3½ oz/100 g fresh Chinese egg noodles
1 tsp seeded chopped chile
1 tbsp/15 ml sesame oil
fresh coriander leaves

1 tbsp scallions
salt and pepper

For the guinea fowl breasts:
2 guinea fowl breasts (with skin)
5½ oz/150 g fresh Chinese egg noodles
½ red pepper
4 baby corn cobs
8 dried shiitake mushrooms
2 Chinese cabbage leaves
3½ tbsp/50 ml cooking juices from meat

For the marinade:
fresh coriander leaves
1 garlic clove
1 tsp ground ginger
1 tbsp/15 ml oyster sauce

Despite its frightful screeching, the guinea fowl has made itself welcome in the farmyard as well as at the most distinguished tables since the 17th century. The guinea fowl is not very large, but one weighing 2–3 lb/1–1½ kg is plenty for 4 people.

Typically, André Jaeger, has recommended an exotic variation on the guinea fowl, for which he uses ingredients that are comparatively unfamiliar in most of Europe. The breasts have to be removed, the skin and sinews carefully trimmed from the thighs and the fat removed. The breasts are marinated for 24 hours with finely chopped coriander leaves (which are also known as cilantro and Chinese parsley). This seasoning with its sophisticated aroma gives an extra nuance to the flesh of the guinea fowl. Brown the breasts very briefly in hot oil, to give them a nice color while preserving their tenderness.

This method can also be used for many other kinds of poultry, as long as their flavor goes well with the Asian spices.

1. Remove the breasts with their skin and place in the marinade for 24 hours. Remove the thighs; bone and remove sinews and fat. Soak the dried mushrooms in water. Chop the liver finely, and mix with the black bean sauce and parsley. For the pastry, pour 3½ tbsp/50 ml of boiling water over the flour and add a pinch of salt; make this into a smooth paste and set aside to rest.

2. Roll out the pastry and cut out circles 3 ½ in/8 cm in diameter. On each circle, place a teaspoonful of the liver stuffing, then close the edges by pinching together. Brown these dumplings in oil, then add ½ in/1 cm water. Cover and complete the cooking by steaming.

à l'Asiatique

3. Cut the thigh meat into pieces, then chop the scallions and chile finely and mix with the other ingredients. Roll some uncooked noodles around 1 tbsp of this mixture, forming a nest. Brown in hot oil and keep warm.

4. Peel the red pepper and cut into thin strips. Cut the Chinese cabbage into ¼ in/1 cm strips. Cook the mushrooms in the water in which they were soaked. Braise the pepper and cabbage strips, mushrooms, and halved baby corn lightly. Boil and refresh the noodles, brown the guinea fowl breasts in hot oil and set aside to rest. Slice the breasts and serve with the noodles, garnished with oyster sauce and the meat stock.

Preparation time: 30 minutes
Cooking time: 20 minutes
Difficulty: ★★

Serves 4

2 squab
4 slices raw foie gras, about 1¾ oz/50 g
4 fresh truffles, about ⅓ oz/10 g
3½ oz/100 g lean bacon
1 Savoy cabbage

2 onions
1 carrot
1 garlic clove
1 egg yolk
10½ oz/300 g puff pastry (see basic recipes)
1 cup/250 g butter
1¼ cups/300 ml veal stock
olive oil
thyme
bay leaves
salt and pepper

Roger Jaloux often uses puff pastry to provide a culinary surprise for his guests, as in this recipe.

Our chef has a great liking for game birds and excels in the preparation of quail, grouse, partridge and squab. He never tires of developing new recipes. Not all squab live up to his standards: the birds should have bright eyes and have been properly plucked. If you have to do this, don't tear out the feathers by force, but first gently remove the breast feathers, then those of the wings and finally the thigh feathers. This process is rather tedious but necessary to keep the skin intact. The squab has no gall bladder, but the crop and gizzard should be removed, any remaining feathers singed off and the breast meat carved off as carefully as possible.

For the puff pastry, you have two choices. You can make it yourself, allowing sufficient resting time after each turn of the pastry, or—if time is of the essence—fall back on frozen pastry, preferably all-butter. Despite some reser-vations, it is usually good enough in quality. In either case, make sure you have a large enough quantity before you begin to make this dish.

1. Prepare the squab, remove the breast meat, bone the thighs, and season with salt and pepper.

2. Choose some handsome-looking Savoy cabbage leaves and wash them, cut into thin strips, blanch in salted water and refresh. Brown the onions and bacon in butter, and add the cabbage strips. Braise for about 12 minutes. Make a sauce with the bones and veal stock.

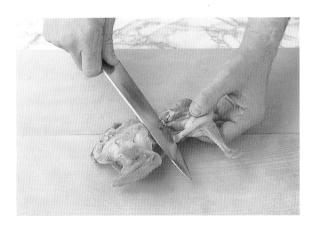

Puff Pastry

3. When the cabbage has cooled, lay a circle of pastry on baking parchment, and place on this a squab thigh. On top of this place a squab breast, a slice of foie gras and a slice of truffle. Finish with a heaping tbsp of cabbage. Repeat for three more portions.

4. Close up the pastry, paint with egg yolk and bake in a 390 °F/200 °C oven for about 20 minutes. Place 1 on each plate, cutting each pastry pocket in half and pouring on some sauce. More braised cabbage can be served as an accompaniment.

Braised Calf's Cheek

Preparation time: 20 minutes
Cooking time: 2 hours
Difficulty: ★★

Serves 4

8 calves' cheeks
1 green cabbage
¾ cup/100 g Puy lentils
4 carrots
2 shallots
½ head of garlic

2 onions
½ bay leaf
1 sprig of thyme
2 tbsp/30 g goose fat
2 tbsp/30 g butter
2 cups/500 ml dry white wine
4 cups/1 l veal stock
wine vinegar
3½ tbsp/50 ml olive oil
1 bunch of parsley
salt and pepper

Calf's cheek, with its pale pink flesh, is very suitable for braising. It is tender and should be simmered slowly over low heat, and should be turned at intervals to ensure even cooking. Once the meat is cooked it can be kept for 3 days. It will have even more flavor if prepared in advance and reheated before serving.

Wash and blanch a sufficient amount of cabbage leaves large enough to wrap a calf's cheek in. Make sure that the leaves don't tear, as they will have to contain some sauce as well.

The green Puy lentil, which carries a governmental seal of quality, is a true delicacy. The lentils should be well soaked in cold water before cooking. As they give off a lot of impurities while cooking, the pot should be skimmed several times. All in all, it takes some time to prepare this delicious autumn dish.

1. Brown the calves' cheeks in goose fat, beginning with the fatty side. Then add the garlic with a mirepoix of onions and 2 carrots. Add the veal stock and white wine, season with salt and pepper, cover, and braise for about 2 hours in a 300 °F/150 °C oven.

2. Wash the cabbage, then blanch in salted water. Refresh and drain. Put the lentils in a pan and cover with cold water. Chop the rest of the carrots finely and add to the pan. Add the thyme and bay leaf and simmer for 20–25 minutes over low heat.

with Lentil Vinaigrette

3. After braising the cheeks, remove from the pan, then strain the juices and reduce to the desired consistency. Wrap each cheek with some sauce in a cabbage leaf. Then wrap in aluminum foil, and reheat by steaming before serving.

4. Prepare a vinaigrette with wine vinegar, olive oil, salt and pepper. Drain the lentils and mix with the shallots and chopped parsley. Stir in the vinaigrette. Place a mound of lentils on each plate and place on top a braised calf's cheek, drizzled with butter. Pour the sauce around and serve.

Rabbit with Carrot Sauce,

Preparation time: 30 minutes
Cooking time: 25 minutes
Difficulty: ★★★

Serves 4

1 rabbit, about 3½ lb/1.5 kg
4 large carrots
1¾ lb/800 g new potatoes
1 bunch of flat-leaf parsley
juice of 1 lemon
1 tbsp goose fat
melted butter
salt and pepper

For the rabbit stock:
bones and trimmings of the rabbit
4 mushrooms
2 garlic cloves
1 onion
2 shallots
1 carrot
¾ cup/200 ml white wine
1 cup/250 ml veal stock
1 sprig of thyme
1 bay leaf

The rabbit was introduced to France in the Middle Ages to compensate for the lack of wild game there. It soon settled into its new surroundings and began to reproduce with its well-known speed. The*lapin de garenne* appeared in the seventeenth century, and then the domestic rabbit. Despite what you see in cartoons, rabbits do not live solely on carrots, but on alfalfa and other cereals, such as wheat and barley.

A good-size rabbit weighs 3½–4 lb/1.5–2 kg. Its flesh should be a fine, robust pink, covered by a very thin membrane. It is best to buy a whole rabbit and then cut it up carefully yourself, so the bones do not splinter. Patrick Jeffroy recommends blanching the rabbit meat beforehand in the stock, so it does not dry out. This makes the flesh much more tender.

The carrot sauce is a true tribute to this nutritious root vegetable. Varieties of carrot are distinguished according to color and shape.

If you want a change from potatoes, you can use Jerusalem artichokes, young turnips, or even crosnes ("Japanese artichokes").

1. Cut the rabbit into serving pieces. First remove the thighs, then the forelegs, and cut the rest of the rabbit into equal-size pieces. Remove the membrane, sinews, and fat. Season with salt and pepper. Set aside the kidneys and liver. Keep the bones and trimmings for the preparation of the stock.

2. For the sauce: lightly brown the bones and trimmings. Add a mirepoix made from the stock vegetables, with thyme and bay leaf. Add quartered mushrooms. Next, add the white wine, then the veal stock. Simmer for 20–25 minutes, occasionally skimming off the foam. Reduce the sauce and strain.

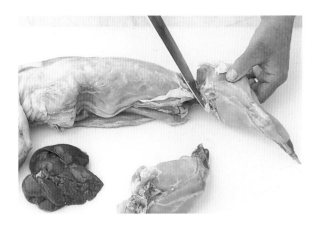

Potatoes, and Parsley

3. Brown the rabbit in goose fat until golden, then braise for about 20 minutes. Brown the liver and kidneys as well. Drain the meat and keep warm. Purée the carrot and add the lemon juice, then put through a fine strainer. Wash and peel the potatoes and boil in water, but do not allow them to become too soft.

4. Pour off the excess fat from the pan and add the carrot juice and some of the stock. Season with salt and pepper. Brown the potatoes in melted butter, then glaze the potatoes with the rest of the stock. Add parsley and arrange on each plate. Whisk some butter into the sauce and pour it over the rabbit.

Preparation time: *45 minutes*
Cooking time: *1 hour 30 minutes*
Difficulty: ★

Serves 4

1 young guinea fowl, about 3⅓ lb/1½ kg
7 oz/200 g boudin noir, or other blood sausage
6½ tbsp/100 g goose fat
4 potato pancakes

2 generous lbs/1 kg sauerkraut
1 red bell pepper
1 onion
2 garlic cloves
1¼ cup/300 ml white wine (such as Alsatian Riesling)
1 tbsp/10 g sweet Hungarian paprika
juniper berries
2 bay leaves
salt and pepper

Sauerkraut is the showpiece of Alsatian cuisine. Émile Jung has created a new variation, with guinea fowl, which is very popular for its delicate and flavorful meat. There is no better preparation for the guinea fowl than simply to sauté it with salt and pepper.

Sauerkraut is made from finely shredded white cabbage, which is salted and fermented; it becomes very nourishing as a result of this method of preservation. In Germany, a number of "sauerkraut cutters" would cut the cabbage for the women to prepare for their families during the winter.

Today, sauerkraut is available everywhere, raw or cooked, and even canned. The last-mentioned is not a good solution, as canned sauerkraut can have a metallic aftertaste. If you buy it raw, you must rinse it in cold water to get rid of the excess sourness and salt. The water should only just cover it during cooking, because too much water would dilute the flavor. As accompaniments, paprika and red pepper add further piquancy.

1. Carefully wash the sauerkraut twice. Then braise the finely chopped onion and garlic in 3½ tbsp/50 g of goose fat. Season the guinea fowl with salt and pepper. Roast for about 30 minutes in a 390 °F/200 °C oven. Keep warm.

2. When the onion and garlic are translucent, add the sauerkraut, juniper berries, and bay leaves, pour the wine over the mixture, and simmer, covered, for 1½ hours over low heat.

Sauerkraut and Red Pepper

3. Dice the red pepper and braise for 10 minutes in 3½ tbsp/50 g of goose fat. Add the paprika and stir over low heat. Keep warm. Poach the blood sausage for 15 minutes over low heat, then set aside.

4. Add the diced pepper to the sauerkraut. Divide the guinea fowl into four portions. Arrange some sauerkraut and a portion of guinea fowl on each plate, and garnish with a small piece of blood sausage and a pancake made from potato, grated and fried in goose fat.

Preparation time: 1 hour
Cooking time: 1 hour
Difficulty: ☆

Serves 4

1⅓ lb/600 g beef tenderloin, in 1 piece
14 oz/400 g potatoes
7 oz/200 g turnips
3½ oz/100 g white of leek
7 oz/200 g Savoy cabbage
3½ oz/100 g carrots
1 onion
3 tbsp/50 g grated horseradish

1 cup/250 ml white wine (such as Alsatian Riesling)
3 cups/750 ml white stock
salt and pepper

For the marinade:
1 cup/250 ml white wine (such as Alsatian Riesling)
2 carrots
2 onions
garlic cloves
1 bouquet garni
peppercorns

During the 19th century, housewives from Alsace prepared the traditional version of this country recipe in the morning using 3 kinds of meat—lamb, beef and pork, which had been marinated overnight in white wine. The vegetables were added in the morning and the mixture taken to the baker, who would cook it in a cool oven from 10 a.m. until noon, so it would be ready for the midday meal for the entire family.

Here Émile Jung suggests preparing beef tenderloin in this way. The meat must be marinated overnight. In the morning, simmer the vegetables until tender (you can also add celery to those listed). The young white turnips, which are rich in vitamins and minerals, are very appropriate. The "baeckeoffe" should be braised over low heat, and the meat must remain pink in the center.

The regional characteristics of this dish include the use of grated horseradish. This large root from the Cruciferae family has a very pronounced flavor and should be grated at the last possible moment, so that the essential oils, similar to those of mustard, do not dissipate. In France, horseradish is sometimes known as "German mustard," a justifiable term considering the extent to which it is used in German cuisine.

1. Marinate the meat overnight with the sliced onions, the halved garlic cloves, the diagonally cut carrots, the bouquet garni and a few white peppercorns, and a cup of white wine.

2. Slice the potatoes, leek, turnips, carrots, and onion, blanch the Savoy cabbage and cut into thin strips. Cook all the vegetables in a braising pan with the white stock and the white wine for 30 minutes.

Beef Tenderloin

3. Add the vegetables to the beef, cover and cook for 30 minutes. Remove the meat and set aside to rest for 10 minutes, then cut into 8 slices. Arrange the vegetables on the plates, alternating according to type and color.

4. Using a ladle, form the cabbage into mounds and place on the plates. Reduce the cooking juices and pour on top of the vegetables. Place two slices of beef on top of the vegetables on each plate. Season with coarse salt and garnish with horseradish before serving.

Preparation time: 2 hours
Cooking time: 15 minutes
Difficulty: ★

Serves 4

1¾ lb/800 g rack of suckling pig
7 oz/200 g pork loin
7 oz/200 g pork caul (if available)
⅔ cup/200 g potato purée
1 generous lb/500 g potatoes

1 Savoy cabbage
finely diced celery, carrot, onion and leek
1 cup/250 ml chicken stock
1 cup/250 g butter
4 tsp/20 ml beer
2 cups/500 ml cream
1 egg white
thyme
rosemary
salt and pepper

It is probably no surprise that the combination of suckling pig and beer is widely popular in Germany, and it gives sparkle to many a festive occasion.

Experience has shown Dieter Kaufmann that a suckling pig of 6 to 8 lb/3 to 4 kg, which can be cooked in one piece, is the best to use. The most delicious part is the saddle, and it is even better when prepared a few days in advance. To give the meat a good color, it should be cooked slowly; allow a good 2 hours for a whole suckling pig, less if you are cooking only the saddle. If you are unable to get suckling pig, you can use the same method with pork tenderloin or spring lamb.

Dieter Kaufmann uses Altbier from Düsseldorf, a light brown beer with a low alcohol content that goes well with the other ingredients. This beer is a good match for the potato dumplings.

If you cannot obtain pork caul, brush the cabbage-wrapped pork with olive oil and baste during cooking.

Your guests will rave about this combination of suckling pig and beer.

1. Remove the skin and fat from the pork and French the ribs. Finely grind the pork and work in the cream and egg white and 1 tbsp of diced vegetables browned in butter. Season the stuffing to taste. Blanch and dry the cabbage, and remove the veins from the leaves.

2. Season the rack of pork and spread with stuffing. Cut the remaining cabbage into thin strips, blanch and braise in butter. Prepare the potato purée.

in Beer Sauce

3. Wrap the rack in the cabbage leaves and then in the pork caul (if used). Brown in an ovenproof skillet, then roast for 6–7 minutes in a 430 °F/220 °C oven.

4. Brown the bones and skin of the rack with the rest of the diced vegetables. Deglaze with beer. Add a ladleful of chicken stock, reduce, then stir in some butter. Put some sauce on each plate, then arrange a portion of potato purée and the cabbage on the plate alongside the meat.

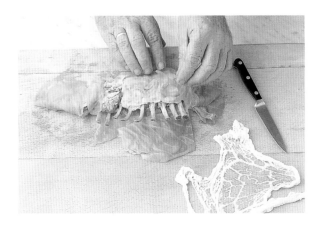

Sweet and Sour

Preparation time: 1 hour 30 minutes
Cooking time: 20 minutes
Difficulty: ★★

Serves 4

2 generous lb/1 kg beef tenderloin, in 1 piece
1 generous lb/500 g chopped veal bones
2 cups/250 g dried Zanté currants
red cabbage
diced carrot and celery
⅔ cup/150 ml sugar-beet or cane syrup
2 cups/500 ml crème fraîche
6½ tbsp/100 ml peanut oil
3½ tbsp/50 g sugar
salt and pepper

For the marinade:
4 cups/1 l vinegar
2 cups/500 ml water

6 onions
3 bay leaves
2–3 cloves
juniper berries
3½ tbsp/50 g salt
3½ tbsp/50 g sugar

For the bread dumplings:
4–6 day-old rolls
1 cup/250 ml beef stock
1 cup/250 ml milk
1¾ oz/50 g lean bacon
1 onion
2 eggs
2 tbsp/30 g butter
bread crumbs
salt, nutmeg, chervil

To make traditional sauerbraten, it used to be necessary to marinate the meat for 2 weeks, and it took several hours to cook. Here, Dieter Kaufmann suggests a less time-consuming variation, with a tender cut of meat marinating in vinegar for only 6–8 hours (longer would mask the flavor of the meat). Then the tenderloin is browned very quickly so it is cooked only medium-rare.

It is better to prepare the sauce in advance, because you might not have time to do so just before serving. The originality of this recipe relies on the use of *Rübensirup*, sugar-beet syrup, a specialty of the Rhineland, where a great deal of sugar-beet is grown. Dieter Kaufmann remembers helping himself to sugar-beets from a truck just after the war, and eating bread spread with sugar-beet syrup.

In order to follow tradition even further, this beef tenderloin is served with Kaufmann's unbeatable dumplings. They are usually made from day-old rolls and can be seasoned in various ways according to taste. The lean bacon and onions recommended here can easily be replaced with mushrooms such as chanterelles, or any other ingredient that will add flavor.

Among poorer families, rabbit was often substituted for beef; you could try this alternative, which has a finesse of its own.

1. Mix the vinegar with the water. Place the beef in a nonreactive dish with the other marinade ingredients and cover with the liquid. Marinate for 8 hours in the refrigerator.

2. Brown the chopped onions and lean bacon in butter. Remove from the heat and mix with diced rolls, milk, chervil, eggs, salt and pepper. Let rest for 1 hour. Shred the red cabbage and braise in butter with a pinch of sugar.

Beef Tenderloin

3. Brown the beef, turning several times, for about 20 minutes with the veal bones and the vegetables from the marinade. Remove the beef and let rest. Deglaze with half of the liquid from the marinade, reduce and add the sugar-beet syrup and crème fraîche. Boil for a few minutes, then strain and add the raisins.

4. Form bread dumplings about the size of a golf ball. Poach for 6–7 minutes in boiling salted water. Place 3 slices of beef on each plate, and garnish with dumplings, sauce and some red cabbage.

Preparation time: 20 minutes
Cooking time: 10 minutes
Difficulty: ☆

Serves 4

14 oz/400 g smoked reindeer
12 eggs

8 tsp/40 g butter
6½ tbsp/100 ml crème fraîche
fresh thyme
salt and pepper

For the garnish (optional):
bleak roes (the bleak is a small river fish)

In Sweden, hospitality is a time-honored tradition. The rocky roads and the harsh Scandinavian climate meant that wanderers were always welcomed into the home. In every home a fortifying buffet would be ready and waiting—the so-called *aquavitbord* of herring, various types of bread, cheeses and, of course, various spirits. Later these buffets were given the name of smorgasbord, and other ingredients were added, such as smoked reindeer meat.

Reindeer are raised by the Sami people and are a real delicacy. The meat has a very strong flavor and the milk of the female reindeer is highly esteemed and is used for making cheese. However, populations are slowly diminishing, to a great extent because the reindeer is hardly used any more as a draft animal.

There are many ways to prepare reindeer: roasted, with a creamy sauce, or as steak with morels and cream. Here the smoked reindeer steaks are briefly browned in the pan.

The accompaniment of scrambled eggs slightly softens the powerful flavor of the meat. Potatoes or cranberry sauce would also fulfill this function. If your butcher is unable to obtain supplies from near the Arctic Circle, you can use the same method for smoked venison.

1. For the scrambled eggs, mix the eggs, crème fraîche, salt and pepper.

2. Melt the butter in a pan and add the egg mixture. Stir with a wooden spoon until done.

from Lapland

3. Add fresh thyme.

4. Cut the smoked reindeer meat into thin slices. Brown the sliced meat quickly, without fat. Put the scrambled eggs in the center of each plate, arrange the reindeer slices around them, and top, if you wish and can obtain it, with bleak roe.

Corned Brisket of Beef with

Preparation time: 45 minutes
Cooking time: 3 hours
Difficulty: ★★

Serves 4

2 generous lb/1 kg corned beef brisket
7 oz/200 g new potatoes
1 bunch of small carrots
4 small leeks
7 oz/200 g Savoy cabbage

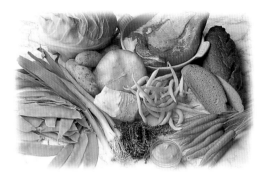

7 oz/200 g turnips
7 oz/200 g snow peas
7 oz/200 g wax beans
1 bunch of fresh thyme
1 piece of horseradish
Dijon mustard
rye bread
butter
bouquet garni
salt and pepper

Until recent times, the wide, open spaces of Sweden made travel and communications difficult and fostered the development of elaborate ways of preserving food, including salting meat. Our chef explains the process: the beef must be marinated for 4–6 days in an 18 percent salt solution with the addition of saltpeter, and kept cool. The meat must then be rinsed before cooking. To avoid an unwelcome surprise, it is advisable to taste the cooking water and to change it if it still tastes too salty, because this shows that the meat still carries too much evidence of its method of preservation.

If you do not have time to salt the beef yourself, buy it already salted, and cook it in a flavorful stock, so the meat becomes nicely tender and can be eaten "with a spoon," as the saying goes. Use the leaner part of the brisket, and cut thick slices out of the side part.

To bring out the full flavor of the meat, Örjan Klein uses strongly flavored horseradish, whose pungent aroma will delight you. But serve it separately, so that your guests can help themselves.

1. Place the brisket in boiling water with the bouquet garni and return to a boil. Simmer for 2½–3 hours, until the flesh is fork-tender, skimming the froth from time to time. Remove the meat and reserve the cooking liquid. Weight the meat with a heavy can or clean brick and let it rest overnight in the refrigerator.

2. Prepare the vegetables, cook separately in salted water, refresh. Reheat with some butter just before serving.

Vegetables and Horseradish

3. Cut the brisket into thick slices and reheat in the cooking liquid.

4. Arrange the meat and all the vegetables decoratively on a serving dish. Serve with rye bread, mustard, grated horseradish and thyme.

Loin of Lamb with

Preparation time: *1 hour 15 minutes*
Cooking time: *1 hour 15 minutes*
Difficulty: ★★★

Serves 4

2 loin roasts of lamb
4 dates
8 Belgian endive
8 shallots

1 tbsp mustard
4 cups/1 l lamb stock
¼ cup/60 ml red wine vinegar
2 cups/500 ml port
fresh mint leaves
4 star anise
1 tbsp sugar
1 tbsp butter
salt and pepper

The combination of lamb and dried fruit is a favorite one in Morocco, and in Europe, lamb is often spiced "in the traditional manner" with coarse mustard. Here both traditions are united.

The boned loin, which is stuffed and rolled, should first be browned for about 10 minutes to render the fat. The main cooking is then done in the oven on a small bed of potato. Don't forget to allow the meat to rest a little after cooking, in order to regain all its tenderness.

The date originally came from North Africa and the Middle East. It contains phosphorus and calcium, and its use in gastronomy is no longer confined to desserts. According to legend, the date grove of Marrakech grew up from the date pits that the workers discarded while building the royal city.

1. Bone the lamb and trim excess fat. Remove the flaps of meat from the sides and trim excess fat from them. Lightly pound the flaps to produce thin slices. Pit and purée the dates and mix with the mustard.

2. Spread the date and mustard mixture over the flaps of meat. Wrap a piece of loin and a piece of tenderloin in each flap, then tie into cylinders.

Dates and Mustard Seeds

3. Braise the finely chopped shallots, deglaze with the red wine vinegar and reduce until the liquid has disappeared. Deglaze again with the port and reduce again. Add the lamb stock, star anise and some mint leaves. Simmer, strain and keep warm.

4. Separate the endive leaves and blanch. Braise them in butter and sugar over moderate heat until golden. Brown the lamb and cook until medium-rare. Let the meat rest, then cut into 1 in/2 cm thick slices. Put some sauce on each of the plates and arrange 4 lamb slices and some endive on them.

Guinea Fowl with Kidneys,

Preparation time: *45 minutes*
Cooking time: *20 minutes*
Difficulty: ★★

Serves 4

4 boneless guinea fowl breasts
1 veal kidney
7 oz/200 g spinach
1 tbsp shallots, chopped
1 garlic clove
3–5 oz/100–150 g pork caul (if available)
4 tsp/20 g butter

oil
salt and pepper

For the vegetable mixture:
2 rutabagas
2 carrots
1 oz/30 g smoked bacon
6½ tbsp/100 ml brown veal stock
1 tbsp shallots, chopped
¾ cup/200 ml cream
4 tsp/20 g butter
salt and pepper

The guinea fowl is very popular in Switzerland, where it is stuffed like a chicken. This colorful gallinaceous bird from Africa, which in ancient times was known as "Numidian" or "Carthaginian chicken," is here prepared with veal kidney, which is firm and white, still enveloped in fat. The guinea fowl should be juicy and plump, with the skin still on the breasts.

Oour chef recommends a farmyard guinea fowl, or a young bird whose carcass is still quite soft. According to tradition, the bird should be allowed to rest for two days before cooking because it tastes even better then.

The kidney is browned in hot oil to make it firmer for stuffing. Instead of spinach, ytou can make the stuffing with finely chopped cabbage if you prefer.

The garnish consists of rutabaga, which remains firm when cooked and is very digestibl, teamed with carrots and diced bacon. You can replace the rutabagas with turnips or even kohlrabi, if you prefer. The vegetable mixture requires very careful preparation. It is cooked in two stages, which should be brief so the vegetables are cooked evenly.

1. Cut the kidney into strips about ½ in/1 cm wide, season with salt and pepper, and brown very briefly in hot oil. Set aside. Braise the chopped shallot in butter, add the spinach, season and add half a garlic clove. Mix well and remove from the pan.

2. Butterfly the guinea fowl breasts, season, and pound lightly. Place on each a few cooked spinach leaves, 1–2 strips of kidney, and a few more spinach leaves. Fold the meat over the stuffing. Wrap each in a piece of pork caul that has previously been soaked in water (if you don't have pork caul, brush with olive oil and baste frequently during roasting). Set aside.

Rutabagas and Carrots

3. Peel the rutabagas and carrots, cut into ⅛ in/3–4 mm slices and cook separately and briefly in salt water; they will be cooked again in the cream. Braise the chopped shallots and the diced bacon in butter, deglaze with the veal stock, reduce a little and then add the vegetables and the cream.

4. Simmer the vegetables for a further 10 minutes, so the flavors can mingle well. Brown the stuffed breasts in an ovenproof skillet, then roast for 7 minutes in an oven at 485 °F/250 °C. Let rest for 5 minutes, then slice and arrange on each plate with some rutabagas and carrots.

Preparation time:	45 minutes
Cooking time:	45 minutes
Difficulty:	✹✹

Serves 4

2 young squab, about 1 generous lb/500 g
3½ oz/100 g raw foie gras

1 oz/30 g truffles
3½ oz/100g oyster mushrooms
4 potatoes
1 egg yolk
9 tbsp/140 g butter
¾ cup/200 ml truffle juice
¾ cup/200 ml chicken stock
salt and ground pepper

In certain parts of France, squab is a traditional Christmas dish, served with the flesh still pink, with a glass or two of Bordeaux.

In Burgundy, and particularly in Morvan, the squab, like its parents, is fed on maize, wheat, and peas. According to the best breeders, it is this diet that makes the birds' flesh so delicate and tasty. Despite the hardness of its food, it has a fragile beak. At the end of its short life (28 days), the squab averages about 14 oz/400 g.

The pink flesh must be browned in a skillet for 15 minutes before being wrapped in the pastry and baked in the oven. This quarter of an hour is essential to allow the heat to disperse evenly throughout the meat. Squab does not tolerate very long treatment, so both cooking times are short.

Instead of the truffle sauce you can, of course, prepare a different sauce. A well-balanced mixture of two dessert wines, such as Madeira and port, reduced until practically no liquid remains and to which butter is added, will enrich this dish with a very intense aroma. If you make the sauce in the morning, you will gain both time and also flavor. There is another interesting variation on this dish, using noisettes of lamb, prepared in the form of rolls.

1. Prepare the squab, cut off the wing tips and the neck. Cut each squab into 4 serving pieces. Heat the butter in an ovenproof skillet and brown the squab lightly on all sides, basting frequently. Then roast for 8 minutes in a 430 °F/220 °C oven.

2. Keep the squab pieces warm. Paint the birds with egg yolk. Peel 4 potatoes, hollow them with an apple-corer, and boil or steam until tender.

with Truffles

3. Roll each squab piece in finely chopped truffles, then reheat them in the oven. Drain the potatoes and fill with a purée of liver and chopped truffles.

4. Reduce the truffle juice by half and add the chicken stock. Put some sauce on each plate and arrange a wing, a thigh, some oyster mushrooms and 2 potato halves on top.

Preparation time: 45 minutes
Cooking time: 25 minutes
Difficulty: ★★

Serves 4

1 chicken, about 4½ lb/2 kg
1¾ oz/50 g fresh chanterelles
½ cup/50 g corn kernels
12 baby leeks

6½ tbsp/100g butter
2 cups/500 ml onion juice, made by juicing 5 medium onions
6½ tbsp/100 ml chicken stock
chives
salt and pepper

For the syrup:
2 tbsp/25 g sugar
3½ tbsp/50 ml water

For a long time the flesh of poultry was considered to be lean, and so people were occasionally allowed to eat it on fasting days, when meat was normally forbidden.

Following the basic revolution in taste that occurred during the Renaissance, poultry came into its own in gastronomy. Highly regarded birds include the poulard, a chicken 7–8 months old that has not yet laid any eggs and is especially fattened to produce a very delicate flesh. Bresse poultry is of particularly high quality: each bird has plenty of room in which to wander, and is fed on maize and milk.

The stuffed chicken rolls can be prepared in advance, so the meat will absorb the flavor of the stuffing ingredients. Because of their thickness, the chicken thighs should be steamed for 10 minutes in advance before they are cooked with the wings.

Corn goes excellently with chicken and is thus an ideal accompaniment. Onions are a basic cooking ingredient whose character is well suited to making stock for a sauce.

For a slightly sharper taste, in the hunting season you can substitute pheasant for Bresse chicken.

1. Prepare the chicken: remove and bone the breasts, wings and thighs. With a meat mallet, lightly pound the chicken pieces until flat. Cook the leeks in salted water. Lightly cook the corn in butter and set aside.

2. Finely chop the chicken breast meat and the mushrooms. Season and prepare as stuffing. Stuff the thighs and wings with this mixture, roll up and tie. Wrap in aluminum foil and refrigerate.

Caramelized Onion Sauce

3. Reduce the onion juice by half. Prepare a light caramel with sugar and water. Add the onion juice and simmer for 15 minutes, or until reduced to about ½ cup/125 ml. Whisk in the butter and chicken stock, then season to taste.

4. Steam the thighs for 10 minutes, basting frequently, then brown in a skillet with the wings. Divide the thighs in half, and slice the wings. Garnish with corn, small pieces of leek, chives and sauce.

Ragout of Duck

Preparation time: 45 minutes
Cooking time: 1 hour
Difficulty: ★★

Serves 4

1 large duck, 6½—7½ lb/3–3½ kg
1 generous lb/500 g red cabbage
1¾ oz/50 g smoked bacon
4 turnips
6 plums

1¾ oz/50 g flour
3 tbsp/45 g duck fat or oil
1⅔ cup/400 ml red wine
red wine vinegar
1 sprig of thyme
salt and pepper

For the sauce:
1 onion
½ celery rib
2 garlic cloves

In Denmark, November 11 is the Feast of the Duck. Duck with apples or with red cabbage and plums is the traditional St. Martin's Day dinner.

Our chef advises you to use a good wine for the sauce. The accompanying vegetables have been chosen with care, and you should make sure that the balance of flavors is preserved. Note that the breast meat, legs, and skin are all coo-

ked separately to bring out the best in each. Finally, the bacon gives the dish a smoky character, which is the way the Danes like it.

The red cabbage, whose slightly sweet taste goes well with this dish, can be prepared in advance with vinegar. In Denmark the custom at Christmas is to serve glazed potatoes as an accompaniment.

1. Remove the breasts and legs from the duck. Bone the thighs. Skin the breasts and cut each into 4 slices. Dice the smoked bacon. Peel the turnips and cut each into six pieces. Pit the plums and cut each into 2–3 pieces.

2. Brown the duck skin in a skillet until crisp. Set aside the fat. Cook the turnips in salted water with 1 tbsp/15 g of duck fat. Add the plums and slowly heat until the water has evaporated. Make a sauce from the carcasses and leg bones and coarsely chopped vegetables.

with Red Cabbage

3. Brown the boned duck meat and the smoked bacon in duck fat scented with thyme. Pour off the fat and stir in the flour. Turn the pieces of meat and add the red wine and duck stock. Cover and simmer over very low heat for 15 minutes. Then remove the meat, strain the liquid and reduce. Return the meat to the sauce.

4. Braise the red cabbage with duck fat; season and add the red wine vinegar. Serve the meat with the cabbage and turnips, and pour the sauce on top.

Roast Breast of Veal

Preparation time: *1 hour*
Cooking time: *1 hour 30 minutes*
Difficulty: ★★

Serves 4

3⅓ lb/1½ kg boned breast of veal
1 bouquet garni
1 small onion stuffed with a clove
1 sprig of parsley
celery leaves
salt and pepper

For the baked apples:
3 apples
1 onion, chopped

¼ celeriac
¾ cup/200 ml veal stock
1 tsp ground mustard seeds
1 tbsp/15 ml vinegar
1 tsp Dijon mustard
1 tsp curry powder
2 tbsp/30 g butter
chives

For the beet salad:
2 raw, medium-sized beets
1 garlic clove
1 chopped shallot
5 tbsp/75 ml salad oil
juice of ½ lemon
salt and white pepper

Breast of veal is a somewhat neglected cut in the United States, but it is one of the most economical cuts of veal and is delicious and succulent if prepared carefully.

The accompaniments for this recipe are in accordance with Danish tradition, according to which potatoes are often served with apples. Choose new potatoes or a variety such as Yukon gold, which will go superbly with this mustard-scented roast.

Celeriac, also known as celery root, is also wonderful with apples and with the flavor of curry. The beet salad, also a Scandinavian specialty, completes this dish—with its profusion of root vegetables—to perfection.

1. *Cover the meat with water, add salt, and simmer with the vegetables, skimming off the froth from time to time.*

2. *After 1½ hours, remove the meat, season lightly with salt, cover with a sheet of plastic wrap and press under a heavy object, such as a baking sheet weighted with a couple of cans of tomatoes. Strain the stock and reduce until the required consistency is obtained. Cut the beets into thin slices and marinate with oil, lemon juice, garlic, chopped shallots and pepper.*

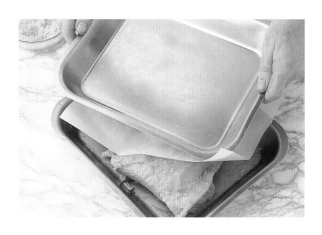

with Apples and Beets

3. Cut the unpeeled apples and the peeled celeriac into 2 in/5 mm cubes. Braise the onions in butter with the curry powder and mustard seed. Deglaze with vinegar and mustard. Add some of the cooking stock, reduce and strain. Whisk in the butter and set aside.

4. Reheat the meat in a little of the stock, then slice. Sauté the celeriac and apple cubes over high heat, mix with the sauce and season. Serve the beet salad separately.

Chicken with Artichokes,

Preparation time: 30 minutes
Cooking time: 15 minutes
Difficulty: ✳

Serves 4

4 chicken breasts with the 1st joint of the wings
4 small artichokes

2 fennel bulbs
4 sun-dried tomatoes
¾ cup/200 ml olive oil
4 tsp/20 ml balsamic vinegar
4 sprigs of rosemary
parsley leaves
salt and pepper

In Italy the art of drying tomatoes is passed on from generation to generation. First the halved tomatoes are dried in the sun on long strings, then they are steeped in olive oil with herbs.

For this recipe, use tomatoes, fennel and artichokes that are as fresh as you can get them. If possible, you should use the small purple artichokes of Southern Europe. They can be eaten raw or cooked.

The chicken breasts should come from good-quality poultry; preferably free-range and organically raised. It is worth it to seek out a good chicken supplier.

Balsamic vinegar from Modena, matured for many years in a succession of barrels, is an excellent product, whose inimitable flavor will enrich your dish. Rosemary has a typically robust Mediterranean character, and should therefore be used with discretion.

1. Chop the fennel, artichokes and dried tomatoes. Braise in a ceramic casserole with olive oil and rosemary, but do not brown.

2. Season the chicken breasts and add to the vegetables. Add a little water. Bring to a boil, cover the pot and place in a 430 °F/220 °C oven for 6–7 minutes.

Fennel and Tomatoes

3. Remove the chicken breasts and cut into thin slices. Completely reduce the cooking liquid over medium heat.

4. Add the parsley to the vegetables and deglaze with balsamic vinegar. Arrange the vegetables in the center of the serving dish and place the chicken breast on top. Pour some oil over it and garnish with rosemary.

Loin of Lamb with Fennel

Preparation time: *1 hour*
Cooking time: *30 minutes*
Difficulty: *★★*

Serves 4

1 loin roast of lamb, about 3⅓ lb/1½ kg
3 fennel bulbs
4 tomatoes

1 zucchini
½ head of garlic
1¾ oz/50 g black olives
10 tbsp/150 g butter
¾ cup/200 ml olive oil
¾ cup/200 ml chicken stock
lamb stock
3 tbsp/20 g star anise
salt and pepper

There is hardly an animal more intimately connected with mystical and religious traditions than the lamb. The Easter lamb is the incarnation of purity and the newborn lamb the embodiment of innocence.

The flesh of the lamb reared entirely on its mother's milk is particularly beloved by connoisseurs. The loin is a flavorful and tender cut of meat. The roasting should be carefully monitored, as lamb does not respond well to over-cooking.

Star anise is not related to aniseed. It has a distinctive star shape and a powerful anise flavor. It is also used to make tea. The flavor of anise occurs in fennel as well.

1. Remove and wash the outer layers of the fennel, and hollow small "boats" out of the hearts. Poach the hearts in salted water for about 10 minutes with 1 star anise.

2. Take three-quarters of the unpeeled garlic, the outer layers of the fennel and the peeled, quartered tomatoes and simmer for 15–20 minutes in chicken stock. Roast the lamb in a 450 °F/230 °C oven for 20–25 minutes.

Tomatoes and Star Anise Sauce

3. Pit the olives. Dice the zucchini, the olives, and the trimmings from the fennel hearts. Braise these vegetables in olive oil with the rest of the finely chopped garlic.

4. Strain the stock and whisk in the butter. Place mounds of the vegetable stuffing on the fennel hearts and top each one with a quartered tomato. Arrange the vegetable "boats" on the plates. Reheat in the oven. Remove the lamb and carve into noisettes. Arrange on each plate in a star shape with the vegetable "boats" and pour the sauce over them.

Calf's Sweetbreads with

Preparation time: 1 hour
Cooking time: 40 minutes
Difficulty: ★★

Serves 4

1 veal kidney
2 calf's sweetbreads
3 Belgian endive
1 truffle
2 tbsp/30 ml truffle juice
¾ cup/200 ml cream
1 egg

6½ tbsp/100g butter
flour
salt and pepper

For braising the sweetbreads:
butter
½ onion
1 carrot
1 sprig of thyme
1 bay leaf
¾ cup/200 ml red port
¾ cup/200 ml beef stock
¾ cup/200 ml veal stock

The sweetbread or thymus gland is a transient gift of nature, because it disappears as the animal matures. Its flesh is pale and, when fresh, odorless. It is a somewhat time-consuming process to remove the residual blood and other impurities that the sweetbread may contain. For this reason Michel Libotte recommends blanching it on the morning before you make this dish.

Libotte demonstrates his loyalty to the specialties of his native Belgium by giving the main role in this dish to Belgian endive. The concerted efforts of growers have made it possible to enjoy it all year round. There are early and late varieties of this vegetable in addition to the main crop, which is available from September to February.

If Belgian endive is too bitter for you (although this can be prevented by removing the core), you can replace it with fresh celery.

1. Soak and blanch the sweetbreads and then remove the thin surrounding membrane. Season and dredge in flour.

2. Brown the sweetbreads in butter until golden, then add diced onion, carrot, and thyme and bay leaf. Braise for a few minutes, then deglaze with the port, the beef stock and three quarters of the veal stock. Braise in a 350 °F/180 °C oven for 15 minutes. Halve the Belgian endive lengthwise, trim off the ends and cook in butter.

Kidneys and Belgian Endive

3. Finely chop the truffle, braise in butter and deglaze with truffle juice and the remaining veal stock. Add the cooked endive and continue to braise. Prepare a hollandaise sauce: beat an egg yolk with some lukewarm water and whisk in melted butter.

4. Truss and season the kidney. Brown in butter until golden and then transfer to a 350 °F/180 °C oven for 15 minutes, turning once. Let rest, and then slice both the kidney and sweetbreads. Reduce the cooking juices from the sweetbreads, add half the cream, and whisk in the butter, then strain. Add the rest of the cream, lightly beaten, and a tbsp of hollandaise sauce . Sauce each portion and briefly glaze under a broiler.

Preparation time: *1 hour*
Cooking time: *45 minutes*
Difficulty: ☆☆

Serves 4

6½ lb/3 kg loin of suckling pig, with kidney
1 banana
½ lemon
2 apples (such as Golden Delicious)
¾ oz/20 g fresh cranberries

2 sheets of filo pastry
¾ cup/200 ml grapeseed oil
⅔ cup/150 ml olive oil
⅔ cup/150 ml pork stock (prepared from the bones)

¾ cup/200 ml veal stock
1 tbsp/20 g honey
4 tsp/20 g sugar

butter
salt and pepper

For the stuffing:
the pig's kidney
½ cup/50 g bread crumbs
1 tbsp/10 g green peppercorns
1 tbsp/10 g chopped parsley

For the spicy sauce:
6 tbsp/40 g spices (curry powder, cinnamon, caraway, coriander and ginger)
⅔ cup/150 ml pork stock (prepared from the bones)
¾ cup/200 ml veal stock

The suckling pig has white and remarkably tender flesh. An animal 4–8 weeks old is just right for this dish, whose apparently complicated preparation should not put you off. The suckling pig has been appreciated since the Middle Ages and provides the most delicious meals. Even its skin—cut into thin strips and browned—is tasty.

Boning the pork is challenging but not impossible; if it frightens you, have your butcher do it. Brush olive oil onto the skin before putting the meat in the oven, and regularly baste the meat with its own juices, to make its skin crisper. Before serving, allow the meat to rest for a few minutes so that it will be juicier.

The stuffing can be seasoned either: dried green peppercorns, which have to be soaked before use, or with brined green peppercorns, which should be first rinsed in cold water.

For the fruit accompaniment, you might consider replacing the apples and bananas with a few thin slices of pineapple.

1. Bone the pork, leaving the eye of the loin and belly flaps intact. Reserve the kidneys, and use the bones and trimmings to prepare the stock.

2. Cut the banana in 2 in/4 cm long strips. Marinate for at least 30 minutes in grapeseed oil with a little lemon juice. Quarter each sheet of filo pastry and wrap around the banana strips. Dice the apples, add sugar and lemon juice, and caramelize lightly in butter.

Honey with a Spicy Sauce

3. Stuff the pork with a mixture of pepper, bread crumbs, chopped parsley and kidney; roll up and truss. Rub the skin with butter and olive oil and roast for 45 minutes in the oven. Then remove the string. Brush with honey and allow to caramelize lightly on the top rack of the oven.

4. Pour off the fat from the roasting pan. Add the spices, deglaze with the pork and veal stocks, and reduce. Strain and then whisk in the butter. Brown the pastry-wrapped bananas in butter. Cut the pork into ¼ in/½ cm thick slices, and arrange on each plate 2–3 slices of pork, 2 banana strips, 2 tbsp/30 ml apples and some cranberries. Pour sauce on top.

Preparation time: *1 hour*
Cooking time: *2 hours 30 minutes*
Difficulty: ★★

Serves 4

3⅓ lb/1½ kg smoked shoulder of pork (calas)
3½ oz/100g smoked bacon
pork rind
4½ lb/2 kg fresh fava beans
1 generous lb/500 g potatoes
1 tbsp tomato paste

2 leeks
1 carrot
1 bouquet garni
3 garlic cloves
2 tbsp/40 g flour
3½ tbsp/50 g butter
parsley
thyme
bay leaves
savory
salt and pepper

This dish is very popular in Luxembourg—it could almost be called a national dish. "Judd mat galardebounen" is eaten all year round and is an example of the simultaneously rustic and lavish cuisine enthusiastically represented by Léa Linster, winner of the Bocuse d'Or prize for 1989. In view of the small size of the country, it is not surprising that there was once a great shortage of grain there, so that they had to be replaced by other staples such as potatoes and fava beans.

Fava beans appear in the markets of the Grand Duchy, and elsewhere, in early spring. This is the best time to can them for year round eating. Once they have been skinned—the skins give them a bitter taste—fava beans go very well with the herb savory. If necessary, savory can be replaced with thyme. Savory is valued for its beneficial effect on the digestion, which explains its frequent use in dishes containing beans and lentils.

It used to be customary to prepare this dish on the day after a festive meal, where plenty of chicken and veal had been served; pork was considered as a pleasant "penance." Today it is on the menus of several restaurants in Luxembourg.

1. Put the pork with the carrot, one leek and the bouquet garni in a big pan of water and cook for about 2½ hours. Cut the bacon into small dice and brown in a frying pan. Peel and quarter the potatoes and boil in salted water.

2. Shell and skin the fava beans and boil in salted water. For the sauce, prepare sauté diced leek, a sprig of thyme, a bay leaf, some pork rind cut into pieces and the garlic. Deglaze with cooking water from the pork, add tomato paste and savory. Reduce and strain.

Pork with Fava Beans

3. Brown the flour very lightly in butter, add the sauce and stir well. Simmer for 10 minutes and whisk in some butter.

4. Slice the pork, then place on the serving dish with the potatoes, sprinkled with parsley. Scatter the browned bacon dice on top. Reheat the fava beans in butter and serve separately in a bowl with the sauce.

Preparation time: 1 hour
Cooking time: 2 hours
Difficulty: ★★

Serves 4

3⅓ lb/1½ kg tripe
2 eggs
3½ tbsp/100 g flour
2 cups/200 g bread crumbs

For the sauce:
remainder of the tripe
pork rind, cut in pieces
1 shallot

2 tomatoes
1 onion
1 carrot
½ celeriac
½ leek
7 oz/200 g potatoes
3½ tbsp/50 g butter
4 gherkins
1 tsp/5 ml tomato paste
2 cups/500 ml chicken stock
6½ tbsp/100 ml Madeira
1 cup/250 ml dry white wine
2 cloves
thyme, bay leaf, parsley
salt and pepper

This traditional dish is known as "Kuddelfleck" in Luxembourg. For this recipe Léa Linster recommends the upper part of the stomach, which you should be able to buy cooked. It needs to be cooked for a further 2 hours and then cut into small pieces, covered with bread crumbs and fried. If the tripe has not been blanched beforehand, simply allow twice as long for the preparation.

Choose tripe of good quality, which will stay tender. The slices must be cut absolutely straight.

The sauce can be prepared according to your own taste. Our chef uses white wine and Madeira; these produce a brown sauce with an exquisite flavor, which will flavor the potatoes, which should be of a floury variety.

This dish is recommended for a winter meal, which is when it used to be prepared before the invention of the refrigerator. When the cattle were slaughtered, the parts that would deteriorate the soonest were eaten first.

1. For the sauce, brown the skin of the tripe; the pork rind; diced carrots, onions and celeriac; and thyme and bay leaf. Deglaze with the wine and Madeira, and reduce. Add the chicken stock and tomato paste and reduce until thickened. Strain and whisk in the butter.

2. Cook the tripe with soup vegetables in water for 2 hours. Strain, let cool, and cut into diamond shapes. Coat in flour, egg yolk and, finally, bread crumbs. Dice the gherkins and the peeled and seeded tomatoes.

Luxembourgeoise

3. Brown the tripe in butter over medium heat until golden.

4. Boil the potatoes in salted water, then pass through a potato ricer. Finally add the gherkin and tomato dice to the sauce, season and let cool. On each plate, put 2 pieces of tripe, some potato and a big spoonful of sauce. Garnish with a few parsley leaves that have been braised in butter.

Lamb in a Pastry

Preparation time: 2 hours
Cooking time: 1 hour 30 minutes
Difficulty: ✴✴

Serves 4

1 saddle of lamb, about 3⅓ lb/1½ kg
17½ oz/500 g bread dough
1 handful of hay
flour

For the potato topping:
1¾ lb/800 g potatoes
7 oz/200 g dried cèpes
3 garlic cloves
2 cups/500 ml cream

1 pinch of nutmeg
salt and pepper

For the juniper berry and ginger mixture:
1 tbsp/10 g juniper berries
3 tbsp/20 g ginger
dried peel of 1 orange
salt and pepper

Vegetables (according to season):
10 carrots with greens
10 turnips with greens
7 oz/200 g peas
3½ oz/100 g green beans
10½ oz/300 g fava beans

In the art of cookery, one should combine new ideas with techniques developed through the centuries. Régis Marcon, following a regional tradition, recommends soaking the cèpes overnight in lukewarm water; next day you will find at the bottom of the container a number of particles of earth or sand that have come loose from the mushrooms. Incidentally, this method also produces a well-flavored stock.

You should choose a handsome piece of saddle of lamb with a very white layer of fat, which guarantees its fres-

hness. Preference should be given to very young lambs, preferably milk-fed lambs. You should truss the meat firmly so it retains its shape after preparation, and brown it evenly before wrapping in the crust. The meat will be tender and full of flavor if you roast it so that it remains pink inside.

The preparation involves scented hay. The dough preserves the flavor of the meat and makes it exceptionally juicy, as you will see when the crust is opened.

1. Soak the cèpes for 24 hours. Brown the saddle of lamb without fat in a pan for a few minutes, season with salt and pepper, then set aside.

2. Spread out the bread dough by hand, and place the hay in the center. Put the browned meat on the hay, and wrap the dough around it. Sprinkle with flour. Roast in a 450 °F/230 °C oven for 45 minutes.

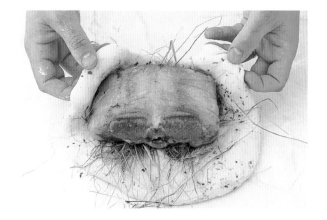

Crust with Cèpes

3. Peel and wash the potatoes and cut in thin slices. Reduce by half the water in which the cèpes were soaked. Add 2 crushed garlic cloves, cream, salt, pepper, and nutmeg, and strain. In a baking dish, arrange alternate layers of potato slices and chopped cèpes, pour sauce over them, and bake at 400 °F/210 °C for 1½ hours.

4. For the juniper berry and ginger mixture, cut the rest of the garlic into thin slices and mix with half the juniper berries and the dried orange peel. Crush all these ingredients with a rolling pin. Add the rest of the juniper berries, the ginger and the pepper. Just before serving, reduce the lamb stock, whisk in the butter, and season. Place slices of lamb on each plate. Garnish with the vegetables, which have been browned in butter, and pour some sauce on each plate before serving.

Twice-cooked Duck

Preparation time: 1 hour
Cooking time: 1 hour
Difficulty: ✭

Serves 4

4 duck legs
4 cups/1 kg duck fat (or oil)
1¾ oz/50 g bacon
14 oz/400 g Puy lentils
8 garlic cloves
thyme, bay leaf
2 tsp honey

4 tsp/20 g sugar
2 tbsp/30 g butter
6½ tbsp/100 ml wine vinegar
2 cups/500 ml chicken stock
1 tbsp/20 g ground star anise
1 bouquet garni
zest of 1 orange
salt and pepper

For the finely diced vegetables:
3½ tbsp/50 g carrots
3½ tbsp/50 g celery
3½ tbsp/50 g onion

In this dish, the preparation of the lentils is particularly important. If they are cooked for too short a time, they remain hard and flavorless; if for too long, they turn into a thick, indigestible mush.

For centuries lentils were considered poor people's food. Today, now that we know that they are rich in nutrients, we treat them with greater respect. The famous Puy lentils, which are protected by a government seal of quality, are cultivated in Velay in France, a region with fertile volcanic soil. Their color is a beautiful dark green with dashes of blue, and they go extremely well with the flavor of duck.

The double cooking of the duck described here requires a certain amount of patience. In order to obtain fine legs, Régis Marcon likes to choose free-range Barbary ducks. If you cook the meat for a long time over low heat, it will have an even pinkness and will preserve its volume and its fine flavor.

If you want to substitute squab for duck, you can use exactly the same method. This dish is especially popular in the autumn. It is served hot and can be kept in the refrigerator for 2–3 days.

1. The day before, season the duck legs with sugar, salt, pepper, thyme and bay leaf. Refrigerate overnight. Heat 3½ cups/900 g of duck fat, bring to a boil, add the duck legs and simmer, completely covered with fat, for 1 hour over low heat. Put the lentils into cold water and blanch. Finely dice the carrots, onions and celery.

2. Brown the vegetables for 5 minutes in the remaining duck fat, add the bouquet garni and the lentils, and add 1½ cups/350 ml water. Bring to a boil and simmer for 30 minutes, reserve the cooking water with a few lentils, and add half the chicken stock. Season, cook for 10 minutes more over low heat, purée in a blender, and add to the remaining lentils.

with Puy Lentils

3. Caramelize 1 tsp honey, then deglaze with the wine vinegar until a syrupy consistency is obtained. Add 1 cup/250 ml chicken stock, and reduce by one quarter. Add the orange peel. Remove from the heat and whisk in the butter.

4. Peel the garlic and blanch 3 times in boiling water for 2 minutes each time. Caramelize for 5 minutes with the rest of the honey and a pat of butter. Roll each garlic clove in a thin slice of bacon. Brown the duck legs in a skillet, then finish cooking in a 250 °F/120 °C oven for about 45 minutes. Place a pile of lentils on each plate, place a sliced duck leg on top, and pour a little sauce around the plate. As a garnish, wrap a tbsp of lentils in thin slices of bacon and place on the plates.

Loin of Veal

Preparation time: *8 hours*
Cooking time: *2 hours 30 minutes*
Difficulty: ★★★

Serves 4

1 loin of veal (5 ribs)
7 oz/200 g veal (for the purée)
2 generous lb/1 kg large mushrooms
1 bouquet garni
1 large leek
2 carrots
3½ oz/100 g dried black morels
12 cèpes (caps only)
bones and trimmings of the veal
calf's feet

½ cup white wine
4½ lb/2 kg firm potatoes
1 veal kidney
Madeira

14 cèpes (caps only)
2 each carrots, turnips, tomatoes
some onions, cloves garlic, shallots
cream
5½ oz/150 g raw duck foie gras
cardamom juice
1 small leek
1¾ oz/50 g morels
2 calf's sweetbreads
2 cups/500 ml chicken stock
10 tbsp/150 g butter
2 cups/500 ml puréed mushrooms
4 egg whites
white bread crumbs
olive oil
salt and pepper

For this recipe, Régis Marcon received, from the hands of the master Paul Bocuse himself, the Bocuse d'Or award for 1995—a prize that acknowledged the ability and talent of a modest but very gifted cook.

The rich accompaniment deserves special mention. The veal in a mantle of cèpes is stuffed with a purée of veal and mushrooms, and duck foie gras glazed with cardamom juice. The whole dish is further garnished with the famous skewered meat from Le Puy, in which calf's sweetbreads alternate with morels in a mantle of deep-fried egg white and puréed mushroom. It is also served with potatoes stuffed with pink kidneys.

Régis Marcon dedicates this dish to his mentor, the lady Margaridou.

1. Remove sinews and fat from the loin of veal, French the ribs ends, and make a hole through the center with a sharpening steel. Stuff with part of the puréed veal and finely chopped mushrooms; garnish with leek, carrots and morels. Cover with purée and slices of cèpes, and roast for 15 minutes at 300 °F/150 °C, then for 2 hours at 210 °F/100 °C (until it reaches 145 °F/62 °C inside), basting regularly.

2. For the potatoes with cèpes: brown the bones and trimmings. Add the calves' feet and 1 glass of white wine, and prepare as usual for a sauce. Cut the potatoes to look like the stems of cèpes, hollow out and prepare small balls from them. Roast in the oven with the above sauce, and stuff with pink kidney dice. Place on top the heads of cèpes glazed in butter.

Margaridou

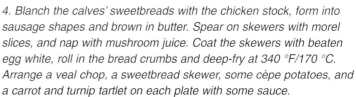

3. For the vegetable tartlets: using four 2 in/4 cm molds, fill them with slices of carrots and turnips cut into tear shapes; on the bottom of each mold place some stuffing made with diced tomatoes, onions, garlic, shallots and cream, and lay on top a slice of duck foie gras, browned and glazed with cardamom juice. Cover with some julienne of leek and a few morels.

4. Blanch the calves' sweetbreads with the chicken stock, form into sausage shapes and brown in butter. Spear on skewers with morel slices, and nap with mushroom juice. Coat the skewers with beaten egg white, roll in the bread crumbs and deep-fry at 340 °F/170 °C. Arrange a veal chop, a sweetbread skewer, some cèpe potatoes, and a carrot and turnip tartlet on each plate with some sauce.

Roast Shoulder of Lamb

Preparation time:	30 minutes
Cooking time:	16 minutes
Difficulty:	★★

Serves 4

1 shoulder of lamb, about 3⅓ lb/1½ kg
40 carrots with greens
1 large potato

10½ oz/300 g flat-leaf parsley
3 tbsp/30 g coriander
3 tbsp/30 g basil
3 tbsp/30 g chervil
5 tbsp/70 g butter
1¼ cups/300 ml lamb stock
2 tbsp honey
olive oil
salt and pepper

Potatoes cut into rose shapes are a true family tradition in the French department of Savoie, where they are often served with coffee. In the 19th century, about 100 years after their introduction into Central Europe, these potatoes fried in pork fat were a luxury item at festive dinners, where even their skins were greatly prized. These "potato roses" not only add a Savoyard note to this dish but form a very original garnish.

Lamb is considered a symbol of purity, and for centuries it has been associated with a series of mystical traditions; in the three great monotheistic religions—Judaism, Christianity and Islam—it is traditionally part of the most important religious feasts of each year.

Young lamb is best suited for this. The flesh should be firm and glossy, yet feel tender. The shoulder is a very tender joint with a small amount of fat. It is easy to prepare, and better value than the leg or rib. Make sure that that it has some time to rest after cooking, before it is carved.

To achieve a balance between the various flavors, it is best to use fresh herbs, which have a fuller flavor, and add cayenne pepper if you want to give a Mediterranean flavor to your dish.

1. Place the shoulder of lamb on your work surface and trim off the superfluous fat. Remove the stalks from the herbs, wash them, and cook for 5 minutes in boiling salted water. Drain well, purée and pass through a fine sieve. Peel the carrots, leaving 1 in/2 cm of the greens attached, cook for 5–6 minutes in salted water, and refresh in ice cold water.

2. Reduce the lamb stock, stir in butter and add the herb purée, then season and keep warm. Heat some olive oil in a pan. Season the lamb with salt and pepper, brown, then roast for 16 minutes in a 390 °F/200 °C oven, turning it after the first 8 minutes. Set aside to rest on a rack covered with aluminum foil.

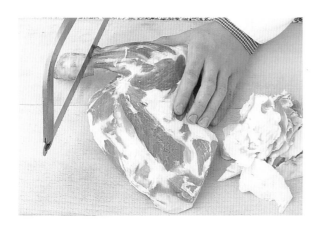

with Potato Roses

3. Put 2 tbsp of honey in a pan and heat until golden brown. Add the carrots and some butter and season. Place the shoulder of lamb in the center of the serving dish with the carrots at the side. Pour some of the herb sauce on top and serve the rest in a sauce-boat.

4. Peel a large potato, and cut into a long, thin strip. Roll up this strip into a rose shape. Plunge into oil heated to 354 °F/179 °C. Remove when browned and drain on paper towels to remove the excess oil; season with salt and serve with the lamb.

Oxtail Parmentier

Preparation time: 30 minutes
Cooking time: 20 minutes
Difficulty: ★

Serves 4

2 oxtails
1 generous lb/500 g potatoes (such as
Charlotte or Yukon gold)

5¼ oz/150 g truffles
aromatic garnish for oxtail
5 tbsp/70 g butter
6½ tbsp/100 ml whole milk or half and half
truffle juice
fine salt
ground pepper
coarse salt

Our chef tells us that this dish, which he calls "Parmentier de Raymonde," was a favorite recipe of his mother's.

Choose a firm, waxy potato such as Yukon gold or, if you can find it, Charlotte, which Guy Martin particularly likes for its juiciness, tenderness and flavor. It is medium-sized, uniformly rounded and has a golden-yellow skin and gleaming yellow flesh. It stands up well to roasting and does not turn dark.

The oxtail should be glossy and red, and, after boning, provide a generous amount of meat. Its taste can be intensified by adding hearty stock to the cooking water.

If you see that the fibers of the meat are separating during cooking, press it together after draining.

The truffle slices create a very decorative effect, but if you cannot obtain whole truffles, you can use chopped truffles or even truffle juice to add subtlety to the purée.

1. The day before, braise the oxtail, keep back 3½ tbsp/50 ml of the cooking water and slowly reduce by half. After cooking, loosen the meat from the bones.

2. On the day of preparation, boil the potatoes and make a purée with ⅓ cup/80 g of butter, the milk, half the truffle juice and a third of the chopped truffles. Season to taste and keep warm in a bain-marie. Make sure that the purée does not become liquid.

with Truffles

3. Cut one third of the truffles into thin slices, and chop up the rest. Put the reduced sauce, the truffle juice and 4 tsp/20 g of butter in a pan. Season and keep warm. Warm up the oxtail with 2–3 tbsp of water.

4. Place on the serving dish four metal rings, 3 in/7 cm in diameter and 1½ in/3 cm high. Fill with alternating layers of oxtail and purée, finishing with the truffle slices. Pour over 2 tbsp of the hot sauce and sprinkle with a few grains of coarse salt. The parmentier can also be prepared in 1 deep dish.

Preparation time: 1 hour
Cooking time: 50 minutes
Difficulty: ★★

Serves 4

1 kid, about 6½ lb/3 kg
8 small onions
24 small potatoes
2 garlic cloves
olive oil
salt and pepper

To pour on:
3½ tbsp/50 ml vinho verde (Portuguese white wine)
¾ cup/200 ml water

For the paprika paste:
2 garlic cloves
1 tsp ground sweet paprika
6½ tbsp/100 ml brandy or cognac
6½ tbsp/100 ml olive oil
1 bay leaf
parsley

For the chopped spinach:
1 generous lb/500 g spinach
3 garlic cloves
1 tsp flour
3½ tbsp/50 ml olive oil
vinegar

In the flat regions of Portugal, lamb is the meat of choice, while in the mountainous areas of the North, it is kid. In the villages of the Sao Jao Porto area, the Portuguese white wine Vinho Verde is served with roast kid. But the most distinguished type of preparation is found in the university city of Coimbra, where the shanks are used in the famous dish "chanfana de cabro." If the characteristic flavor of kid is too strong for you, you can replace it with a milk-fed lamb.

Roast the meat very slowly, at a moderate heat. Stay near the oven for the whole time and—most important—do not forget to "give the dish a chill" about every 15 minutes.

(This is an expression used in northern Portugal, which refers to the rush of air caused every time you open the oven door to baste the meat.)

This Portuguese-style kid, with a crisp golden-brown skin, has a very special flavor, which comes from the paprika and brandy mixture with which you have marinated the meat.

The dish can be served with a medley of small spring vegetables, as one does with navarin of lamb, instead of the garlicky spinach recommended here by our chef.

1. Remove sinews and fat from the kid, quarter it and cut out the leg, loin, saddle and shoulder.

2. Chop the garlic finely, mix with the paprika, brandy and olive oil, add parsley and bay leaf, and stir until creamy. Prepare the potatoes and onions for the accompaniment. Peel them and place in a baking pan. Add chopped garlic, olive oil, salt and pepper. Bake in a 350 °F/ 180 °C oven for 20 minutes.

Roast Kid

3. Spread the paprika mixture over the meat and refrigerate for about 1 hour. Roast the kid in a 320 °F/160 °C oven. Every 15 minutes, baste with a mixture of white wine and water. Remove from oven, deglaze with some water, and strain.

4. Cook the spinach in bubbling salted water, refresh, strain and chop. Shortly before serving, braise the garlic in olive oil and add the chopped spinach. Dust with the flour, stir, add a little vinegar and serve hot. On each plate arrange one slice of each cut of the meat, add the vegetables and pour sauce on top.

Roast Blood Sausage and

Preparation time: 1 hour
Cooking time: 30 minutes
Difficulty: ★★

Serves 4

4 quails, including hearts and livers
4 thin slices of duck foie gras
1 blood sausage, about 5¼ oz/150 g
2 egg yolks
7 tbsp/50 g flour
½ cup/50 g bread crumbs
1 shallot
parsley
borage blossoms
1 sprig of marjoram
6½ tbsp/100 g butter

6½ tbsp/100 ml chicken stock
2 tsp balsamic vinegar
salt and pepper

For the celery:
1 bunch of celery, about 14 oz/400 g
1 tsp chopped shallot
¾ oz/20 g smoked bacon
4 tsp/20 ml dry vermouth (Noilly Prat)
¾ cup/200 ml heavy cream
3½ tbsp/50 g butter
½ tsp flour
salt and white pepper

For the purée:
14 oz/400 g potatoes
¼ cup/60 ml milk
4 tsp/20 g butter
⅓ cup/80 ml heavy cream

The German love for charcuterie is no secret. Dieter Müller offers us a very tasty recipe for blood sausage with truffles; it is made from calf's head and sweetbreads, contains some cocoa, and is served with a delicious potato purée.

To give the potato purée the right consistency, you should use floury potatoes; our chef prefers Bintje or Urgenta. Be generous in adding butter and cream to the purée, to make it light and fluffy and a wonderful match for the other ingredients in the dish.

The garnish should, of course, be typically German. Dieter Müller highlights a single vegetable. According to taste, you can choose leek, spinach, celery or *Rübstiel*-whose flavor is similar to that of cabbage. This will produce a colorful and very sophisticated dish, further refined with a few drops of balsamic vinegar.

1. Slice the blood sausage and coat the slices with egg and then flour. Peel, wash, cook and purée the potatoes, beat in the butter, add plenty of cream and hot milk, and then season. For the sauce, reduce the chicken stock and balsamic vinegar in a pan until it has a syrupy consistency.

2. Wash the celery leaves well, and using only the most delicate leaves, chop finely, blanch and refresh in ice water. Brown the chopped shallot and 1 tsp diced smoked bacon in butter, sprinkle with ½ tsp flour, and add the vermouth and the double cream. Cook for 4–5 minutes until it has thickened, then whisk in the butter. Add the blanched strips of celery and reheat.

Quail with Balsamic Sauce

3. Remove the quail legs, remove the livers and cut into dice. Brown in butter with the chopped shallot and parsley. Add some chicken stock, cook for 2–3 minutes, and season. Brown the legs in melted butter and garnish with the diced liver. Broil on the top rack of the oven. Season and brown the thin slices of foie gras.

4. Brown the bread-crumbed slices of blood sausage in melted butter, and briefly cook the quails' hearts in the hot pan. Place on each plate 1 tbsp potato purée and 1 tbsp diced celery, then lay on top one slice of blood sausage and one of liver, and on the other side 1 quail leg and 1 quail heart. Pour the sauce over, and garnish with marjoram and borage blossoms.

Preparation time: 2 hours
Cooking time: 30 minutes
Difficulty: ★★

Serves 4

3½ oz/100 g venison
1 oz/30 g goose liver
¾ oz/20 g each bacon, morels, shiitake
mushrooms and chanterelles
2½ tbsp/40 ml cream
2 tsp/10 ml port
thyme, rosemary, salt and pepper

For the red cabbage:
1 red cabbage
2 apples (such as Golden Delicious)
2 shallots, 1 chile

4 tsp/20 g butter
2 cloves
2 cups/500 ml red wine
4 juniper berries
sugar, salt, white peppercorns

For the gingerbread sauce:
1¾ oz/50 g gingerbread
2 cups/500 ml venison stock
1 cup/250 ml red wine
2½ tbsp/40 ml port
6 juniper berries, thyme

For the crèpinettes:
4 medallions of venison, about 3½ oz/100 g each
pork caul
peanut oil. salt and pepper

For the spinach spätzle:
3½ oz/100 g young spinach
⅓ cup/160 g flour
3 eggs
1 tbsp water, salt

For a successful sauce, use unsweetened or only slightly sweetened gingerbread.

Venison takes center stage in this recipe; during the hunting season it is almost always to be found on restaurant menus. The flesh of a young deer should be cooked when quite fresh; it does not need to be hung and certainly not to be marinated. Take a saddle of venison from which you cut out the tenderloins. With the skin, fat, cream and spicy mushrooms you can prepare a firm, tasty stuffing that is wrapped up in pork caul (if you can't obtain this, brush the meat with oil and baste). You can replace the venison with rabbit or young pigeon, if you prefer.

"Spätzle" can be made in various colors. For this recipe they are colored green with spinach.

1. Chop the mushrooms finely, dice the liver and brown together. Dice the venison and bacon, season and purée in a food processor. Add the liver, port, juniper berries, rosemary, thyme, and cream. Brown the venison tenderloins on both sides and immediately transfer to a cool place. Place a medallion of venison on each piece of caul, spread stuffing on top to a thickness of ¾ in/2 cm, and roll up.

2. For the gingerbread sauce, mix the venison stock, port, red wine, thyme, juniper berries and the crushed gingerbread. Reduce by half. Strain. Return to the heat and reduce to a syrupy consistency. Blanch the large leaves of red cabbage and put aside for the roulade.

with Gingerbread Sauce

3. Cut the cabbage heart into thin strips. Peel the apples, cut into thin slices and mix with the cloves, chile, juniper berries, wine and cabbage. Marinate for 48 hours. Braise the shallots in butter, add the marinated red cabbage and 1 tbsp of sugar, season with salt, cover and braise in the oven for 25–30 minutes. Roll up in the cabbage leaves.

4. Cook the spinach in salted water, refresh and squeeze out excess liquid. Purée, and add the flour, eggs, and 1 tbsp water. Knead the mixture thoroughly in a bowl. Form into "spätzle" and poach in plenty of boiling salted water. Refresh and reheat in the pan with some butter. Arrange on the plates with the venison and sauce.

Preparation time: 45 minutes
Cooking time: 45 minutes
Difficulty: ★ ★

Serves 4

1 saddle of kid
1 eggplant
1 tomato
8¾ oz/250 g chanterelles
10½ oz/300g wild mushrooms
3 large potatoes
1⅔ cup/400 ml lamb stock
olive oil
garlic

basil
salt and ground pepper

For the garlic purée:
3½ oz/100 g garlic
1 cup/250 ml milk
1 pinch of salt

For the herb stuffing:
2 cups/500 ml mushrooms
⅓ cup/30 g bread crumbs
4 anchovy fillets
chopped herbs: chives, sage, basil, fresh
thyme, rosemary, tarragon, savory, parsley

If milk-fed kid is stuffed with truffles and roasted with herbs, its exceptional tenderness comes into its own. And this is the whole secret about choosing kid: it must come from an animal which is neither too fat nor too big, as an older kid will have a very strong flavor. Our chef prefers kid meat from Provence. The saddle is best suited to this recipe.

For the herb and garlic stuffing, the garlic should be treated carefully. Blanch it several times to remove all the bitterness, before adding it to the bread crumb mixture. Then you will need to prepare a balanced mixture

of the various herbs, which is not as simple as one might think. For example, sage is much stronger than tarragon and basil, whose flavors complement each other. If you then add chives and parsley as well, you will need a certain flair to produce the right combination.

The potato pancakes remind our chef of the days when he worked with Alain Chapel, and used to combine them with truffles. Now, his interests have turned to Mediterranean cuisine, which is why he makes them with eggplant and thyme.

1. For the garlic purée, blanch the sliced garlic in water 4 times, then cook them in salted milk for 30 minutes. Strain and purée them. Add the ingredients for the herb stuffing with some oil, the ground pepper and salt. Mix and set aside to cool. Cut the tenderloins from the saddle of kid.

2. Cut the mushrooms into thin shreds. With a mandoline, cut the potatoes into shreds and dry in a kitchen towel. Mix with the mushrooms. Cut the eggplant into large dice, brown in olive oil with the unpeeled garlic, and keep warm.

in a Mantle of Herbs

3. Heat some olive oil in a nonstick pan, form the strips of potato and mushrooms into small pancakes and brown on both sides. Peel the tomatoes, dice them, and braise in a pan with olive oil, basil, salt and pepper.

4. Quickly brown the seasoned tenderloins in a pan and then spread with the herb stuffing to a thickness of ¼ in/½ cm. Broil for 5–6 minutes on the top rack of the oven. Put the meat on the plates with its juices, and arrange around them the eggplant, tomatoes, potato pancakes, and mushrooms.

Catalan Cockerel with

Preparation time: 1 hour 15 minutes
Cooking time: 1 hour 10 minutes
Difficulty: ★★

Serves 4

1 cockerel with comb
8 fresh sea-cucumbers
4 shrimp heads
8 whole shrimp
2 sea urchins
1 large potato
½ tbsp red bell pepper, roasted, peeled, and diced
6½ tbsp/100 ml white wine
1 cup/250 ml chicken stock

3½ tbsp/50 ml heavy cream
olive oil
1 tomato

For the braised vegetables and herbs:
1 tomato
1 onion
1 leek
1 celery rib
1 garlic clove
bay leaf, thyme
pinch of saffron threads

Recommended accompaniment:
4½ oz/120 g fresh pasta

This new example of an eternal triangle combines poultry, shellfish and a very unusual type of seafood. This is a sea cucumber, an echinoderm from the depths of the sea, almost cylindrical in shape. It is native to all the oceans, but is eaten mainly in Asia and the Pacific area, where it is often sold dried. It should be browned very briskly with garlic to prevent its juices from escaping.

No praise can be too high for Catalan poultry. Our chef uses the sturdy prizewinning cockerels from Prat, near Barcelona. The color and texture of the cockscomb gives

the dish an unusual twist. A Chinatown market can supply you with a locally raised equivalent.

The shrimp are served in Catalan style, that is, the tails peeled but complete with their heads.

The preparation times for the ingredients are all different, and you must be very careful to observe them: 1 hour for the cockerel, but only one minute for the shrimp. Finally, the sea urchins' strong flavor of iodine will enrich this delicious poultry dish with a whiff of the sea.

1. Cut the cockerel into 8–10 parts. Cut the cockscomb into 4 pieces. Brown the vegetables and herbs in a braising pan big enough to hold the cockerel as well. Remove the vegetables and set aside.

2. Brown the cockerel pieces in olive oil, then put the vegetables and cockscomb back in the pan with the saffron.

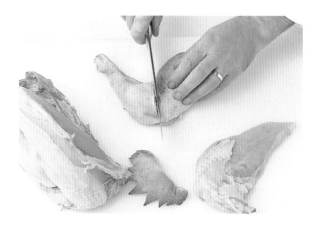

Sea Cucumber and Shrimp

3. Deglaze with white wine and reduce by half. Add the stock, the tomato and the shrimp heads. Cover and simmer for about 1 hour.

4. Brown the sea cucumbers 5 minutes before serving. At the last minute, add the whole shrimp (with tails peeled), the sea urchins and the chopped red pepper. For the sauce, reduce the stock, strain, and add salt, white pepper and heavy cream. Serve with fresh pasta.

Preparation time: *45 minutes*
Cooking time: *15 minutes*
Difficulty: ★★

Serves 4

1 chicken, about 3⅓ lb/1½ kg
14 oz/400 g fresh morels
4½ oz/120 g green asparagus tips

2 shallots
3½ tbsp/50 g butter
1 cup/250 ml chicken stock
2 cups/500 ml cream
½ cup/125 ml dry white wine
flour
tarragon
salt
freshly ground pepper

The ancient Romans had sacred hens, whose feeding was carefully supervised, and they were used to determine the prophecies of the augurs. So a good chicken can only be a sign of good luck.

In the Burgundian countryside, there are a number of farms where the famous Bresse chicken is raised. It is recognized by the label "*volaille de Bresse*," which guarantees its origin. A special chicken is always worthy of special preparation, so you should choose a suitable ena-meled iron pan, which will distribute the heat evenly.

Failing a Bresse chicken, use a free-range grain-fed farm bird, preferably one that has been raised organically.

In addition, you will want to have fresh morels. You may substitute dried morels, which should be soaked for 30 minutes hours; their soaking water is the ideal basis for the mushroom stock.

1. Prepare and quarter the chicken and render its fat. Brown the giblets (not the liver) and backbone in chicken fat, deglaze with wine and add the chicken stock. Simmer for 20 minutes and add the cream. Strain and reserve. Cook the asparagus in boiling salted water, then refresh. Toss with melted butter, season and keep warm in the oven.

2. Brown the seasoned and lightly floured chicken pieces in chicken fat in a casserole. Roast in a 350 °F/180 °C oven for 10 minutes, skin-side down. Remove the wings, keep warm, and roast the thighs for a further 10 minutes.

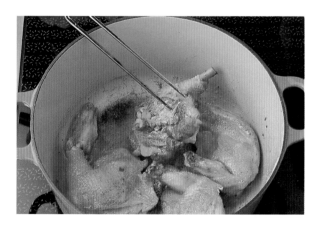

Sauce and Asparagus

3. Carefully wash and dry the morels. Put the roasting juices from the chicken, the chopped shallots and the morels into a pan. Braise lightly and season with salt and pepper. Add the cream sauce until everything is coated. Simmer over low heat for 5 minutes.

4. Add the morels to the pan containing the chicken pieces. Simmer for a few minutes and season to taste. On each plate, place a chicken piece and around it the asparagus and morels. Pour the morel sauce on top. Garnish with tarragon leaves.

Chicken and Frogs'

Preparation time: 30 minutes
Cooking time: 20 minutes
Difficulty: ★★

Serves 4

4 chicken thighs
10 pairs frogs' legs

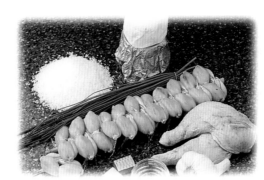

12 garlic cloves, unpeeled
3 shallots
6½ tbsp/100 ml rich chicken stock
1 cup white port
13 tbsp/200 g butter
1 bunch of chives
salt and pepper
¾ cup/200 g coarse salt

Frogs live in cool, damp places. Only the thighs of the frog are eaten; they have quite a delicate flavor. Choose frogs' legs of medium size, which are juicier and have more flavor. Don't cook them for too long, or the flesh will grow mushy and lose its fine flavor.

When you cook the unpeeled garlic in the oven, stick closely to the recommended temperature, so that the aroma will be preserved.

You can replace the chicken thighs with duck breast or "osso buco" made from turkey legs, if you wish.

1. Divide each chicken leg into 2. Season with salt and pepper, and brown in a deep pan. Add the three shallots, chopped.

2. Pour off the fat from the pan and deglaze with white port. Add the chicken stock and simmer for 12 minutes.

Legs with Garlic

3. Cover the bottom of a baking dish with coarse salt. Lay on top the unpeeled garlic cloves and put in a 350 °F/180 °C oven. Keep warm after cooking. Season and sauté the frogs' legs, then scatter chopped chives over them.

4. Dry the chicken pieces with paper towels and keep warm. Reduce the sauce and stir in the butter. Strain and season to taste. Place the chicken pieces in the center of each plate and arrange alternating frogs' legs and garlic cloves in a circle around them. Pour the sauce over before serving.

Guinea Fowl with

Preparation time: 2 hours
Cooking time: 15 minutes
Difficulty: ★★

Serves 4

1 guinea fowl
4 small turnips with greens
1 shallot
1 pork caul
2 slices white bread, soaked in milk
2 eggs
10 tbsp/150 g butter

1 tbsp/15 ml oil
salt and pepper

For the finely diced vegetables:
3 carrots
1 fennel bulb
3 celery ribs

For the brown stock:
carcass of the guinea fowl
diced carrots, onions, and celery
salt and pepper

The French name for the guinea fowl is *pintade*, the painted one, because of its speckled plumage. Its delicate flesh can be prepared in many different ways. A guinea fowl can be recognized from quite a long distance away because of its very loud screeching.

Our chef raves about the tiny spring vegetables from his native Nantes region. He especially recommends the turnips, which should be used in this recipe along with their greens. As with many other baby vegetables, the turnips only need to be scrubbed, not peeled.

If you use the pork caul, don't forget to soak it before use, to remove all impurities. Then the guinea fowl fillets can be wrapped in it and browned in the pan, turning frequently.

1. Bone the guinea fowl. For the stuffing, finely chop the thigh meat and the white bread which has been soaked in milk. Finely chop the carrots, fennel and 1 celery rib. Braise these vegetables in butter with the chopped shallot, season with salt and pepper. Add the eggs and mix.

2. Make a brown stock with the guinea fowl carcass, 1 carrot, 1 celery rib and 1 finely diced onion. When it is ready, strain and reduce. Season with salt and pepper. Cut each guinea fowl breast into 16 thin scaloppini; gently pound them flat.

Spring Vegetables

3. With a pastry bag, pipe 1 tsp of stuffing onto each guinea fowl scaloppini and wrap in a piece of the softened pork caul, making small parcels.

4. Cut the remaining celery rib into 32 small sticks. Boil in salted water and set aside. Steam the turnips. Brown the stuffed guinea fowl parcels in a little oil and butter, turning frequently. Put some sauce on each plate, place a turnip in the center, drizzling some melted butter on top to make it shine. Arrange guinea fowl parcels and celery sticks alternately in a circle around the turnip.

Grouse with Savoy Cabbage

Preparation time: 1 hour 10 minutes
Cooking time: 45 minutes
Difficulty: ★★

Serves 4

2 grouse
4 thin slices of pork fat or fatback
1 cup/120 g diced vegetables (celery, carrots, shallots, mushrooms)
2½ tbsp/40 ml grapeseed oil
6 ½ tbsp/100 ml red wine
1 tbsp/20 ml port
1¼ cups/300 ml game or chicken stock
2 tbsp/30 g butter
5 juniper berries, crushed
5 peppercorns, ground

1 sage leaf, 1 sprig of thyme
¼ bay leaf
1 tbsp green peppercorns
salt and pepper

For the vegetables:
1¾ lb/800 g Savoy cabbage
3½ oz/100 g diced bacon
1 shallot
1 lemon
6½ tbsp/100 ml vegetable stock
¾ cup/200 ml heavy cream
1 pinch of nutmeg, butter

For the caramelized apples:
4 apples
2 tbsp sugar
6½ tbsp/100 ml white wine (such as Riesling)
6½ tbsp/100 ml Gewürztraminer or similar wine
20 threads of saffron

In England and Scotland the grouse is highly prized, and the "Glorious 12th" of August is celebrated as the first day of the shooting season. Despite the British enthusiasm for grouse, it is little known in other countries; if necessary, it can be replaced by pheasant or guinea fowl.

Living in the remote moors of England and Scotland, the grouse lives chiefly on heather; its delicately gamy taste is slightly reminiscent of pheasant or partridge. Don't roast it for too long. It should remain pink inside. Let it rest for a little while after roasting; this will make it even more tender.

For the vegetable accompaniment, take a crisp cabbage, blanch it and then plunge it into cold water to remove the slight taste of sulfur which some people dislike.

Put the vegetable garnish on the plate first, and carve the grouse just before serving. Serve this dish very hot, with a little sauce.

1. Cut the Savoy cabbage into thin strips. Blanch in salted water, and refresh in cold water; braise the chopped shallots and diced bacon in butter. Add the cabbage, season with salt and pepper, add a pinch of nutmeg and a few dashes of lemon juice. Add some vegetable stock, cover and cook until nearly all the liquid has evaporated. Finally add the cream.

2. Prepare the grouse for cooking, season inside and out with salt and pepper. Cover the breast with pork fat and tie securely. Heat the grapeseed oil in a pan. Dice the vegetables and brown them quickly in the oil with the herbs and spices. Place the grouse on the vegetables, breast down.

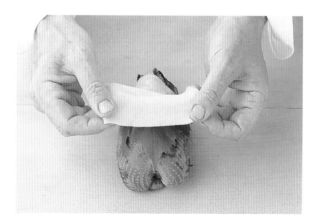

and Caramelized Apples

3. Put the grouse in a preheated 390 °F/200 °C oven; turn after 8 minutes, baste with wine and port, and then cover. Roast for an additional 10 minutes, turning again after 5 minutes; the meat should stay pink inside. Let the grouse rest; deglaze the roasting pan with the game stock, reduce, strain and whisk in the butter. Add the rinsed green peppercorns and season to taste.

4. Peel and core the apples and cut each into 8 pieces. Use a small shallow pan to make a light caramel. Add the two wines and the saffron and reduce by half. Poach the apples. Reheat the cabbage. On each plate, place some cabbage, with slices of grouse on top, and pour on some sauce.

Salad of Venison with

Preparation time: 45 minutes
Cooking time: 50 minutes
Difficulty: ★★

Serves 4

1¾ lb/800 g loin of venison
2 kohlrabi (or turnips)
3½ tbsp/50 g butter
1 tbsp/20 ml balsamic vinegar
1 tbsp/20 ml hazelnut oil
7 tbsp/50 g hazelnuts, shelled
¾ cup/75 g seasonal salad greens
1 bunch of thyme
parsley
salt and freshly ground pepper

To poach the truffle:
1 truffle (1¾ oz/50 g)
3½ tbsp/50 ml red wine
3½ tbsp/50 ml chicken stock

For the game stock:
3½ oz/100 g carrots and celery
2 shallots
¾ oz/20 g mushrooms
6 juniper berries, chopped
6 black peppercorns
½ bay leaf
6½ tbsp/100 ml robust red wine
¾ cup/200 ml Madeira
¾ cup/200 ml cognac
6½ tbsp/100 ml reduced game stock

Little distinction is made in the kitchen between the red deer and the roe deer, although they are easily distinguished when seen in the wild. The roe deer is generally considered the most appealing of forest animals. Their flavor is best at 10–12 months old. In Europe, they are usually eaten during the hunting season, from September to December.

Horst Petermann, who lives near the Black Forest, benefits from the Swiss privilege of hunting during the summer too. The flesh of the young roe deer, which is a beautiful dark red in color, can be marinated for a day or two in crushed juniper berries and some olive oil.

This makes it more tender and gives it a slightly peppery note.

The accompaniment of truffle and kohlrabi has a powerful flavor, which superbly complements the taste of game. Take a fresh, firm truffle, which can be peeled if you prefer, but should not be washed. Kohlrabi is very popular in Eastern Europe, and may have a green or purplish skin. You can use turnips instead if you like.

If you want to try this recipe outside of the deer-hunting season, our chef recommends using a bird such as squab or guinea fowl.

1 Bone and trim the venison, and refrigerate until ½ hour before needed. Chop up the bones for the stock.

2. For the game stock, brown the bones and trimmings in a pan and add the finely chopped vegetables and the mushrooms. Flambé with cognac, deglaze with Madeira and wine; add the herbs and spices and the game stock. Simmer for 45 minutes over low heat; strain and carefully remove the fat.

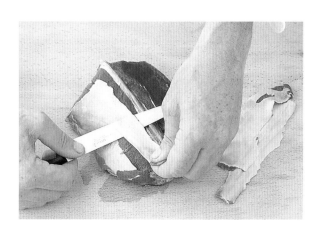

Truffles and Kohlrabi

3. Brown the venison in butter for 5 minutes; it should remain underdone. Keep warm. Poach the truffle in stock and red wine, and cut into thin strips. Peel the kohlrabi and cook in salted water, leaving them crisp, and then cut into thin strips.

4. For the vinaigrette, put the truffle juice in the pan in which the venison fillets were browned. Reduce by half; add the hazelnut oil and the vinegar. Put the truffle and kohlrabi strips in a salad bowl. Chop the hazelnuts, brown in butter and place on top, covering with the vinaigrette. Garnish the venison with thyme and parsley and serve with the salad.

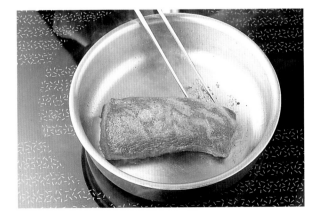

Loin of Rabbit with

Preparation time: 1 hour
Cooking time: 1 hour
Difficulty: ★★

Serves 4

2 saddles of rabbit
1 cup/250 g Puy lentils
3 large carrots
1 leek, white part only
2 shallots
1 bouquet garni
6 tbsp/90 g butter

2 tbsp cream
flat-leaf parsley
salt and freshly ground pepper

For the sauce:
12 oz/350 g rabbit bones
1 onion
1 carrot
1 garlic clove
1 tbsp tomato paste
1¼ cups/300 ml white wine
1¼ cups/300 ml water
oil

Rabbit has the reputation of being dry, but in fact it can be nice and juicy, as long as it is browned gently in plenty of butter, and turned from time to time.

Apart from the preparation of the rabbit you should also take great care with the sauce. It must be well reduced to be successful. It should have a robust taste—if it is too bland, add some herbs to enhance the flavor.

The green Puy lentil is one of the best types of lentil, grown in the volcanic region of Velay in France, and rich in iron and vitamins. In this recipe, the lentils should not be cooked to the *al dente* stage, but until they have opened and become quite soft. They will form a fine contrast to the other vegetables, the carrots and leek, which should remain crisp and crunchy.

1. Cut the white part of the leek into ½ in/1 cm wide strips. Cook in salted water, refresh and drain. Peel the carrots, dice one and cut the other into balls, and boil in salted water. Chop the shallots finely.

2. Remove any fat and sinews from the rabbit saddles and cut the meat into chunks. For the sauce, cut up the bones and the forelegs of the rabbits. Brown in oil. Finely chop the onion and carrots, and add the garlic. Brown while stirring continuously; pour off the fat and return to the heat. Deglaze with white wine and add water and the tomato paste.

Lentils and Carrots

3. Simmer for 30 minutes over low heat. Braise the chopped shallots, then add the carrots, the cooked lentils, 2 tbsp cream, 2 tbsp rabbit stock, and 2 tbsp/30 g of butter. Simmer very lightly until thickened, and season to taste.

4. Season the rabbit pieces and fry lightly in butter, turning continually so that they do not become brown; cook for 6 minutes over a low heat. Sauté the carrot balls and the leek strips in butter. Allow the rest of the rabbit stock to boil for 1 minute over high heat, then whisk in 8 tsp/40 g of butter. Season to taste and garnish with parsley.

Veal Tenderloin with

Preparation time: 1 hour
Cooking time: 1 hour
Difficulty: ★★

Serves 4

14 oz/400 g center cut of veal tenderloin
4 pieces of marrow bone
4 cups/1 l chicken stock

For the vinaigrette:
1 bunch of watercress
3 shallots
4 cornichons
1 tbsp capers
2 anchovy fillets in oil

2 sprigs of parsley
2 sprigs of tarragon
1 sprig of basil
4 tbsp walnut oil
2 tbsp wine vinegar

For the garnish:
4 artichoke hearts
4 carrots
4 broccoli florets
4 sprigs of parsley
bicarbonate of soda
butter
watercress
salt and freshly ground pepper

When choosing veal, the French look for the seal of good quality. For this dish, the chef, Roland Pierroz, uses a calf raised solely on milk. He takes the most tender cut of the fillet, the tenderloin, which should be served medium rare. However, it is not always easy to buy veal tenderloin, and you can substitute boned loin of veal.

An Italian-style vinegar-based sauce, like those served with bollito misto, is ideal for this dish. The capers and cornichons give it a tart flavor. The anchovy fillets form a fine contrast to the delicate meat, and the flavors of all these ingredients, which are apparently so different, are harmoniously blended by the walnut oil.

This oil goes very well with watercress, which can be replaced with spinach if necessary. You can also use other vegetables for this recipe, such as poached leeks, cauliflower and turnips, all appropriate with boiled meat.

1. Remove fat and sinews from the veal and tie into a neat cylinder. Prepare the artichoke hearts and cut the carrots into olive shapes. Steam separately. Blanch the broccoli in boiling salted water with a pinch of bicarbonate of soda. Refresh and set aside. Blanch the watercress for 5 minutes in boiling salted water, refresh, and squeeze out excess water.

2. Purée the watercress in a blender, and put through a sieve. Peel the shallots and chop coarsely. Purée in the blender with the parsley, tarragon, capers, cornichons, and anchovies. In a bowl, stir together walnut oil, vinegar, salt and pepper, then stir in the watercress purée, which will give it a lovely green color.

Herb Vinaigrette

3. In a saucepan, bring the chicken stock to a boil. Simmer the marrow bones, diagonally cut, for 5 minutes in boiling salted water. Put the veal in the stock and poach for 10–12 minutes at a simmer; the meat must remain pink in the center.

4. Stuff the artichoke hearts with carrots and broccoli florets and reheat by steaming. Season. Cut the veal into 1 in/2 cm thick slices. Arrange the meat and a slice of marrow bone in the center of each plate, and next to it an artichoke heart. Sprinkle coarse salt over the meat and pour on some of the herb vinaigrette.

Preparation time: 1 hour
Cooking time: 20 minutes
Difficulty: ★★

Serves 4

2 ducks
2 apples
7 oz/200 g snow peas
1 small celeriac
oil
salt and coarse salt
white pepper

For the sauce:
1¼ cups/300 ml duck stock
1 tbsp sherry vinegar
½ tbsp nut oil
1 tbsp/22 g honey
¼ cup/60 g butter
2 cardamom seeds
2 pieces of mace blades
pinch of nutmeg
pinch of curry powder

The duck, highly esteemed even in classical times, is a widespread species—both as a wild bird living in the wild and as a domestic bird. There are a number of varieties including the Barbary, the mallard, and the ubiquitous Pekin ("Long Island") duck.

For this recipe you need fleshy birds with plump breasts. The breasts should first be browned skin-side down to give them a nice color and to allow the fat to escape. It can be served either whole or carved into thin slices.

The Pourcel brothers practice a modern, vigorous cuisine, which is aware of its roots. Their restaurant is among the best in Montpellier, which was formerly a center of the spice trade for the whole Mediterranean region.

Not everyone knows that mace is nothing more than the outside layer that surrounds the nutmeg. Although the blade and the nut come from the same plant, they have quite different flavors. Cardamom and curry powder complete the delicious medley of spices that give this dish its particular character.

1. Peel, core and dice the apples. Braise in a little water and 1 tbsp/15 g of butter, to produce a compote. Keep warm. Peel the celeriac, slice thinly and deep-fry in hot oil, then season and set aside.

2. Trim the snow peas, cook in plenty of boiling salted water, and refresh. Reheat the celeriac chips in the oven.

Spicy Sauce

3. Brown the duck breasts in a pan until golden. Turn, and roast in a 350 °F/180 °C oven for 10 minutes. Reheat the snow peas in butter.

4. Pour the fat from the pan. Return to the heat and add the honey. Caramelize slightly and deglaze with vinegar. Then reduce almost completely. Add the duck stock, the nut oil and the spices. Reduce and stir in the rest of the butter; season. Arrange on each plate first the vegetables, then the duck, and pour the sauce over.

Guinea Fowl with

Preparation time: 2 hours
Cooking time: 30 minutes
Difficulty: ★★★

Serves 4

2 young guinea fowl
1 egg white
tarragon, flat-leaf parsley, garlic
butter

For the sauce:
½ cup/120 g butter
1 oz/30 g sugar lumps rubbed with lemon peel
6½ tbsp/100 ml lemon juice
6½ tbsp/100 ml white wine

¾ cup/200 ml chicken stock
6½ tbsp/100 ml brown veal stock
chives, garlic

To finish the sauce:
1½ oz/40 g lemon slices
½ oz/15 g lemon peel preserved in salt
¾ oz/20 g sun-dried tomatoes
1 tsp/7 g tarragon
1 tsp/7 g green peppercorns

For the "panisses":
½ cup/250 g chickpea flour
1 tbsp olive oil
4 cups/1 l salted water
butter

The flesh of guinea fowl can sometimes dry out during roasting, and Stéphane Raimbault deals with this risk by first steaming and then grilling. This keeps the meat tender and delicious, particularly if you wrap the breasts in aluminum foil before steaming.

The sauce made from preserved lemons can take a long time to prepare. Raimbault preserves his lemons for 3–4 weeks.

The word *panisses* indicates that this is a typically Provençal dish. These fried cakes of corn or chickpea flour are similar to the Corsican *panizze* and can be eaten in a sweet or savory form. They are best cooked just before serving, in a mixture of olive oil and butter.

You can easily adapt this guinea fowl recipe to most other kinds of game bird. Our chef notes the passing of the seasons throughout the year with different kinds of birds, but always keeps this dish on the menu at his restaurant.

1. Bring 2 cups/500 ml of water to boil with oil and salt. Stir the chickpea flour into the other 2 cups/500 ml of water, then pour the mixture into the boiling water and cook for 10 minutes, stirring continuously. Pour into a buttered terrine, allow to cool and cut into triangles. Just before serving, fry in a mixture of olive oil and butter.

2. Prepare the guinea fowl, remove the legs and save for another occasion. Remove the breasts, and cut pockets into each. Remove the small sinews from the "tenders," dip into egg white and coat in a mixture of chopped tarragon and parsley. Stuff each breast with its own "tender," wrap in foil and steam, then grill.

Lemon Sauce

3. Cut up the carcasses, brown in butter, and add the crushed garlic, the chopped chives, the lemon sugar cubes, and the lemon juice. Add the white wine and the chicken stock, reduce by a quarter and add the brown veal stock. Strain. Add the remaining sauce ingredients and the butter, and mix gently.

4. On each plate, place a guinea fowl breast cut into 3 sections, and place beside them the fried panisses. Pour the sauce around before serving.

Pork Tenderloin withBoulangère

Preparation time: 1 hour 30 minutes
Cooking time: 1 hour
Difficulty: ★★

Serves 4

1 pork tenderloin, about 1¼ lb/600 g
1⅓ oz/40 g smoked bacon
6½ tbsp/100 g brown pork stock
tomatoes
1⅓ oz/40 g lemon zest, chopped
garlic, sage
flat-leaf parsley
olive oil
salt and pepper

For the garnish:
6 very small artichokes
1 generous lb/500 g potatoes
1 lemon
2 tbsp tomato paste
5¼ oz/150 g small onions
3½ tbsp/50 g butter
1 cup/250 ml white chicken stock
olive oil
garlic
bouquet garni
saffron
parsley
salt and pepper

This recipe almost amounts to a family reunion, as pork, potatoes, and sage often meet in the same recipe.

The pork in this recipe could be replaced by a veal tenderloin. The dish acquires its full flavor from the addition of chicken stock with herbs and spices. Those suggested here—garlic, saffron and a bouquet garni—can be replaced by others if you desire.

The combination of meat, potatoes, tomatoes and artichokes is a particularly attractive one, and the strong flavor of Provençal sage goes superbly with pork and veal.

In this recipe Stephane Raimbault uses the Provençal artichokes known as *poivrade*, which are frequently eaten raw. In Provence, artichokes are also used as a kind of barometer. They are hung on a door and one can tell from the opening and closing of the leaves whether there will be sunshine or rain.

1. Finely chop the onions and braise in butter. Finely chop the potatoes and mix with the onions. Place in an ovenproof dish rubbed with garlic. The layer of potato and onion should be ¾ in/1½ cm thick. Cover with the chicken stock in which garlic, a bouquet garni and saffron have previously been infused. Bake in a 390 °F/220 °C oven. Sprinkle with chopped parsley before serving.

2. Prepare the artichokes and cook in salted water with some lemon juice. Slice and brown in olive oil and butter, then add with the tomato paste.

Potatoes and Artichokes

3. Remove fat and sinews from the pork and truss. Season and brown with the bacon, garlic, herbs and the peeled, seeded and finely diced tomatoes. When cooked, keep warm for 10 minutes. Meanwhile, deglaze the pan with the pork stock, strain and add the chopped lemon peel, the chopped sage, and the olive oil.

4. Place a metal ring in the center of the plate, and layer inside it first some artichokes, then overlapping pork slices, and finally the boulangère potatoes, from which you have cut a circle of the same size with a similar ring. Pour the sauce around and serve.

Duck with

Preparation time: 35 minutes
Cooking time: 3 hours 30 minutes
Difficulty: ★★

Serves 4

4 duck legs
fat from the duck carcass
½ cup/125 ml stock

For the marinade:
4 tbsp chopped fresh ginger
2 garlic cloves
2 tbsp white peppercorns
1 tsp ground star anise
8 tbsp coarse sea salt

For the garnish:
½ cucumber
1 bunch of chives

For the sauce:
1 cup/250 ml duck stock
2 tsp ginger
4 star anise
2 shallots
2 tsp/15 g honey
2 tsp/15 ml hoisin sauce
pinch of cayenne pepper
soy sauce as required

For this type of preparation you should choose a fine plump duck. When cooking the duck, look out for the moment when the meat starts to pull away from the bone—at that point the duck should be taken off the heat. The legs should be completely covered with duck fat during cooking. If the duck's own fat is not enough, you can add peanut oil.

Finally you should broil or grill the duck to crisp the skin. You can achieve the same effect by putting the duck in a 430 °F/220 °C oven for five minutes in a heavy skillet, skin-side down. Separate the legs at the joint to present them attractively.

The choice of Chinese spices is based on Paul Rankin's long experience. Star anise and ginger form the basis of this medley; their sharpness can be softened with some soy sauce. The chives used for the garnish are a kitchen herb that has been grown in China for many centuries.

1. Marinate the duck legs for 24 hours, distributing the spices and seasonings evenly over them. Render fat and skin from the ducks with ½ cup/125 ml of stock; simmer for about 2 hours, until the fat becomes clear. Strain and set aside for the preparation of the duck legs.

2. Peel the cucumber, and cut ribbons from it with a potato peeler. Finely chop the chives. For the sauce, braise the shallots and ginger in some duck fat, brown lightly, and add the other ingredients. Simmer until it thickens, and season to taste with soy sauce.

Chinese Spices

3. Rinse the duck legs well to remove excess salt and spices. Put in the pan with the duck fat to cover and simmer for about 1½ hours over low heat. Set aside to cool in the duck fat. Just before serving, broil the legs, skin side up, to make them golden-brown and crisp.

4. Arrange the cucumber strips on the warmed plates, place the duck legs on top, and distribute the chives over them. Finally pour the sauce around.

Preparation time: 20 minutes
Cooking time: 1 hour 30 minutes
Difficulty: ✶

Serves 4

3⅓ lb/1½ kg lamb (shoulder or neck)
8 oz/225 g potatoes

8 oz/225 g carrots
8 oz/225 g leeks
8 oz/225 g small onions
2 sprigs of thyme
1 bunch of fresh parsley
1 cup/250 ml heavy cream
1 tsp/5 g butter
salt and pepper

Lamb is now used for this traditional Irish dish, which was formerly based on mutton. It used to be a meal for poor people; it was prepared in one big pot and combined with various vegetables according to the taste and pocket of the housewife.

The best meat comes from lambs that are more than 5 months old and that already have a distinctive taste. The shoulder and neck, right next to the bone, have a particularly good flavor and can stand long cooking.

Potatoes grow successfully in both quality and quantity in Irish soil. Potatoes were grown there for the first time as early as the 16th century, from New World seedlings plundered from captured Spanish ships, and it is now a staple.

The French sometimes describe the leek as "poor man's asparagus." It has, however, made itself welcome in the kitchens of great chefs, and lends its subtle taste to this stew, just right for serving on cold winter evenings.

1. Prepare the lamb and cut into large cubes, discarding the thin layer of fat around the meat. Put the meat in a large pan with water and a little salt. Bring to a boil, skim off the scum and fat from the surface, and simmer for 30 minutes.

2. Peel the potatoes and cut into large pieces. Put half of them in the pan and simmer for another 30 minutes, then stir vigorously so that the potatoes disintegrate.

Stew

3. Add the rest of the potatoes and the other vegetables, and simmer for a further 30 minutes, until the meat and potatoes are thoroughly cooked.

4. Heat the heavy cream with the butter, and add, with the chopped parsley and thyme. Heat briefly and serve.

Preparation time: 45 minutes
Cooking time: 45 minutes
Difficulty: ★

Serves 4

1 chicken, about 4½ lb/2 kg
1 sheet of firm pork fat or strips of blanched bacon
7 oz/200 g oyster mushrooms

1 shallot
1 carrot
1 leek
½ celery rib
4 tsp/20 g butter
1⅔ cups/400 ml crème fraîche
¾ cup/200 ml white wine
salt and pepper
chicken stock

The *géline* chicken, preferred by our chef for this dish, is a cross between the black chickens of the Touraine district of France and the *langshan* chicken, another black variety, which originally comes from China. It is mainly raised in Touraine, where it has been admired since the Middle Ages. Nowhere could this variety be better celebrated than in the Rabelais' native region; the giants in his novels eat massive quantities of chicken at their banquets.

The chicken is roasted in 430–460 °F/220–240 °C oven. It should be protected from the heat by covering the breast with a thin sheet of fat or strips of bacon, which will also give extra flavor to the meat. A short rest after roasting lets the meat become more tender, and improves the taste even further.

Cultivated oyster mushrooms are now available all year round. They are grown on wood or specially prepared bales of straw. Use smaller mushrooms for this dish. These contain less water, and their distinctive taste serves to bring out that of the chicken.

If you like, you can use a guinea fowl instead of chicken.

1. Finely dice the carrot, leek and celery. Braise the oyster mushrooms in a little butter; season with salt and pepper. Mix with the finely chopped shallot.

2. Prepare the chicken for roasting; season with salt and pepper, and cover with the fat or bacon before trussing. Roast for 40 minutes in a preheated oven, then cover and let rest for 15 minutes.

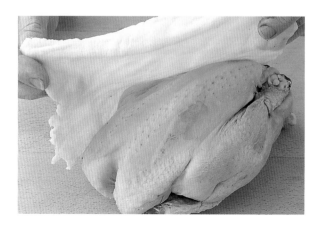

Oyster Mushrooms

3. Brown the diced vegetables brunoise in the roasting pan. Pour off the fat and deglaze with white wine. Reduce until practically no liquid is left. Add crème fraîche and reduce.

4. Strain the sauce and season to taste. Remove the chicken from the pan, carve and place the pieces in the center of each plate. Pour the sauce on top and arrange the mushrooms around the chicken pieces.

Calf's Sweetbreads

Preparation time: 45 minutes
Cooking time: 20 minutes
Difficulty: ★★

Serves 4

4 calf's sweetbreads, about 5¼ oz/150 g

12 verbena leaves
6½ tbsp/100 ml verbena tea
2 generous lb/1 kg green asparagus
2 tbsp veal demiglace
butter
salt and pepper

The calf's sweetbreads should be snow-white. If there are still traces of blood, soak them in cold water and refrigerate the evening before preparation.

Meanwhile you can prepare an infusion from the strongly scented, almost peppery verbena leaves, which are also used for the famous liqueur from Le Puy. The verbena forms the connection between the sweetbreads and green asparagus, whose taste it is intended to complement rather than overpower. Here, as always, it is a question of balance, which must be carefully observed.

The asparagus must be fresh and crisp. Poach it for just a few minutes, so it stays al dente, then toss it carefully in butter. If you are unable to get good asparagus, you can substitute lightly braised chanterelle mushrooms.

The *glace* is a strongly reduced meat stock, which gels after it has been cooled. It is used to intensify the flavor of sauces, because it is highly concentrated. A *demiglace* is simply a partly reduced stock with a thick consistency.

1. Blanch and refresh the sweetbreads, removing the outer skin. Brown them in butter in an ovenproof dish, and season.

2. Add the verbena tea, cover and braise for 10 minutes in the oven at 350 °F/180 °C.

with Verbena Butter

3. Cook the asparagus in boiling salted water until just crisp; drain and toss in butter with the verbena leaves.

4. Brown the sweetbreads once again in butter. Add the demiglace and reduce, then stir in the remaining butter. Place on each plate some asparagus tips, and next to them the sweetbreads with the sauce, which has been seasoned to taste.

Tenderloin of Beef with

Preparation time: 30 minutes
Cooking time: 10 minutes
Difficulty: ★★

Serves 4

4 beef tenderloin steaks, about 6 oz/170 g each
8 slices marrow bone slices (1½ in/3 cm long,
2¾ in/6 cm in diameter)
3½ tbsp/50 g butter
3½ tbsp/50 ml oil
allspice

For the sauce:
3 cups/750 ml red wine
1 carrot
1 onion

4 shallots
3½ tbsp/50 g flour
⅓ cup/80 g butter
1 bay leaf

1 sprig of thyme
pepper

For the potato rosettes:
7 oz/200 g potatoes
6½ tbsp/100 g melted butter
salt

For the potato purée with truffles:
7 oz/200 g potatoes
4½ tbsp/70 ml cream
3½ tbsp/50 g butter
2 tbsp/30 ml milk
½ oz/10 g truffle
3½ tbsp/50 g butter for the sauce
salt and pepper

The flesh of Charolais cattle is irresistible; it is one of the best meats in the world. Our chef, who comes from the Ardèche region, adores it and has created a suitable recipe, which also includes bone marrow. Charolais cattle are known for their huge size. The tenderloins from these animals can weigh up to 8¾ lb/4 kg. Here, the seasoned steaks are pan-fried, initially over high heat, then over low heat. The meat must be browned evenly on all sides and repeatedly basted with its own juices during cooking.

Allspice is a dried, red-brown berry that comes mainly from Jamaica. For the sauce, use a red wine rich in tannin. With this feast of flavors, you might be worried that the delicate taste of the bone-marrow will be overwhelmed. In fact its chief role in this recipe is to provide a little variation in texture.

1. Braise the finely chopped onion, carrot, and shallots in butter. Add thyme, bay leaf, and pepper, dust with flour, allow to cook for 2 minutes and add the red wine. Simmer, gradually reducing to ¾ cup/200 ml.

2. Wash and peel all the potatoes (14 oz/400 g altogether). Boil half of them and prepare a purée with the cream, butter, milk, and finely chopped truffles. Cut the remaining potatoes into thin slices.

Allspice and Bone-marrow

3. For the potato rosettes, arrange the raw potato slices in a buttered nonstick pan in a rosette shape, and brown in melted butter. Season the steaks with salt and allspice, and cook in butter and oil.

4. Soak 4 of the marrow-bone slices in cool water and remove the marrow from each. Gently cook in butter. Poach the remaining pieces of marrow bone. Place the steaks on the marrow bones, and top with the potato rosettes and pieces of marrow. Serve with the potato purée. Finally, pour on the sauce. Garnish with thyme and bay leaves.

Duck Breast

Preparation time: 30 minutes
Cooking time: 1 hour 30 minutes
Difficulty: ★★

Serves 4

4 duck breasts, about 8¾ oz/250 g
½ tsp/2 g curry powder
½ tsp/2 g apple pie spice
½ tsp/2 g ground star anise
3 tbsp/50 g honey
3½ tbsp/50 g butter
4 tsp sherry vinegar
¾ cup/200 ml duck stock or brown veal stock
salt and pepper

For the candied figs:
4 figs
4 tsp/20 g butter

1 tbsp/20 g honey
salt and pepper

For the gratin savoyard:
14 oz/400 g potatoes
1¾ oz/50 g fresh cèpes
1¾ oz/50 g fresh chanterelles
2 garlic cloves
¾ cup/200 ml milk
¾ cup/200 ml cream
4 tsp/20 ml peanut oil
3½ tbsp/50 g butter
1¾ oz/50 g cheese (such as Beaufort or Swiss gruyère)

For the garnish:
sage, chives, coarse salt

When Michel Rochedy came to Savoie in 1963, he discovered many similarities to his native region of Ardèche. Both are known for their arid landscape, and despite the infertile soil, similar culinary traditions have developed in these mountainous regions.

The quality of the potatoes is decisive in this recipe; our chef prefers Belle de Fontenay, but a variety such as Yukon gold will do just as well. Michel Rochedy thinks that the fine, delicate chanterelle has a "feminine" character and the cèpe adds a "sharp masculine" note to this dish. If you can only get other mushrooms, prepare them in exactly the same way. Fry them in hot peanut oil, drain them well and pat them dry, to get rid of all excess fat.

The gratin acquires its typical Savoyard character from the Beaufort cheese, which is almost without holes. The best French Beauforts are labeled "Haute Montagne."

1. For the gratin, peel and wash the potatoes, and slice. Peel and wash the mushrooms and brown in peanut oil. Heat the milk with the cream and the crushed garlic. Add the potatoes and simmer for 12 minutes, or until the potatoes are tender. Layer them in a baking dish with the cheese and mushrooms. Bake in 320 °F/160 °C oven for 30 minutes, top with additional grated cheese and brown in the oven.

2. Cut the figs in half, brown in butter, and season with salt and pepper. When they are nicely browned, add the 1 tbsp/20 g honey and cook until the honey forms a candy coating on the figs.

with Candied Figs

3. Caramelize the 3½ tbsp/50 g of honey in a flat pan over high heat. Deglaze with 4 tsp/20 ml sherry vinegar, and add the curry powder, star anise and apple pie spice. Cook for 1 minute, then add the stock. Reduce and season to taste with salt and pepper. Stir 3½ tbsp/50 g butter into the sauce.

4. Brown the duck breasts in a skillet without butter, for 10 minutes on the skin-side and 5 minutes on the flesh side. Cut each duck breast in half and arrange on each plate with the gratin; place 2 fig halves on top of the gratin. Garnish with a sage leaf and chives. Pour the sauce over and season the meat with a little coarse salt.

Preparation time: 30 minutes
Cooking time: 2 hours
Difficulty: ★★

Serves 4

For the calf's head:
½ calf's head
1 onion 1 clove
1 carrot 1 leek 1 celery rib
6½ tbsp/100 ml white wine vinegar
¾ cup/200 ml white wine
3 sprigs of parsley 1 sprig of thyme
1 bay leaf salt and pepper

For the tortellini à la savoyarde:
2¾ oz/80 g pasta dough
2¾ oz/80 g tripe, cooked

1 bunch of wild celery (or 1 tbsp chopped celery leaves)
¼ bunch of hyssop or 1 tbsp chopped parsley
1½ oz/40 g cheese (such as Beaufort or Swiss Gruyère) salt and pepper

For the garnish and the sauce:
2 carrots
1 leek
2 shallots
1 egg
⅓ cup/40 g capers
7 tbsp/100 g butter
4 tsp/20 ml sherry vinegar
2½ tbsp/40 ml truffle juice
¼ oz/8 g truffles
salt and pepper

For the final garnish:
½ bunch of chives
¼ bunch of chervil
12 chervil stems

Michel Rochedy learned his culinary skill from his mother, the best cook he has ever known. Here he prepares a calf's head such as he once ate at Jacques Pic's restaurant in Valence. It had the slightly tart taste that develops from long simmering in the traditional style. Rochedy believes that the best calves are to be found in his native Ardèche. These are calves that have grown up with their mothers and been reared exclusively on their milk. The head is juicy and full of flavor; you can check with a needle during cooking to see if it is done. When you buy the tripe, try to get a mixture of crisp and gelatinous parts, which will form a good contrast. The right

effect is provided by a typical Savoyard cheese, such as the robust Beaufort, although other alpine cheese may be substituted.

It is said that tortellini originated from the passionate love of a pasta seller for one of the young girls he employed. One day, while peeping through the keyhole into her room, he could see only her navel, which inspired him to create a new shape of pasta. This original version is also seasoned with two mountain plants, wild celery and hyssop. (But you can use ordinary celery leaves and flat-leaf parsley instead.)

1. For the pasta, form a well in ¾ cup of flour and add 1 beaten egg. Knead using the palm of your hand until the eggs and flour are well mixed. The dough should be soft but not sticky. Knead for a few minutes more, wrap in foil and let rest for an hour.

2. Soak the calf's head overnight and cut into 2-inch/4-cm thick pieces. Blanch and refresh them, then simmer with the garnish and other ingredients for 2 hours. Cover with a cloth during cooking, so that the meat does not darken.

Tripe à la Savoyarde

3. Peel and wash the carrots and leek and cut into thin strips. Finely chop the shallots and hard-cook the egg. Chop the yolk and white separately. Cut 4 nice slices from the truffle and chop the rest finely. Roll out the dough and cut out rounds, add a stuffing of tripe, cheese, chopped celery leaves, and hyssop, prepare the tortellini as shown, and poach them.

4. Reduce the water in which the calf's head was cooked, add the truffle juice and the sherry vinegar, and then whisk in the butter, in small pieces. Arrange the pieces of calf's head on the plate, place some tortellini alongside, pour over the sauce, sprinkle the truffle, chives, chervil, chopped egg white and yolk on top, and garnish with slices of truffle.

Saddle of Rabbit

Preparation time: 15 minutes
Cooking time: 20 minutes
Difficulty: ★

Serves 4

4 saddles of rabbit, with kidneys
1 generous lb/500 g rhubarb

20 scallions
10 tbsp/150 g butter
6½ tbsp/100 ml stock made from the rabbit bones and trimmings
sherry vinegar
oil
confectioners' sugar
salt and pepper

The rabbits for this recipe should weigh about 3⅓ lb/1.5 kg; one that is too young will not have developed enough flavor, even if its flesh is firm and white.

The rhubarb compote may perhaps confuse people used to seeing rhubarb only in desserts. It is true that the red stalks of this plant are used mostly for desserts, but they have been used in medicine for their astringent, stimulating and laxative effects. Also, Joël Roy believes that rhubarb goes extremely well with white fish (such as pike and turbot), and tender, delicate meats. The stems should be firm and crisp and not too fibrous; yielding a nice smooth compote with a subtle flavor.

This dish is best prepared in spring, when the rhubarb is still young.

1. Bone the saddles of rabbit, each yielding 2 loins and 2 tenderloins. Make a stock with the bones and trimmings.

2. Peel the rhubarb and cut in pieces. Peel the scallions and cook for 5 minutes in a mixture of butter, salt and a little water.

with Rhubarb

3. Braise the rhubarb with a nice piece of butter, some confectioners' sugar and salt, until it is soft. Crush with a fork.

4. Season the rabbit with salt and pepper and brown the loins for 5 minutes in butter and oil. Add the tenderloins, cook for 2 minutes, then add the kidneys and cook for 1 minute more. Reduce the rabbit stock and stir in butter. Add a few dashes of sherry vinegar before serving.

Preparation time: 30 minutes
Cooking time: 50 minutes
Difficulty: ★★★

Serves 4

4 young partridges
10½ oz/300 g turnips
8 shallots
1 pork caul (see note on page 32)
5 tsp/25 g butter
6½ tbsp/100 ml olive oil
parsley

For the game butter:
heart and liver of partridge
1 shallot, chopped

butter
curry powder
salt and pepper

For the marinade:
1 cup/250 ml white wine
4 cups/1 l olive oil
2 cups/500 ml sherry vinegar
1 cup/250 ml water
2 tsp/10 g salt
1½ tsp/5 g peppercorns

For the sauce:
the partridge carcasses, chopped
2½ oz/75 g leek
3 tbsp/25 g chopped parsley
1 onion
3½ oz/100 g turnips
4 cups/1 l water or chicken stock
1 cup/250 ml white wine
salt and pepper

As soon as the hunting season begins, the partridge, and particularly the red variety, becomes a favorite meal for Spaniards. Young partridge can be found from the beginning of the hunting season up to 11 November.

Despite his Catalonian origins, Santi Santamaria prefers the Scottish partridge, which has a distinctive gamy taste (they are imported to the United States). This recipe is inspired by a very old traditional method of preparation, the Spanish marinade called *escabèche*. A special taste is given to the partridge by a new element, turnips. Buy very hard, absolutely fresh and unblemished turnips.

Santamaria is actually not a lover of pork caul and uses it only when absolutely necessary. It contains a great deal of fat, which affects the other ingredients.

1. Prepare the partridges; remove the breasts (both sides in 1 piece) and legs, bone the legs. For the game butter, soak the livers and hearts in water overnight. Drain, dry and trim; brown in a small saucepan with the chopped shallot. Strain and mix with the butter. Finally, season with curry powder, salt and pepper.

2. Take the ingredients for the marinade, the unpeeled shallots, the turnips and the partridge legs and simmer them for 40 minutes over low heat. Drain well. Braise the turnips for a little longer, then keep warm. For the sauce, crush the carcasses and brown them in oil with the onion, some parsley, 2½ oz/75 g of leek and 3½ oz/100 g of turnips. Deglaze with wine and water or chicken stock, season with salt and pepper and simmer over low heat.

"en Escabèche"

3. Season the inside of the breasts, and spread with the game butter, keeping some of the butter for the sauce. Strain the sauce. Reduce by half and thicken with the rest of the game butter, then strain again.

4. Fold up the pieces of breast and wrap in the pork caul, if used. Spread some butter over it and cook in a 375 °F/190 °C oven for 7 minutes. Season the braised legs with salt and pepper and fry to a golden brown. Remove the pork caul and place the pieces of partridge in the center of each plate. Add the marinated shallots and browned turnips. Pour the sauce on top and serve garnished with parsley.

Preparation time:	*1 hour*
Cooking time:	*2 hours*
Difficulty:	★★

Serves 4

7 oz/200 g dried white beans
1 head of cabbage
½ oz/10 g truffles
truffle juice
olive oil
salt and pepper

For the sausages:
2 generous lbs/1 kg calf's sweetbreads
750 g smoked belly of pork
3½ oz/100 g goose liver
sausage casings

With these sausages, Santi Santamaria refines traditional Catalan cuisine in his own special way: the classic sausage and beans becomes a sophisticated dish with the addition of calf's sweetbreads, foie gras, and truffles.

Santamaria prefers to use the small, white beans from Ganxet. The beans should be soaked for 24 hours before you cook them. If any beans are left over after the meal, you can use them to make a lovely, thick soup.

The sweetbreads should be absolutely fresh and light in color, and have no remaining traces of blood or sinews.

Don't cook them for too long, to preserve their juicy, fragrant character.

As you will see, this recipe combines very simple ingredients such as belly of pork, cabbage and beans, with more refined ones such as calf's sweetbreads and foie gras. This is a good opportunity for you to demonstrate your culinary skills by combining these varied ingredients harmoniously. You can make your task easier with certain variations: the truffles can be replaced by herbs of your choice, as truffles are not always easy to find and are also quite expensive.

1. Blanch and refresh the sweetbreads, clean them, and coarsely chop them with the pork. Finely chop the foie gras and truffle. Mix all together and season.

2. Cook the beans, which have been soaked overnight, for 2 hours over low heat in plenty of water. With the help of a funnel, make sausages 6/ n/15 cm long from the stuffing, and refrigerate.

with Truffles and Beans

3. Wash the cabbage leaves, blanch, refresh and cut into thin slices. Braise in oil in a pan.

4. Prick the sausages and poach them for 8–10 minutes in some of the water in which the beans were cooked. For the sauce, reduce the truffle juice and the cooking water, strain and stir in butter. Arrange one sausage per person in soup bowls, and add beans and cabbage to each bowl, and top with sauce.

Preparation time: 20 minutes
Cooking time: 10 minutes
Difficulty: ★

Serves 4

2 duck breasts
1 generous lb/500 g pumpkin or winter squash

10 tbsp/150 g butter
juice of 1 lemon
¼ cup/60 ml cognac
¼ cup/60 ml red wine
balsamic vinegar
vegetable stock
shallots
rosemary
salt and pepper

Balsamic vinegar, which originated in Modena in the Italian province of Emilia, makes a marked contribution to the success of this recipe. Aged balsamic vinegar is very expensive, because it takes several years to produce. The juice of white grapes, which is exclusively used to produce it, first ferments naturally and is then laid down for a very long time, in a progression of small barrels made from different types of wood.

When it is ready to be sold, balsamic vinegar is brown in color and has an intense smell and a well-balanced sweet-sour taste. Inexpensive balsamic vinegar is made in a very different way. In and around Modena, the *palio degli aceti* is held every year; this is a competition among the best vinegars in which the best producers of balsamic vinegar are chosen.

The preparation of the sauce is not altogether straightforward. The various stages (the addition of cognac and wine, then of balsamic vinegar, and the reduction) should be carried out attentively. You need to allow enough time for the preparation.

You can also vary the type of bird you prepare in this way: squab, quail or guinea-fowl can be substituted.

1. Put the shallots in a pan with butter and stock, and bring to a boil. Cut the pumpkin into small slices and brown in butter.

2. Score the fat of the duck breasts. Heat butter in a skillet with some rosemary. Briefly brown the breasts on both sides so that they remain nice and juicy.

Balsamic Vinegar

3. With the duck breasts still in the pan, deglaze with cognac. Add the lemon juice, red wine, rosemary, and salt and pepper, then reduce.

4. Add the balsamic vinegar and reduce by about three-quarters. Remove the meat from the pan. Strain the sauce and season to taste. Serve with the slices of pumpkin, and pour the sauce over.

Pigs' Feet

Preparation time: 45 minutes
Cooking time: 2 hours
Difficulty: ✶

Serves 4

8 pigs' feet
1 carrot
2 onions
1 celery rib
1 small Savoy cabbage
2 garlic cloves
3½ tbsp/50 g butter
6½ tbsp/100 ml dry white wine

1 tbsp tomato paste
4 cups/1 l meat or vegetable stock
3½ tbsp/50 ml olive oil, cold-pressed
nutmeg
cinnamon
cloves
salt and pepper

For the pre-cooking of the pigs' feet:
1 carrot
1 onion
1 celery rib
parsley
salt and pepper

This recipe of peasant origin used to be served with polenta to farmers after a long day working in the fields. It was also popular with large families.

Pork is still popular today, and is consumed in large quantities.

Nadia Santini recommends choosing pigs' feet that are not too large, because these have the best flavor. They are first washed in cold water and simmered with aromatic vegetables, then allowed to cool so the meat becomes firm. Then the meat is carefully removed from the bones.

Santini points out that you can also use calves' feet or oxtail for this dish. As an accompaniment, she recommends polenta or fresh pasta (penne or rigatoni).

1. Place the well-washed pigs' feet in a saucepan with carrot, onions, celery, parsley and salt and pepper. Add water to cover and simmer gently for 1 hour, or until the meat is tender. Let them cool in the cooking liquid.

2. Finely chop the carrot, onion and celery and braise in a large saucepan in butter and oil.

Cassoëula

3. Add garlic, white wine, cabbage leaves and tomato paste and bring to boil.

4. Remove the meat from the pigs' feet and add to the pan with the cabbage leaves; add the stock and all other ingredients and simmer until everything is cooked through. Arrange on the plates and serve.

Duck

Preparation time: *45 minutes*
Cooking time: *1 hour 30 minutes*
Difficulty: ★★

Serves 4

1¾ cups/400 g long-grain rice

For the garlic butter:
6½ tbsp/100 g butter
4 garlic cloves

For the marinade:
2 ducks
1 onion

1 orange
1 lemon
2 cups/500 ml white wine
1 bunch of parsley
6 black peppercorns
salt

To prepare the duck:
1 leek
1 celery rib
1 Spanish-style chorizo sausage
3½ oz/100 g lightly smoked slab bacon
5 black peppercorns
salt

This traditional and very popular dish is very typical of Portugal. The duck and its many varieties has always excited the imagination of Portuguese chefs, and as a result there are hundreds of recipes for duck.

To prevent the duck from drying out, Maria Santos Gomes bones the duck halfway through the cooking and layers it with rice. You will be delighted with the result, because this helps the various flavors to mingle. Here Gomes uses an unpretentious accompaniment: chorizo and bacon, which should not be too fatty or too piquant—this applies particularly to the chorizo, which can be quite pungent. The flavor provides an additional nuance of taste.

Use long-grain white rice for this dish, rather than brown, and take care not to overcook it.

1. Clean and truss the ducks, and marinate for about 3 hours in white wine, parsley and water, with orange and lemon zest. Then put them in a pan with the chorizo, bacon, leek, celery, peppercorns and salt. Cover with water and simmer for 1½ hours.

2. Then spread the duck with a mixture of butter and crushed garlic. Roast for 30 minutes in a 375 °F/190 °C oven until golden brown. Meanwhile skim the fat from the water used to cook the ducks and cook the rice in it.

with Rice

3. Remove the ducks from the oven, allow to cool, and remove all the meat. Cut the breasts into thin strips.

4. Put a layer of rice in an ovenproof dish, then a layer of duck meat, then another layer of rice, and so on, until all the rice and duck meat have been used up. Finally lay the sliced chorizo and diced bacon on top. Return to the oven for 10 minutes and serve hot.

Chicken and Crab

Preparation time: 15 minutes
Cooking time: 30 minutes
Difficulty: ★★

Serves 4

2 chicken breasts
16 crayfish
5½ oz/150 g pistachio nuts

½ cup/100 g rice
1 egg
¾ cup/200 ml crème fraîche
1 onion
6½ tbsp/100 g butter
6½ tbsp/100 ml ouzo
6½ tbsp/100 ml white wine
bouquet garni
salt and pepper

The island of Aegina, which lies opposite the harbor of Athens, was an important trading center from the 8th to the 5th centuries, B.C., and it is still famous for its pistachios. Many Greek desserts, cakes, stuffings and soups are garnished with pistachio nuts. Pistachios are very nutritious, but fragile to cook with, and should be handled with care. They will make this dish crisper, more colorful and more aromatic.

In our recipe you can put chopped pistachios into the crayfish stock, but make sure that it has stopped boiling. Add them only towards the end and let them infuse for a short time before you strain the stock.

For this recipe you should choose a chicken with tender flesh and not cook it for too long, lest the breasts become tough.

The typically Greek ouzo sauce has a very refreshing effect. Instead of ouzo, you can use aniseed to flavor the sauce. The chicken can be replaced by rabbit, and if desired you can use almonds instead of pistachios.

1. Butterfly the chicken breasts, carefully press them flat, and save the "tenders" and trimmings for the stuffing. Season with salt and pepper, and marinate for 10 minutes in ouzo. Chop the pistachios and set some of them aside.

2. Purée the chicken trimmings in a food processor; add the egg, 6½ tbsp/100 ml crème fraîche and salt and pepper. Divide this paste among the chicken breasts. Wash the crayfish. Prepare a fumet from 8 of the heads, all of the shells and the finely chopped onions.

with Pistachio Sauce

3. Lay a crayfish tail on each chicken breast, and sprinkle with an even layer of chopped pistachios. Roll up, wrap in aluminum foil and poach for 15–20 minutes. Meanwhile, cook the rice and keep it warm.

4. Add the remaining pistachios to the crayfish fumet. Reduce, add crème fraîche, reduce again, add the ouzo, and strain. Brown the remaining crayfish in butter and deglaze with the wine. Place a few slices of stuffed chicken breast on each plate and pour fumet over them. Serve a cone of rice and herbs on each plate.

Pork Tenderloin with Graviera

Preparation time: 45 minutes
Cooking time: 40 minutes
Difficulty: ★★

Serves 4

1¾ lb/800 g pork tenderloin
7 oz/200 g Greek graviera cheese
1 cup/100 g walnuts
⅔ cup/80 g raisins
30 small shallots
8 potatoes
6½ tbsp/100 ml white Samos wine
¼ cup/50 ml olive oil
cinnamon

For the sauce:
2¼ lb/1 kg pork bones
1–2 medium carrots
1 small leek
1 celery rib
1 onion
1 tsp tomato paste
⅔ cup/150 ml red wine
¾ cup/200 ml sweet Samos wine
6½ tsp/100 ml olive oil
bouquet garni
chervil leaves
salt and pepper

The island of Samos is one of the Greek island group in the Aegean called the Sporades. Muscat wine from Samos has been popular in Europe for centuries, and it turns up in this example of modern Greek cuisine, in which Nikolaos Sarantos combines it with pork tenderloin.

The sweetness of the wine balances the tartness of the other ingredients of the sauce. Leave a little fat on the pork tenderloin; when you brown it, it will form a little crust which will become crisper in the oven and will taste delicious.

The combination of Samos wine and pork is rounded off by the graviera, a hard cheese with a fruity taste, usually enjoyed with olives, golden raisins, or currants. It is made from a mixture of sheep's and cows' milk. Its structure is similar to that of Parmesan, and it is easily recognized by its rind. For this recipe it is melted in wine and mixed with dried fruits; this transforms it into an exquisite accompaniment and an exciting new taste. But be careful when browning the stuffed tenderloins not to let the melted cheese escape: tie the meat carefully to prevent this.

1. Melt the cheese in the wine with the raisins and walnuts. Cool and form into a roll, then refrigerate. Butterfly the tenderloin lengthwise, season, sprinkle with a little Samos wine, scatter chopped walnuts and raisins on it, and lay a slice of the cheese mixture on top.

2. Fold and tie up the tenderloin, and brown briskly in a pan with some olive oil. Deglaze with Samos wine and roast for 15 minutes in a 400 °F/200 °C oven. For the sauce, braise the bones with the finely chopped vegetables, deglaze with the red wine, add water and the bouquet garni, and reduce. Strain, add the Samos wine, and simmer for 5–6 minutes.

and Samos Wine Sauce

3. Braise shallots in oil, pour on some sauce, add cinnamon, and reduce for 20 minutes over a low heat. Boil the potatoes in salted water. Brown them in oil and then add some sauce.

4. Slice the tenderloins. Arrange on each plate with some sauce, some of the braised shallots, garnished with chervil, and some potatoes.

Preparation time: 3 hours
Cooking time: 1 hour 30 minutes
Difficulty: ★★

Serves 4

½ kid (leg, rack, and loin)
4½ oz/120 g liver, kidney, ½ heart
8 garlic cloves
10½ oz/300 g mirepoix of vegetables
6½ tbsp/100 ml olive oil
1¾ cup/375 ml dry white wine
savory, rosemary
3 sage leaves, 1 bay leaf

For the polenta:
1½ cups /200 g instant polenta
1¼ cup/300 ml chicken stock

2 tsp/10 ml olive oil
1½ oz/50 g Parmesan
1 small sprig of thyme, bay leaf
salt and pepper, nutmeg

For the mixed beans:
1 cup/100 g dried white beans
½ cup/50 g borlotti beans
7 oz/200 g green beans
2 tomatoes, ½ leek, 1 carrot, 2 celery ribs
3½ oz/100 g fava beans
2 shallots, 4 garlic cloves
4 sage leaves, 2 bay leaves
savory flat-leaf parsley
4 tsp/20 ml olive oil
salt and pepper

For the stuffing:
1½ oz/40 g kid meat, ¾ oz/20 g chicken
½ egg white, salt and pepper
2 tbsp/30 ml heavy cream
3 basil leaves, garlic
rosemary

Goat's meat usually comes from the male goat, as the female is needed for milk production. The flesh of the kid is more tender and milder in flavor than a lamb's. It makes little difference which cut you choose. Although rib, loin and leg are chosen here, you could just as well use shoulder or neck. The offal is speared on a sprig of rosemary; it is exceptionally tender.

The delicate taste and special tenderness of the meat should be preserved as much as possible, so our chef recommends cooking it slowly and with care, preferably with several different vegetables, which enhance the flavor of the meat. The resulting mixture of meat and vegetable juices can be seasoned at the end of the cooking time with a little white wine, to give it a slight tartness.

Instant polenta is prepared with corn meal that has been pre-cooked by steaming. The dried beans should be soaked in cold water for 24 hours; this makes them more digestible. To thicken the mingled juices of the meat, vegetables and wine, add the olive oil. You will be totally entranced by this dish.

1. Bone the leg and loin, French the rib bones of the loin, and season with salt and pepper. In a food processor, prepare a stuffing with the chicken, kid meat, egg white, heavy cream, salt, pepper and chopped garlic. Add the chopped herbs.

2. Cook the beans separately. Braise the chopped shallot and add the green beans and fava beans, previously cooked in salted water, and finally the chopped herbs. For the polenta: reduce the chicken stock with herbs and strain. Add the instant polenta, cover and set aside for 15 minutes, add the Parmesan, salt, pepper and nutmeg. Spread out on a board, allow to cool, then cut into lozenge shapes, and brown in oil with thyme.

Beans and Polenta

3. Cover the boned meat with basil leaves and spread the stuffing on top. Roll up and truss, and brown in olive oil. Add the garlic and the mirepoix of vegetables and cook, covered, for about 40 minutes. Take out the meat, skim off excess fat, deglaze with white wine, and add the chicken stock. Reduce, strain, and stir in oil; season to taste.

4. Cut the liver, heart and kidneys in pieces, season and brown over high heat in olive oil. Spear the pieces on rosemary stalks and keep warm. On each heated plate, place a piece of polenta, some vegetables, 1 rosemary skewer with the offal, and some sliced meat, and pour the sauce around.

Loin of Venison with

Preparation time: 3 hours
Cooking time: 1 hour 30 minutes
Difficulty: ★★★

Serves 4

2 generous lb/1 kg loin of venison
3½ tbsp/50 g butter
½ apple 10 cranberries

For the black pepper sauce:
venison bones
8¾ oz/250 g mirepoix of vegetables
3½ tbsp/50 ml chicken stock
2 cups/500 ml red Burgundy wine, such as
Crozes Hermitage, 4 tsp/20 g butter
3½ tbsp/50 ml olive oil, rosemary
thyme, black pepper, salt

For the white pepper sauce:
1 tbsp/10 g white pepper, ground
3½ tbsp/50 ml chicken stock
some white wine

4 tsp/20 ml Noilly Prat dry vermouth
⅓ cup/80 ml crème fraîche
2½ tbsp/40 ml heavy cream
1 bay leaf, 1 garlic clove
2 onions, 4 tsp/20 g butter
1 small sprig of thyme, salt

For the celery purée:
1 celeriac, 4 celery ribs
6½ tbsp/100 ml cream
chives, 3½ tbsp/50 g butter, salt

For the potato noodles:
14 oz/400 g potatoes
2 egg yolks, salt, nutmeg
2 tbsp/40 g cornstarch, bread crumbs
chives, 3½ tbsp/50 g butter

Many Germans have made the deer into a sort of cult, whether they themselves go hunting or not. Thus there are many methods of preparation for this exquisite meat. Fritz Schilling himself does not hunt, but he loves venison, of which there is an abundant supply in the Black Forest.

Cook this fine red meat with care, as it must be cooked only briefly over low heat—too much heat and too long a cooking period would make the meat tough. As pepper

goes well with venison, Fritz Schilling has created not one, but two sauces—one using black and one using white pepper. They will surely be a success with your guests.

There are various possibilities in the choice of the cuts of meat. Instead of loin, you could use rib, shoulder or leg with equal success. Wild boar or hare can also be prepared in the same way.

1. Bone the loin. For the black pepper sauce, crush the bones, brown with a mirepoix of vegetables, deglaze with wine, reduce, add chicken stock, bring to a boil, strain, whisk in butter, and season to taste. For the white pepper sauce: braise onions with white pepper, add white wine, chicken stock, vermouth and spices. Add crème fraîche and heavy cream, purée in a blender, strain and season to taste.

2. For the celery purée: peel the celery, and cut into 1½ in/3 cm pieces. Blanch in salted water. Make a purée of the celeriac. Stuff the celery with this, and tie 2 pieces together with a chive. Just before serving, reheat in butter. Brown the venison tenderloins in butter for 3 minutes until cooked to rare.

Two Pepper Sauces

3. Potato noodles: boil the potatoes in their skins, peel, rice and stir in egg yolk and cornstarch; season with nutmeg and salt. Roll into thick noodles and cook in salted water. Drain. Toast the bread crumbs briefly in butter, add the noodles and toss them in the bread crumbs.

4. Poach the apple and garnish with cranberries. Pour white pepper sauce on each plate, and pour black pepper sauce around it to form a border. Place 2 slices of venison in the middle, and arrange 1 piece of apple, 1 stuffed piece of celery and 3 potato noodles on each plate.

Mixed Casserole

Preparation time: 30 minutes
Cooking time: 1 hour 45 minutes
Difficulty: ★★★

Serves 4

1 generous lb/500 g rib of pork
1 fresh knuckle
8¾ lb/250 g shoulder of pork
1 generous lb/500 g boneless belly of pork
½ pig's cheek
3½ tbsp/75 g acacia honey
3½ oz/100 g onions

8¾ oz/250 g potatoes
3½ oz/100 g carrots
3½ oz/100 g baby onions
1½ cups/350 ml red wine
¾ cup/200 ml sherry vinegar
2 cups/500 ml peanut oil
1¼ cup/300 ml veal stock
1 tbsp/5 g each oregano, ground thyme, savory, sage, ground coriander and ground nutmeg
½ bunch of chives
salt and pepper

Throughout France, the slaughtering of a pig always used to be carried out in combination with festivals and festive meals. Christmas above all offered an opportunity to eat plentifully of those parts of the pig that could not easily be preserved, and that were therefore enjoyed in the form of pies, blood sausages, and other sausages. This custom is still not totally obsolete, and butchers who know how to make use of practically every part of the pig are still much sought after.

Here Jean & Jean-Yves Schillinger introduce a very nutritious dish that can be enjoyed on long winter eve-nings. You can tell from the firmness and color of the flesh whether it is fresh and of good quality. Be careful to observe the various cooking times for the individual cuts, and put them into the pan one after the other—first the shoulder, then the other pieces 10 minutes later. You can use a needle to see whether the meat is cooked—you should feel only a slight resistance when inserting the needle. Don't forget to let the meat rest for a little while before serving. With this rustic dish you should serve a suitable accompaniment, such as sautéed pota-toes.

1. Trim excess fat from all the meat, and brown well in peanut oil. Take the meat out of the pan, pour off the fat and braise the finely chopped vegetables with all the herbs and spices.

2. Add the acacia honey and heat for 2 minutes, then deglaze with sherry vinegar. Return the meat to the pan and add veal stock, red wine and water to cover. Bring to a boil, then put in the oven at 400 °F/200 °C for 1 hour 45 minutes, uncovered.

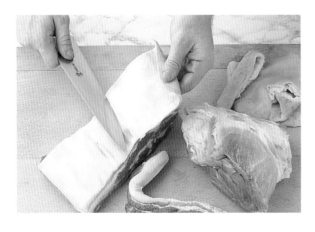

# of Pork

3. Remove all the meat and reduce the stock to the desired consistency. Season to taste. When it has cooled, cut the meat into chunks of equal thickness. Reheat in the sauce before serving.

4. Lightly brown the pearl onions, trim the potatoes to an attractive shape and brown in the pan. Arrange the meat and vegetables in soup dishes and pour sauce over. Scatter finely chopped chives on top.

Breast of Squab

Preparation time: 45 minutes
Cooking time: 20 minutes
Difficulty: ★★★

Serves 4

2 young squab
1½ oz/50 g chicken breast
1½ oz/50 g foie gras of duck
6 oz/160 g mushrooms
½ Chinese cabbage
2 shallots
3½ tbsp/50 g butter
2 cups/500 ml peanut oil
6½ tbsp/100 ml cream
9 oz/250 g puff pastry

1 egg yolk
salt and pepper

For the sauce:
1 oz/30 g carrots, finely sliced
2¾ oz/80 g onions, finely chopped
1 oz/30 g leek, finely sliced
2 tbsp/20 g red currant jelly
1 bay leaf
1 sprig of thyme
2 cups/500 ml red wine
1⅔ cups/400 ml brown veal stock
6½ tbsp/100 ml vinegar
olive oil
salt and pepper

For squab preparations, you could look in cookbooks under either "poultry" or "game": it depends on whether the writer is thinking of farm-raised or wild pigeons. Pigeon was popular in the Middle Ages, and is known later on to have been a favorite dish of Louis XIV. One classic squab dish is squab with peas; Jean Schillinger here suggests a somewhat more elaborate preparation. Here the squab legs are first boned and then stuffed with a chicken breast filling.

For the accompaniment, choose mushrooms according to season. You might opt for fresh morels, cèpes or ordinary mushrooms, which should be thinly sliced and then braised. Cabbage in all its varieties is one of the oldest of vegetables, and goes very well with squab.

To make the pepper sauce less pungent, you can add a little extra red currant jelly at the end of cooking.

1. Prepare the birds. Keep the giblets for the miniature kebabs. Roast the squabs for 10 minutes in a 400 °F/210 °C oven and let them cool. Bone the squab legs. Finely chop the onion, carrot and leek. Set aside.

2. Finely chop the foie gras and chicken breast. Mix and stuff the squab legs with them, and form into a compact shape. Cut the raw Chinese cabbage into thin strips, and the mushrooms into thin slices. Cook the cabbage and mushrooms together in butter.

with Pepper Sauce

3. Roll out and trim the pastry and, using round cutters, cut out 3 circles of different sizes for each serving. Place a stuffed squab leg on each of the medium-sized circles and lay the largest on top, sealing carefully; then place the smallest on top of that as a decoration. Brush with egg yolk and bake for 10 minutes with the oven at 355 °F/180 °C.

4. Brown the finely chopped vegetables in olive oil with the bay leaf and thyme. Deglaze with the red wine. Add the brown veal stock and vinegar. Reduce by two thirds and strain. Finally, add a good red currant jelly. Stir in the butter and season to taste. Brown the giblets in butter and spear on tooth picks.

Crown Roast of Suckling

Preparation time: 1 hour
Cooking time: 50 minutes
Difficulty: ★★★

Serves 4

2 ribs roast suckling pig
1 generous lb/500 g white bread
1 onion fresh sprigs of rosemary
1 bunch of parsley

For the diced vegetables:
1 carrot, 1 onion
1 celery rib, 2 cups/500 ml milk

For the potato purée:
1 generous lb/500 g potatoes

2 apples
dark beer, such as Guinness stout
6½ tbsp/100 g butter

1 garlic clove
salt and pepper

For the sauce:
1 generous lb/500 g bones of the suckling pig
3½ oz/100 g diced vegetables
2 tbsp/30 g tomato paste
4 cups/1 l veal stock
4 cups/1 l chicken stock
¾ cup/200 ml white wine
3½ tbsp/50 g butter
6½ tbsp/100 g honey, salt and pepper

For the garnish:
baby corn, asparagus, carrots, turnips, cherry tomatoes, snow peas, green beans, broccoli, cauliflower, large potatoes

A crown roast is most often made with lamb, but here our chefs use suckling pig of about 17½–23 lb/8–10 kg. An animal that is too large could also be too fatty. Usually, guests are deeply impressed, even before they start to eat, just by the sight of the dish and the ceremony of carving.

For the preparation of the roast, all the rib bones must be carefully scraped clean and covered with aluminum foil before roasting, so the bones do not burn in the oven. The meat is trimmed of its fat, trussed and, if you like, brushed

with honey to make it nice and crisp. For the stuffing, you can achieve wonders with the specified croutons, herbs and onion, but you may want to vary it to taste. The potato purée with dark beer will further enrich your meal with a slightly tart accent.

This impressive roast is surrounded by colorful vegetables, whose variations of flavor combine to produce a harmonious combination. But prepare them just before serving, so they remain hot.

1. Peel the vegetables for the garnish and boil in lightly salted water; put in a pan. Halve 4 potatoes, and pare them to attractive shapes. Blanch, then brown in butter. Make the potato purée with the ingredients as listed.

2. Scrape the meat from the rib bones, and truss in the shape of a crown as shown. Season the roast.

Pig with Spring Vegetables

3. For the stuffing, gently sauté the chopped onion, rosemary and parsley in butter. Add the cubed bread and continue to sauté without browning. For the sauce, brown the bones in a pan, pour off the fat and add the diced vegetables and tomato paste; braise without further browning. Add the wine and reduce by half. Add the veal and chicken stocks, and simmer for 20 minutes.

4. Skim off any scum, strain and reduce by two thirds. Stir in butter and seasoning. Put the roast in an ovenproof dish and fill with the stuffing. Roast for 20–30 minutes in a 400 °F/200 °C oven. Garnish with a sprig of rosemary and serve hot with the vegetables.

Braised Quail with

Preparation time: 1 hour
Cooking time: 20 minutes
Difficulty: ★★★

Serves 4

4 quails
½ oz/15 g duck liver
¼ cup/60 g wild rice, cooked
12 white grapes
¾ oz/20 g truffles
2 shallots
½ white cabbage
12 small turnips
4 cups/1 l veal stock
2 cups/500 ml heavy cream

1½ cups/370 ml champagne
oil
3 tbsp/40 g butter
bread suitable for toasting
fresh thyme
bay leaf
salt and pepper

For the sauce:
1 tomato
4 mushrooms
12 cups/3 l chicken stock
2 cups/300 g diced vegetables (onions, carrots, celery, parsley)
thyme
bay leaf

In this recipe, devised in honor of Prince Edward, our chefs have used the quail that is abundant in England and Scotland.

The Prince himself shoots, and presumably prefers wild to farm-raised quail, even if the latter are a viable alternative out of the hunting season. This recipe can also easily be used for a young squab or poussin. After stuffing, the birds should be well browned on all sides before finishing in the oven.

For an impressive stuffing, use wild rice, which should be soaked the day before. Our chefs naturally choose the "best in the world," Canadian rice, which grows in Manitoba, Ontario, and Saskatchewan. In these old Native American habitats the traditional methods are maintained, and the rice is harvested in canoes.

For the cabbage you need a good dry champagne or high-quality sparkling wine, which will enhance the flavor of the whole dish. The cabbage should be firm, unblemished, and without wilted leaves when you buy it. Blanch it first, then braise it slowly over low heat.

1. Brown the finely chopped shallots and diced duck liver. Add the wild rice, thyme, bay leaf, and truffle, and season. Add some veal stock. Remove from the heat and add the peeled, seeded and quartered grapes.

2. Bone the quail and stuff with the rice mixture. Cut the cabbage into thin strips. Briefly blanch them, cook in an uncovered pan in champagne until the liquid is almost completely reduced. Add the cream and simmer over low heat.

Champagne Cabbage

3. Brown the quails in butter until golden brown on all sides and finish cooking in the oven in a mixture of veal stock and white wine. Prepare the sauce.

4. With pastry cutters, cut decorative shapes out of the bread, deep-fry in oil, and arrange the pieces in the shape of a thistle (as in the photograph), using a very pale caramel to fasten them together and to the plate. Arrange the quail on a bed of cabbage, pour the cooking juices on top, and add three small braised turnips to each plate.

Leg of Venison with

Preparation time: 45 minutes
Cooking time: 30 minutes
Difficulty: ✴

Serves 4

2⅔ lb/1.2 kg leg of venison
1 oz/25 g truffles, cut into strips
1 tsp/5 g truffles, chopped
1¾ oz/50 g black olives, halved and pitted

1½ oz/40 g walnut halves
5½ oz/150 g perciatelle pasta
½ cup/120 g butter
2 tbsp/30 g clarified butter
¾ cup/200 ml heavy cream
2 tsp/10 ml port
3½ tbsp/50 ml stock
3 tsp olive oil
1 pinch of nutmeg
salt and pepper

Venison is particularly popular in the Belgian province of Limburg, which was formerly considered the Cinderella of the kingdom. Roger Souvereyns seasons this very delicate meat with black olives, which go extremely well with this dish.

The tenderest venison comes from a young male animal. Do not marinate it, but allow it to "mature" for a few days if purchased very fresh. The meat should remain pink inside but well browned on the outside. This can be done by browning it first in a pan and then transferring to the oven—cooked this way, it will remain juicy.

Keep strictly to the quantities and proportions of olives and truffles, as otherwise the flavor of the venison could be affected. Slightly bitter Italian olives go very well with this festive dish. You should use black truffles (*Tuber melanosporum*) such as those from the Périgord region of France; these are gathered at the end of February.

The macaroni represents a break by Roger Souvereyns from traditional accompaniments. Make sure that you cook it *al dente* so it will form a contrast to the delicate meat.

1. Prepare the leg of venison; remove all but the thigh bone, trim sinews, and lard with truffles and black olives. Tie with string and season.

2. Brown in a mixture of whole and clarified butter, and then roast for 20 minutes at 355 °F/180 °C, basting frequently. Meanwhile, cook the macaroni in briskly boiling salted water, then refresh. Quickly brown the nuts in clarified butter and drain on paper towels.

Truffles and Black Olives

3. Reduce the cream with the chopped truffle until it thickens; season to taste and add a pinch of nutmeg. Remove the venison from the oven and allow to rest on a plate covered with aluminum foil.

4. Remove fat from the roasting pan, flambé with port, add the stock and reduce by half. Beat in olive oil using a hand-held mixer, and keep warm. Arrange the macaroni on the plate, pour the truffle cream on top, and brown using a salamander or under the broiler.

Preparation time: 1 hour
Cooking time: 2 hours
Difficulty: ★★

Serves 4

4 pigs' feet
24 thick slices of bacon
pork caul (see note on page 32)

For the stuffing:
4 pigs' feet
7 oz/200 g calf's sweetbreads
1 each carrot, turnip, leek
salt and pepper

For the sauce:
bones from pigs' feet

1 each carrot, onion, leek, ripe tomato
1 tbsp paprika
3 cups/750 ml white wine

For the blood sausage mixture:
1 generous lb/500 g blood sausage (*boudin noir*) with onion
3 small shallots
1¾ oz/50 g bacon
2 tsp/10 ml cognac oil

For the herb tubes:
¼ cup/60 g flour
3½ tbsp/50 g butter
⅓–⅔ cup/100–150 ml water
1 egg
chives, chervil, parsley, thyme, chopped

For the braised onions:
¼ cup/60 g butter
4 onions, 1 sprig of thyme
½ bay leaf, salt and pepper

In the Basque country, pork is very highly regarded. This explains why there are so many different pork products there. For centuries the farmers have been keeping pigs and converting their meat to blood sausages, ham, and other sausages. The meat is also eaten fresh, of course, even the rind. There are innumerable kinds of blood sausage and an ever-increasing number of both producers and consumers of this delicacy.

Here the blood sausage is served as an accompaniment, and is basically left as is. Just remove the casing and replace it with a crisp pastry covering.

The pigs' feet, on the other hand, are completely boned, to make it easier to prepare, stuff and cook them. The stuffing is made with calf's sweetbreads, and are sure to produce the desired effect. Braised onions go very well with this dish with their slightly sweet taste, although you could substitute potato purée. The herb tubes could also be served filled with mashed potatoes.

Pedro Subijana is reminded of a regular customer, a surgeon, who gave him a scalpel perfectly suited to boning the pigs' feet. As it happens, Subijana once had dreams of becoming a surgeon...

1. For the stuffing: Boil 4 pigs' feet with vegetables in salted water. Reserve the cooking water. Bone the feet and cut the meat into small pieces. Do the same with the sweetbreads and mix. Chop the onions finely, and cook over very low heat in butter with thyme and bay leaf for 1 hour. Remove herbs and season to taste.

2. Bone the remaining uncooked pigs' feet, press flat, fill with the meat mixture and fold up. Roll in the chopped bacon, wrap in the pork caul, if used, and truss. Otherwise, leave the bacon whole and use to wrap the pigs' feet. Brown in hot oil to a golden brown, pour off the fat and roast for 2 hours at 320 °F/160 °C. Take out of the oven, remove the string and bacon, and loosely cover with aluminum in foil.

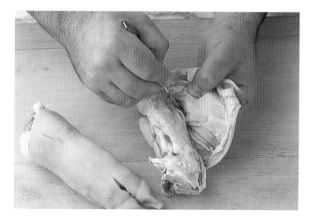

Blood Sausage

3. For the blood sausage mixture, chop the shallots, bacon and mushrooms, and brown. Add the skinned blood sausage and brown. Mix together, season and add cognac. For the sauce, brown the bones with all the vegetables, deglaze with white wine, reduce and add the water used to cook the pigs' feet. Reduce and strain.

4. For the "herb tubes": mix flour, melted butter, egg, herbs and water. Blend together with a wooden spatula, season with salt and pepper. Prepare pancakes with this batter. Cut out squares, and wrap them around tubular molds 1 in/2 cm in diameter and 4 ½ in/10 cm long. Brush with egg and bake in the oven until golden brown. Let cool, and fill with the blood sausage mixture.

Roast Saddle of Hare

Preparation time: 20 minutes
Cooking time: 10 minutes
Difficulty: ★★

Serves 4

2 saddles of hare
oil, rosemary, salt and pepper

For the sauce:
bones of the hare
1 each carrot, onion, leek
1 bouquet garni
flour
peppercorns
3½ tbsp/50 ml cognac
5 tsp/25 ml red wine, water or stock

4 tsp/20 ml hare's blood
butter
salt and pepper

For the red bean purée:
1¼ cup/300 g red beans
1 slice of orange
1 slice of lemon
1 slice of apple
3½ tbsp/50 g sugar
6½ tbsp/100 g butter

For the vegetable garnish:
8 each pearl onions, baby zucchini, new potatoes, baby carrots, Brussels sprouts
1 shallot
thyme

In his constant search for new recipes, Pedro Subijana decided to develop a purée based on red beans. These are known from Latin American cuisine. They have a fine dark red color and are also highly regarded in Spain, where they are valued for their decorative and nutritious qualities.

Pedro Subijana adds fruit to his bean purée, which he serves with roast saddle of hare. The red beans, which are rich in minerals, and are traditionally used for the preparation of a rather thick sauce, are here thickened with hare's blood. The beans should be left overnight to soak

in cold water and then cooked until they are tender.

This purée can be made at different times of year with various kinds of fruit, even with quinces, which Spaniards particularly love.

Use a young hare, weighing less than 6½ lb/3 kg, which will have tender flesh. It is served pink inside, golden-brown on the outside. Carve the meat before serving, as it looks even more appetizing in slices. The sauce should also be thickened with the blood only just before serving, so that it does not coagulate.

1. Season the loins of hare and brown to a golden brown on the flesh side. Remove from the pan, bone and set aside. Just before serving, brown the meat on the other side and cook to rare; cut into slices. Prepare the vegetables for the garnish; brown the potatoes. Trim the vegetables into attractive shapes and cook separately in salted water with a little oil until al dente. Refresh. Leave the zucchini until last; brown and set aside.

2. For the sauce: crush the bones and brown in oil. Add the vegetables and bouquet garni, braise, dust lightly with flour, toast the flour lightly for 2–3 minutes and flambé with cognac. Deglaze with the red wine, reduce, add stock and reduce again. Strain and allow to simmer over low heat.

with Red Bean Purée

3. Just before serving, strain the sauce again, reheat and, off the heat, thicken with the hare's blood. Stir in butter and season to taste.

4. Cook the soaked beans for about 2 hours with sugar, orange, lemon and apple slices. Drain, reserving the cooking water; reserve some of the beans for a garnish and purée the rest. Add butter and if necessary a little of the cooking water. Serve with the hare and baby vegetables.

Quail with Eggplant

Preparation time: 35 minutes
Cooking time: 20 minutes
Difficulty: ★★★

Serves 4

8 quails
2 large eggplants
2 small eggplants
1 zucchini
2 red (bell) peppers
12 cherry tomatoes
2 heads of garlic
1 onion
1 egg
3½ tbsp/50 g flour
7 tbsp/50 g ground almonds

½ cup/100 g bread crumbs
6½ tbsp/100 ml olive oil
salt and pepper

For the basil sauce:
2 sprigs of basil
5½ oz/150 g shallots
½ cup/125 g butter
⅔ cup/150 ml heavy cream
2 tbsp/30 ml white wine

For the white stock:
the quail carcasses
1 each onion, carrot, leek
1 celery rib
1 bouquet garni

Émile Tabourdiau loves the innumerable colors, fragrances and flavors of Provence and here he invites you to unite them in one dish. He created this recipe for a Provençal week at the Hotel Bristol in Paris.

Choose firm, fresh eggplants with smooth and shiny skins. You need large eggplants for the stuffing and smaller ones, which contain less water, to line the mold.

Choose large quails, because they will be easier to bone. Do not fry the breaded quail legs for too long, or they may become dry. Instead of quail, you could substitute a boned rack of lamb.

The basil sauce is typically Provençal and is made from blanched leaves.

1. Thinly slice the small eggplants and brown them. Place ring molds on a baking sheet. Slice the zucchini and braise. Cut circles out of the red pepper and braise in olive oil. Halve the large eggplants, and cook for 15–20 minutes in the oven with some olive oil. Mix their flesh with the chopped and fried onion and some garlic. Prepare a white stock with the quail carcasses and the vegetables

2. Bone the quails, leaving the upper thighs whole and season. Dredge the legs in flour, dip in egg and ground almonds, and deep-fry in hot oil.

and Basil Sauce

3. Braise the chopped shallots in butter, add the white wine and the stock, and reduce. Add the cream and the blanched basil, mix for a couple of minutes and strain. Braise 12 unpeeled garlic cloves in butter. Braise 12 cherry tomatoes. Brown the quail breasts, leaving them pink inside.

4. Line ring molds with the eggplant slices. Put in a layer of stuffing, add 2 quail breasts, fill with more stuffing. Top with rounds of zucchini and bell pepper. Bake at 375 °F/190 °C for 7 minutes. Pour the basil sauce onto the plates and unmold an eggplant charlotte onto each plate. Place the quail legs near the rim of the plate and alternate the garlic cloves and cherry tomatoes in a circle around the plate.

Medallions of Veal

Preparation time: 35 minutes
Cooking time: 25 minutes
Difficulty: ★★★

Serves 4

2 boneless veal loin chops, about 6 oz/160 g each
6 oz/160 g duck foie gras
14 oz/400 g calf's liver, thickly cut
1 pork caul (see note on page 32)

4 slices of puff pastry (see basic recipes)
4 Belgian endive
1 leek (white parts only)
7 oz/200 g purslane
½ cup/125 g butter
6½ tbsp/100 ml veal stock
2 tbsp/30 ml white wine
1 pinch of sugar
1 oz/25 g fresh ginger root
lemon juice
salt and pepper

In this recipe Émile Tabourdiau combines medallions of veal, calf's liver and duck foie gras.

The medallions of veal may be taken from the boned loin, cutting away the skin and fat. The small fillet is not suitable, as the medallions would be be too thick.

The best calf's liver comes from milk-fed calves; it is large and glossy and has a smooth surface. You should remove any residual blood vessels before cutting the liver into slices and browning it in butter (no need to coat in flour first).

A partly browned slice of duck foie gras between the medallions really brings out the best in them, particularly if you cut the foie gras in very thin slices.

As a vegetable accompaniment our chef has come up with little endive tarts. But you can replace them with leek or even celery tarts, if you prefer. Finally, purslane will enhance the visual appeal of your dish with its dark green color. The purslane should be only very lightly braised.

If you like, you can replace the veal with calf's sweetbreads.

1. Brown the veal in butter, and remove when half cooked. Cut in half, press flat, allow to cool slightly and season. Brown the calf's liver, then cut into 4 slices.

2. Form the medallions by alternating slices of veal, foie gras and calves' liver. Wrap in pork caul, or if preferred, brush all over with oil, and roast in the oven at 400 °F/200 °C. Remove and keep warm.

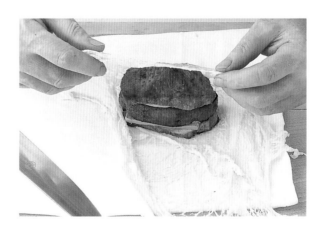

with Duck Foie Gras

3. Add the white wine to the roasting juices, reduce and add the veal stock. Strain and set aside.

4. Put the endive in small round pans and bake with butter, sugar, salt and a few drops of lemon juice. Halfway through cooking, cover with circles of pastry, and return to the oven to finish cooking. Unmold. Cut the leeks into thin strips and braise, adding the ginger, which has been previously cooked in syrup. Braise the purslane in butter. Place a veal medallion, some purslane, and an endive tart on each plate. Nap with sauce and serve.

Saddle of Hare

Preparation time: *1 hour*
Cooking time: *3 hours*
Difficulty: ✶✶

Serves 4

1 saddle of hare, about 600–1¾ lb/800 g
8 cups/2 l robust red wine
4 carrots
4 celery ribs
3 onions
4 tomatoes
5 cloves

cinnamon
6 juniper berries
bay leaves
basil
1 tsp cocoa powder
oil
butter
salt and pepper

For the tomato compote:
2 generous lb/1 kg green tomatoes
3 lemons
1⅔ cup/400 g sugar

Because this recipe includes a double marinade, you must plan to make it well ahead of the time you want to serve it: 32 hours for the tomato compote and 24 hours for the hare marinade.

The mixture of tomatoes, sugar and lemon zest must be stirred every 2–3 hours during the whole period of marination. The green tomatoes will absorb some water, but will still stay crisp. If you cannot get green tomatoes, you could substitute a typically North Italian accompaniment, the piquant *mostarda di frutti* (fruits preserved in mustard syrup), which is produced in Cremona.

The hare should be marinated in a good red wine. The roasting of the hare must be carefully monitored, as the meat can become tough if it is cooked for too long. Venison can be prepared in the same way.

The originality of this dish lies in its use of Oriental spices, and reminds us of the Venetian merchants who conducted an intensive trade in spices in the days of Marco Polo. These spices, formerly weighed against gold, were the focus of lively competition between the chefs of the great houses of the nobility, and still play an important role in Italian cuisne.

1. Place the hare in a large dish with the celery, 2 carrots, 2 onions, 2 tomatoes, cloves, cinnamon, juniper berries, bay leaves and basil, and season with salt and pepper. Pour on 8 cups/2 l of red wine, and marinate for 24 hours.

2. Remove the hare and strain the marinade, discarding the solids and reserving the liquid. Chop the rest of the raw vegetables. Heat oil and butter in a large skillet, add the chopped vegetables and cook for 5 minutes.

with Tomato Compote

3. Add the hare and brown on both sides. Pour on the wine from the marinade, and simmer for 3 hours. Season to taste and add 1 tsp of cocoa powder.

4. For the compote, place the green tomatoes with the sugar and the grated and caramelized lemon peel in a large pan, and bring to boil. Leave to macerate for about 32 hours, until a compote is produced. Cut the saddle of hare into smaller pieces and serve with the vegetables and 1 tbsp of the compote for each person.

Lambs' Feet with

Preparation time: 2 hours
Cooking time: 1 hour 30 minutes
Difficulty: ★★★

Serves 4

20 lambs' feet
¾ cup/200 ml lamb stock
2 generous lb/1 kg lamb bones
7 oz/200 g pork caul (see note on page 32)
2 generous lb/1 kg crayfish
8¾ oz/250 g small dried white beans

2 red (bell) peppers
2 tomatoes
1 head of garlic
2 shallots
1 tsp tomato paste
6½ tbsp/100 g butter
1 cup/250 ml olive oil
3½ tbsp/50 g flour
juice of ½ lemon
1 bunch of parsley
1 bunch of basil
salt and pepper

White beans are the classic accompaniment to leg of lamb and also go very well with lambs' feet. They are not too floury and are very easy to digest. Use the smallest white beans you can find, which keep their shape well when cooked. Even if fresh beans are available, it is better to used dried ones in this recipe.

The crayfish tastes just as delicate and aromatic as its relative, the lobster. Soak them in milk for 2 hours and then rinse thoroughly You can also replace them with lobster.

Choose lambs' feet with white skin and firm flesh, which slightly resists firm pressure. Boning the lambs' feet requires time and patience, as does stuffing them. You should allow plenty of time for these procedures.

The addition of flour, water and above all lemon juice prevents the lamb and vegetables from turning brown. But sift the flour well before you dissolve it in the water.

1. Remove the intestines from the crayfish as shown. Boil in salted water for 5 minutes, then shell the tails.

2. Blanch the lambs' feet and refresh. Prepare a stock with the lamb bones. Blend 3½ tbsp/ 50 g of flour in the cold water and add the juice of half a lemon. Put the mixture in the pan in which the lambs' feet are to be cooked.

White Beans

3. Cook the lambs' feet for about 90 minutes. Set aside to cool in the cooking liquid, then bone. Keep the 16 best-looking pieces and dice the rest. Season with salt, pepper and lamb stock. Add parsley and chopped shallots. Reconstitute 8 of the feet by stuffing with the diced meat. Wrap each foot in the pork caul or brush with oil all over.

4. Braise the lambs' feet in a 275 °F/140 °C oven, basting with 2 cups/500 ml of lamb stock. Cut the peppers into thin strips and braise in olive oil. Put the following together in a pan: the white beans, peppers, tomatoes, tomato paste, garlic and the finely chopped basil. Stir in butter. Serve a few crayfish and 2 lambs' feet with the bean mixture.

Preparation time: 1 hour 30 minutes
Cooking time: 30 minutes
Difficulty: ★★★

Serves 4

1 loin roast of lamb, about 3⅓ lb/1½ kg
2 lamb kidneys
2 zucchini
2 tomatoes

1 head of garlic
1 bunch of parsley
1 bunch of thyme
3½ tbsp/50 g tapenade (see basic recipes)
1 tsp tomato paste
6½ tbsp/100 g butter
4 cups/1 l white wine
1 cup/250 ml olive oil
salt and pepper

The word tapenade comes from the Provençal (*tapeno* and contains, in addition, black olives, garlic and anchovies and olive oil. Tapenade is served with salads, fish and meat dishes. Since the ingredients keep well, it can be prepared in advance. In an airtight container in a cool place it will keep for up to 3 months.

When the lamb has been stuffed with the kidneys, it must be tied up carefully, so it is evenly shaped. This should be done working inward, from the edges to the middle. You can certainly prepare the meat in advance.

1. Season the whole kidneys, and brown for 5 minutes over high heat. Then pierce them so that the excess moisture can escape, halve, and slice. Bone the lamb and butterfly open.

2. Stuff the two sides of the loin with the kidneys. With the bones, prepare a lamb stock, while allowing the white wine to reduce. Carefully roll and tie the meat. Peel, seed and dice the tomatoes, then add to the tapenade with the olive oil and tomato paste.

withTapenade

3. Cut the zucchini into long strips, then blanch for a few minutes. Refresh and drain. Season the lamb stock to taste and add the finely chopped basil, thyme and parsley.

4. Roast the lamb for 20 minutes with garlic, then allow to rest. Pour some sauce onto each plate. Cut the meat into eight slices and place 2 slices on each plate. Arrange the finely chopped tomatoes and the zucchini braised in butter around the plates. Garnish with tapenade.

Dominique Toulousy's

Preparation time: 2 hours
Cooking time: 2 hours 15 minutes
Difficulty: ★

Serves 4

1⅓ lb/600 g white beans
4 pieces confit of duck
4 smoked sausages

4 Toulouse sausages
6½ tbsp/100 g duck fat
3½ oz/100 g fresh pork rind
7 oz/200 g unsmoked bacon
¾ cup/200 ml duck stock
1 carrot
1 onion
10 garlic cloves
2 bunches of thyme and bay leaves
salt and pepper

This is the most famous dish in the cuisine of southwestern France. The word *cassoulet* comes from *cassole*, the earthenware pot in which its preparation is completed. Many variations of this dish are known. One is a simple combination of beans and meat, the cassoulet of the poor; the second is a more refined version with confit of duck and partridge; the third, still more sophisticated, variation also contains pork rind and sausages, which make the dish particularly juicy. This last variation is presented here.

The white beans should be soaked in cold water for 12 hours. The women chefs of the great Toulouse tradition, Dominique Toulousy's aunts and grandmothers, knew that the secret of cassoulet is the long preparation time.

Meat and vegetables are equally important in this dish, and you should follow our chef's instructions precisely. The vegetables for the mirepoix, for example, must be chopped very finely. Otherwise, you just need some patience and should keep to the traditional method— try, for instance, to use an earthenware pot.

Cassoulet is a complete meal in itself, needing no appetizer, and rich desserts are best avoided. If you follow it with a light green salad, your guests will be well satisfied. Cassoulet can be enjoyed all year round.

1. Soak the white beans in cold water for 12 hours. Then blanch the beans and the bacon, cut into large dice. Refresh. Dice the carrot and onion.

2. In a deep pan, braise the diced vegetables with the duck fat. Add the pork rind, bacon, white beans and duck stock. Add thyme, bay leaves and the chopped garlic, and simmer for 90 minutes.

Cassoulet

3. Meanwhile, brown the confit of duck in a pan until golden brown. Add the sausages, brown, and set aside.

4. Put the beans and all the meats into an earthenware casserole. Season to taste and bake for 45 minutes in a 400–450 °F/210–240 °C. Serve hot.

Veal Chops in

Preparation time: 1 hour 30 minutes
Cooking time: 1 hour 40 minutes
Difficulty: ★★★

Serves 4

2 rib veal chops, 2 generous lbs/1 kg each
3⅓ lb/1½ kg fresh cèpes
2 generous lbs/1 kg potatoes

4 garlic cloves
10½ oz/300 g dry toasting bread
13 tbsp/200 g butter
6½ tbsp/100 ml milk
¾ cup/200 ml peanut oil
¾ cup/200 ml crème fraîche or heavy cream
3 bunches of parsley
salt and pepper

Veal chops are a favorite; and here they are wrapped in a crust seasoned with garlic and parsley, which will be even better if prepared the day before. It should be kept refrigerated, so it will be good and firm when you begin preparation. If it is still not firm enough, add some more melted butter and refrigerate again.

The cèpes are prepared by first carefully cleaning and then cutting the stems into small dice. Mix them with garlic and parsley, and add them to the sliced potatoes. Be careful not to cook the potatoes for too long. After

you have browned them quickly over high heat, reduce the heat and continue to cook for another 15 minutes.

The cooking of the chops in the oven demands a certain vigilance, as the meat could dry out if not regularly basted. Keep precisely to the time and temperature given.

The parsley sauce is made with cream or crème fraîche. The parsley is cooked in advance and carefully dried. Both the sauce and the veal chops must be served hot.

1. Remove the crusts from the bread, and dice. Put the bread dice into a bowl with milk, 1 bunch of parsley, chopped, and 3 chopped garlic cloves. Stir in 6½ tbsp/100 g of melted butter, add salt and pepper, and knead until a dough is created. Divide in half and set aside to rest. Wash and cook the potatoes, but do not peel, and cut into ½ in/1 cm thick slices.

2. Roll out the dough between two sheets of foil. Clean the mushrooms, and cut the stems into small dice and the caps into thin slices. Put in a bowl with salt and pepper, mix and marinate for 30 minutes. Brown the veal chops on both sides for 5 minutes, and drain.

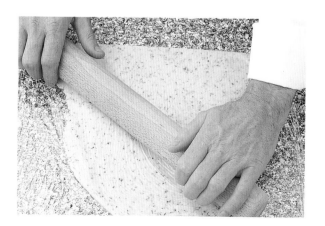

3. Wrap the chops in the bread dough. Chop half a bunch of parsley and the rest of the garlic, and mix with the diced mushroom stems. Brown the potatoes on each side for 5 minutes. Reduce the heat and cook for a further 15 minutes.

4. Brush oil over the bottom of an oven dish, add some butter, cover the chops with mushroom slices, and cook in the oven, first for 10 minutes at 390 °F/200 °C and then another 40 minutes at 300 °F/ 150 °C. Blanch the parsley for 1 minute, refresh, squeeze out excess liquid, boil with the crème fraîche and purée in a blender. Five minutes before the potatoes have finished cooking, add the mixture of garlic, parsley and cèpes, and season.

Rabbit with Cider,

Preparation time: 1 hour
Cooking time: 45 minutes
Difficulty: ✶✶

Serves 4

1 rabbit, about 4½ lb/2 kg
6 very thin slices of smoked bacon
1 pork caul (see note on page 32)
20 pearl onions
8 small leeks
10 turnips
butter
1 bunch of fresh coriander

salt and pepper

For the cider stock:
the rabbit bones
2 apples
1 carrot
1 onion
2 shallots
1 bouquet garni
peelings from the turnips
6½ tbsp/100 g butter
8 cups/2 l hard cider, not too dry
peanut oil

"All parts of the rabbit are good to eat," says Gilles Tournadre, and here he provides proof of this statement. In this dish, all parts of the rabbit are used, and when we see all the goodness that it can provide, we can only be grateful that the rabbit is so efficient at multiplying.

Tournadre would also like to dispel the common prejudice that rabbit meat is too dry. Following his recipe, you can preserve the juicy quality of the meat, but for this you really do need a top-quality rabbit. Once you have found a

good specimen, wrap it carefully in bacon, whose fat keeps the meat juicy and enriches it with an additional nuance of flavor. Use an enameled cast-iron pan and prepare everything over low heat.

For a few decades after World War II, the turnip fell into disfavor. It is high time to return this vitamin-rich vegetable to its rightful status. In this recipe its fine, bitter taste mingles with the sweetness of the cider, a well-known specialty of Normandy.

1. Remove the saddle and legs of the rabbit and bone. Prepare rabbit roulades by wrapping the meat in thin slices of smoked bacon.

2. Proceed in the same way with the legs. Wrap each piece in a piece of pork caul. Cut the turnips into neat shapes and boil in a little water and some butter, then add salt. Prepare the pearl onions and leeks in the same way. Keep the turnip peelings for the sauce.

Turnips and Coriander

3. In a braising pan, brown the crushed rabbit bones with the garnish in peanut oil. Deglaze with the cider. Add the apples, the blanched turnip peelings and the bouquet garni. Simmer for 45 minutes over low heat, strain and reserve the liquid.

4. Brown the rabbit roulades and legs in oil and butter, and cook until done, turning occasionally. Cut into slices and arrange on plates with the turnips, the glazed onions and the leeks. Pour the sauce over and garnish with coriander leaves. This dish can also be garnished with small carrots and chanterelle mushrooms.

Breast of Guinea Fowl with

Preparation time: 45 minutes
Cooking time: 30 minutes
Difficulty: ★★

Serves 4

1 guinea fowl, about 3⅓/1½ kg
4 Belgian endive
diced carrots, celery, onion

1 lemon
5 slices of smoked bacon
6½ tbsp/100 g butter
6½ tbsp/100 ml heavy cream
melted butter
¾ cup/200 ml stock
1 pinch of sugar
salt and pepper

Here Gilles Tournadre introduces a dish that is part of a long tradition of domestic cookery that reflects the wisdom of generations of mothers and grandmothers.

Some cooks complain that guinea fowl easily becomes dry, but true devotees rate it above a poussin or capon.

Tournadre wraps the guinea fowl in foil and poaches it in stock, so that it stays juicy. Then the breasts are reheated in melted butter, and browned at the last moment in fresh butter.

With the lightly salted smoked bacon and the rather bitter endive, the taste of the guinea fowl is given a discreet lift. In winter, you can replace the endive with Brussels sprouts if you wish.

1. Remove the legs from the guinea fowl and save for another use. Remove the breasts and wrap in foil, taking care that the foil does not tear, and then poach in water for 20 minutes.

2. Prepare the stock with the carcass and diced vegetables.

Belgian Endive and Bacon

3. Cut the Belgian endive lengthwise into strips and braise in butter. Then squeeze the juice from a lemon; pour over the endive with a pinch of sugar. Reduce for 5 minutes, add the cream and taste for seasoning. Cut the slices of smoked bacon into very small dice and then blanch them.

4. Remove the guinea fowl breasts and brown them in butter, beginning skin-side down. Baste frequently with the butter from the pan. Brown the diced bacon vigorously in a pan and add the endive. Arrange on a warmed dish and serve.

Preparation time: 1 hour 30 minutes
Cooking time: 40 minutes
Difficulty: ★★

Serves 4

4 boned duck legs
4 slices of cooked ham
meat trimmed from the top of the thighs
fresh pistachios
1 egg yolk
dry white bread
butter

2 sage leaves
parsley
salt and pepper to taste

For the sauce:
4 ladlefuls brown duck stock
½ cup/125 ml white wine
2 tsp balsamic vinegar
1 carrot
1 onion
1 celery rib
some butter

In Piedmont the duck is very popular, and forms the basis of innumerable recipes, in which the breast plays a leading part. But to depart from the beaten track, Luisa Valazza here suggests stuffing the duck's legs. A certain skill in needlework could stand you in good stead when closing up the legs, but don't worry, it is not that difficult.

A duck of 5½ lb/2½ kg will have nice meaty legs. If you like, you can enrich the stuffing with a noble specialty of Piedmont, the white truffle.

If you have time, chop the meat with a knife rather than using a food processor, which produces a uniform but too fine result.

To close the legs after stuffing, you must sew them up with kitchen thread. You can do all this in advance, browning only just before serving. You can check the progress of roasting in the oven with a needle: if the escaping juices run clear, the meat is cooked through. Let it rest for about 10 minutes in a warm place before serving.

1. To make the stuffing, briskly brown the duck meat in butter with sage and the ham cut in strips. Chop in a food processor or with a knife.

2. Mix in a bowl the egg yolk, bread crumbs (soaked in milk and then squeezed to remove excess milk), parsley, pistachios and the duck meat and ham. Season to taste.

Balsamic Vinegar

3. Stuff the boned duck legs and pull the skin over the opening, then sew up with kitchen thread. Put in a pan, brown on all sides, pour off fat, and deglaze with white wine and balsamic vinegar for the sauce.

4. Add the finely chopped vegetables, brown until golden, and add the duck stock. Place in the oven for 30 minutes. Remove the legs and keep warm. Reduce the meat juices until they thicken, add butter and salt. Strain. Remove the thread from the legs. Cut into slices and arrange on plates in a fan shape. Pour sauce over, and garnish with vegetables.

Fondant of Sweetbreads and

Preparation time:	*30 minutes*
Cooking time:	*20 minutes*
Difficulty:	★★

Serves 4

1⅓ lb/600 g calf's sweetbreads
10½ oz/300 g calf's head
3½ oz/100 g black truffles, with juice
8 potatoes
1 pork caul
flour
10 tbsp/150 g butter
6½ tbsp/100 ml milk, whipped until frothy

6½ tbsp/100 ml reduced veal stock
nutmeg
salt
ground black pepper

For the calf's head:
2 leeks
2 onions, studded with cloves
2 carrots
2 celery ribs
1 head of garlic
1 bouquet garni

Calf's head was formerly considered a peasant dish, and was served with heavy sauces. Here Guy Van Cauteren introduces a dish that combines calf's head, calf's sweetbreads and potato purée.

The calf's head should be quite white, and should be soaked overnight in cold salted water. Then the head, without the tongue and brain, is cooked over a low heat for half a day at least, preferably the day before serving, because the meat will then be able to rest and will have more tenderness.

The calf's sweetbreads, or thymus gland, is a delicious ingredient that should be treated with due respect. It certainly deserves the truffle garnish suggested by Van Cauteren. The truffles must be carefully brushed. Canned truffles can be used, but they certainly do not have the robust flavor of fresh ones. The fondants should be regularly basted in the oven, evenly cooked and served hot.

1. Blanch the calf's head in salted water. When it comes to the boil, skim off the scum. Add all the herbs and spices, onions studded with cloves, carrots, celery, a whole head of garlic and the bouquet garni. Put coarse salt into a baking dish, place the unpeeled potatoes on top and bake in a 400 °F/200 °C oven for 45 minutes.

2. Cook the calf's head for 3 to 3½ hours over low heat. Let cool, then chop the meat finely. Soak the sweetbreads, blanch and refresh, then remove the outer skin. Soak the pork caul, then spread out.

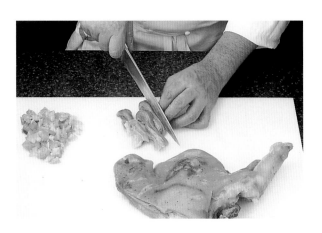

Calf's Head with Potato Purée

3. Cut the sweetbreads into pieces and season. Lay on the pork caul the truffle slices, a few slices of calf's head and some sweetbread. Close up and coat lightly in flour. Repeat for 3 more portions. Brown for a few minutes in a skillet and then put in a 355 °F/180 °C oven for 15 minutes. Deglaze with veal stock and truffle juice and reduce slightly. Season to taste.

4. Stir butter into the sauce and strain. Peel the baked potatoes and crush with a fork; add the whipped milk, butter, salt, pepper and nutmeg. Keep warm. Arrange the fondants on the plates, pour sauce over them and add a helping of potato purée to each.

Preparation time:	*1 hour*
Cooking time:	*1 hour*
Difficulty:	✴✴

Serves 4

1 chicken
4 eggs
4 slices lachsschinken (cured loin of pork)
1 cup/250 g blanched almonds
2 generous lb/1 kg Belgian endive
1 leek
1 cup/250 ml heavy cream
1 cup/250 g butter

white wine vinegar
nutmeg
salt, coarse and fine
ground black pepper
coarsely crushed pepper

For the garnish:
leek
onions studded with cloves
carrots
celery
flat-leaf parsley
garlic
thyme and bay leaf

Choose a chicken 1 year old, or older. The older the bird, the longer it will have to be cooked. With a chicken about 4½ lb/2 kg in weight you will have to allow a minimum of 1 hour. You need only follow Guy Van Cauteren's instructions, with one possible variation: if you add some grated onion to the soup, it will give it a lovely color.

Adding eggs as an accompaniment is an interesting idea. The egg is a nutritious ingredient, rich in minerals. A poached egg is cooked in water with a little vinegar just below boiling point. It requires some skill to ensure that the egg white does not disperse in the water. After 3 minutes, refresh the eggs, trim off any ragged edges and carefully keep them warm in salted water.

The Belgians are proud of their cultivation of endive, which the francophone portion of their population calls *chicon*. You should choose very fresh, white, medium-sized endives; remove them from the oven when translucent and tender. Afterwards, brown them briefly so the residual liquid evaporates.

1. Wash the Belgian endive and put in a pan with butter, salt and nutmeg. Cover the pan with waxed paper and a plate. Bring to a boil, then cook in a 400 °F/200 °C oven for 30 minutes. Blanch the chicken in salted water and refresh.

2. Poach the chicken with the garnish for 1 hour over low heat in a covered pan. Keep the cooking water. Cut the lachsschinken into thin slices and dry-fry them in a pan, then mix with the heavy cream. Set aside. With a pestle, crush the 2 cups/250 g of almonds.

Poached Eggs and Ham

3. Poach the eggs in water with white wine vinegar; refresh. Soak the almonds for 15 minutes in the chicken broth. Dice the Belgian endive finely and add to the broth.

4. Skin the chicken and remove the meat. Cut into small dice and add to the broth. Pour some broth into each soup plate, add a poached egg and the creamed ham. Garnish with a julienne of deep-fried leek.

Preparation time: *30 minutes*
Cooking time: *30 minutes*
Difficulty: ★

Serves 4

1 chicken, about 4½ lb/2 kg
1¼ cup/300 ml heavy cream
10 tbsp/150 g butter
nutmeg
salt, coarse and fine
freshly ground black pepper

For the chicken:
1 leek
1 onion stuck with cloves
2 carrots
white celery
parsley
garlic
thyme
bay leaf

For the garnish:
white part of leek
1 carrot
7 oz/200 g celery root

The people of Belgium have such a devotion to eating good food that in the Middle Ages many streets were named after foods. Even today, towns and villages have retained this tradition, so that tourists are in danger of confusing street names with restaurant menus. The dish called waterzooi is to Belgium what bouillabaisse is to Marseilles, and our chef is particularly fond of it.

This dish is of Flemish origin (the name "water-zooi" is connected to the city of Ghent) and was originally prepared with fish. Eventually, however, chicken came to be preferred.

Do not forget that this dish is supposed to be light, so you should not overdo the heavy cream that is added to the soup. Serve the dish hot and do not keep it any longer than 48 hours—that is, if any is left over.

1. First remove the legs from the chicken and cut them in half, then remove the breasts. Cover the legs and breasts with salted water, bring to a boil, then drain the meat.

2. Finely chop the parsley and set aside. Simmer the chicken, together with the other ingredients, for about 30 minutes over low heat. Remove the chicken from the pan, skin and bone it, then cut into large pieces.

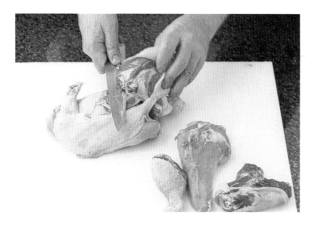

3. Cut the carrots, leek and celery into julienne strips, and cook separately in salted water. Refresh. Strain the water in which the chicken was boiled, and remove the fat.

4. Add the heavy cream, the chicken pieces, and the julienne of vegetables. Heat gently, stir in the butter, and season to taste with nutmeg, salt, and pepper. Serve in warm soup plates, garnished with the parsley leaves.

Duck with Preserved

Preparation time: 45 minutes
Cooking time: 30 minutes
Difficulty: ★★

Serves 4

2 ducklings, 3⅓ lb/1½ kg each
1 raw duck foie gras
16 small fresh figs
3½ oz/100 g mushrooms

2 slices of white bread
¼ cup/60 g butter
¾ cup/200 ml ruby port
¾ cup/200 ml peanut oil
2 tsp/10 g green peppercorns
salt and pepper

For the bigarade sauce:
(see basic recipes)

Fresh ducks should not be bought at the end of the winter, from February to March, but are available for the rest of the year. If you cannot get young ducks with tender flesh and a plump breast, about 3⅓ lb/1½ kg in weight, you may substitute young squabs or, even better, young guinea fowl.

The Seville orange, which is required for the bigarade sauce, is a bitter variety of orange whose thick peel is rich in essential oils. It is used to make orange-flavored liqueurs (Cointreau, Grand Marnier, Curacao) and bitter marmalades. Bigarade sauce goes very well with duck and can be prepared with either veal stock or duck stock. Prepare the sauce the day before and keep it in a cool place,

so the flavors will have a chance to intermingle. The ducks, however, should be browned only just before serving, and the breasts in particular should not be sliced until the last moment, so that the flesh stays juicy.

The fig was already well known in ancient times, when it was prepared in all imaginable ways. The poet Virgil, who knew a great deal about agriculture and cooking, even dedicated several of his writings to them, and these have inspired the method of preserving figs described here. You need about 4 fresh figs per person. Choose purple figs with a skin whose texture and character matches that of the duck. Alternatively, replace them with apples, peaches or apricots.

1. Marinate the figs in the port for 48 hours. Carefully clean the ducklings and season with salt and pepper. Put them in a roasting pan with oil and roast for 30 minutes at 485 °F/250 °C, basting regularly. Remove the ducklings from the oven, remove breasts and legs, and keep warm.

2. Pour off fat from roasting pan, add the finely chopped mushrooms. Brown for 2 minutes at medium heat. Deglaze with 6½ tbsp/100 ml port from the marinade for the figs, then add the bigarade sauce. Reduce by a quarter. Strain finely and stir in the butter.

Figs à la Virgil

3. Heat the figs with the port. Cut the bread into heart shapes and fry in some oil. Cut the foie gras into 4 slices of ¾ oz/20 g each, and brown for 30 seconds on each side. Place on the fried bread slices.

4. Cut the duck breasts into thin slices and arrange in a fan shape on the plates. Surround with figs and a piece of fried bread with foie gras. Pour on the bigarade sauce, and serve hot. Serve the legs as a second course.

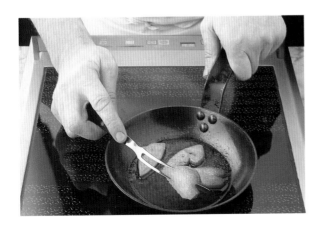

Venison with Cumberland

Preparation time: *20 minutes*
Cooking time: *15 minutes*
Difficulty: ★★

Serves 4

1⅓ lb/600 g saddle of venison (to yield 14 oz/400 g tenderloin)
2 oranges
4 small pears
2 apples

7 oz/200 g muscat grapes
1 lemon
3½ tbsp/50 g cranberries in syrup
4 tsp/20 g ground ginger
3½ tbsp/50 ml white wine vinegar
6½ tbsp/100 ml Cumberland sauce (see basic recipes)
2 cups/500 ml red wine
6½ tbsp/100 g butter
3 tsp/40 g sugar
salt and pepper

The roe deer is usually found in the forests of temperate regions, and is very popular in the hunting season. Its flesh is known for its tenderness, but contracts somewhat during cooking, so the medallions should be cut out and flattened to lengthen the fibers and soften the meat.

Cumberland sauce is a great classic of British cuisine and is traditionally served with game. It accompanies venison with a whole range of fruits. However, you should restrict yourself to fruit that withstands heat well and remains firm during preparation. This includes the pear. Freddy Van Decasserie recommends the Conference (comice) pear, recognizable by its longish shape and pale green skin. It should be small and ripe, but still firm, so that it does not

disintegrate during cooking. A good choice of apple is Golden Delicious. Let the apples cool in their cooking water, so they do not lose their color.

With their sour taste, cranberries form an attractive contrast to the other fruits. These small red berries are a very good accompaniment to game. In the fall you can get them fresh, but they are available in preserved form all year round. Other colorful fruits can be used to enrich this unusual dish, such as mango and papaya to replace the mixture of apples and grapes.

A tenderloin of young wild boar can also be prepared in the same way as the venison.

1. Peel the pears, leaving the stem attached, and poach in lightly sugared red wine. Zest the oranges; peel them and divide into segments. Blanch the zest.

2. Bone the venison, remove the membranes and fat. Cut the tenderloins into 8 medallions. Flatten and season the medallions and brown in 3½ tbsp/50 g butter—they should be pink inside. Keep warm.

Sauce and Winter Fruits

3. Peel the apples and dice, then poach in a light syrup. Peel and seed the grapes, cut in half, warm in 1 tbsp syrup, and mix with the cranberries.

4. Pour off the fat from the pan, heat the sugar quickly and caramelize lightly. Add vinegar, orange, meat juices and Cumberland sauce. Strain, season with ground ginger and salt, and stir in the butter. Add the blanched orange peel. Serve on warmed plates with the venison.

Lambs' Brains, Sweetbreads

Preparation time: 30 minutes
Cooking time: 2 hours
Difficulty: ★★

Serves 4

4 lambs' brains
4 lambs' tongues
1 lb/450 g lambs' sweetbreads
7 oz/200 g carrot
5½ oz/150 g peas

5½ oz/150 g green beans
2 shallots
6½ tbsp/100 g butter
melted butter
¾ cup/200 ml white wine, preferably Jurançon
3½ tbsp/50 ml cognac
8 cups/2 l chicken stock
basil
saffron
salt and pepper

For this dish, there are two white ingredients, the brain and the sweetbreads, and one red, the tongue. You should make sure that they are absolutely fresh, and prepare them without delay. The difficulty of this recipe lies in the different ways of preparing each ingredient. The tongue must be dealt with first; cook it carefully and then cut into small pieces. The brain must be soaked in cold water before the outer membrane is removed, under which residues of blood may still be found; finally, you will have to remove from the sweetbreads all impurities, such as fibers, traces of blood, membranes, and so forth.

In preparing variety meats, you can make use of a few helpful additions. The vinegar, for example, helps the brain and sweetbreads to retain their whiteness. All this preparation can be carried out in advance, so that at the decisive moment you can concentrate on the wine sauce. Geert Van Hecke uses Jurançon, that noble wine from southwestern France that has been deservedly famous since the 16th century; Antoine de Bourbon, King of Navarre, rubbed it on the lips of his infant son Henri, later to be Henri IV.

1. Cook the tongues for 2 hours over low heat in 8 cups/2 l of chicken stock. Remove the tongues, set aside to cool, then remove the skin.

2. Blanch the sweetbreads in lightly salted cold water. Then put the brains into the chicken stock, adding a dash of vinegar, bring to boil and refresh. Reserve the stock. Cut the brains and sweetbreads into pieces, then sauté in melted butter.

3. Add the shallots; deglaze with a small glass of cognac and the wine. Remove the meat and reserve.

4. Add 1⅔ cups/400 ml of the chicken stock to the pan and reduce. Stir in 6½ tbsp/100 g of butter, and add basil and saffron. Arrange everything on plates with some spring vegetables, trimmed attractively and cooked in salted water.

Saddle of Rabbit with

Preparation time: 45 minutes
Cooking time: 30 minutes
Difficulty: ★★★

Serves 4

3 saddles of young rabbit
3½ oz/100 g raw foie gras

1 generous lb/500 g young turnips with greens
7 oz/200 g spinach
2¾ cups/700 ml dark beer
3½ tbsp/50 g butter
3½ tbsp/50 g sugar
1 egg yolk
7 tbsp/50 g ground almonds
salt and pepper

Rabbit meat has long been undervalued. The farm-bred rabbit can be prepared in many ways, such as *hasenpfeffer* (similar to jugged hare), dishes with mustard, and fricassees. Its free-range relative, the wild rabbit, on the other hand, is well suited to frying, grilling, or broiling.

Geert Van Hecke suggests using beer in this novel rabbit dish. In most recipes the majority of ingredients have to be simmered, which takes. This is not necessary here if you use a young rabbit with tender flesh, whose saddle is wrapped in its own skin after boning. The bones are used in preparing the sauce.

As an accompaniment to this fine, tasty meat, there is nothing to beat turnips. If possible, get them with the greens still attached; you can use these for a soup as well. The turnip is a well-known member of the Cruciferae family, containing a high proportion of calcium and vitamin C.

For the sauce, Belgian beer is your best choice. No other country seems to have so many unusual beers as Belgium, and our chef is a beer connoisseur. He particularly recommends Leffe, a beer that is available throughout the world, and which he considers perfectly suited to bring out the flavor of the rabbit.

1. Bone the saddles of rabbit. Brown the bones and deglaze with the beer. Blanch the spinach.

2. Cut the foie gras into ½ in/1 cm sticks, season with salt and pepper. Place spinach leaves and sticks of foie gras on the belly flaps, along with the boned loins. Reserve the tenderloin. Roll up into a sausage, tie and place on aluminum foil.

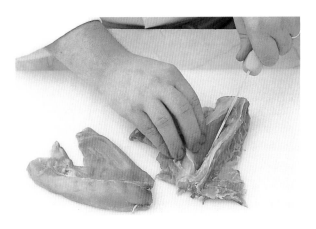

Breaded Mini "Chops"

3. Prepare the turnips, then boil for 30 minutes with 4 tsp/20 g butter and 3½ tbsp/50 g sugar. Steam the saddles of rabbit for 10 minutes. Deglaze with the rabbit stock. Cut the tenderloins into small chunks and insert a piece of bone into each.

4. Reduce the sauce and stir in butter. Brush egg yolk over these mini "chops" and coat with ground almonds. Brown briefly in melted butter. Arrange on the plates with the sauce.

Preparation time: 2 hours
Cooking time: 1 hour 30 minutes
Difficulty: ★★

Serves 4

2 ducklings, 4½ lb/2 kg each
5½ oz/150 g smoked dry-cured ham or prosciutto
1 generous lb/500 g mushrooms

2 generous lbs/1 kg turnips
diced carrots and onions
3 garlic cloves
3½ tbsp/50 g sugar
6½ tbsp/100 g butter
4 cups/1 l chicken stock
2 cups/500 ml Madeira
fresh thyme
bay leaves
salt and pepper

The Chinese discovered the duck and developed the first methods for cooking it over 4,000 years ago. After thousands of years of culinary tradition duck is still considered a top-quality dish and is popular throughout the world. There are many varieties of duck, some of which are preferred for particular dishes.

The flesh of the female duck, and above all that of the duckling, is much more popular than that of the drake. It is more delicate and tasty, and the breasts are plumper. Our chef recommends seasoning the duck, inside and out, the day before, and rubbing it with neutral-tasting oil.

If you have time to extend the preparation over several days, you may by all means roast the duck a day or two ahead, and flambé it with Madeira at the last moment. Port or Banyuls can also be used for this purpose.

For the accompaniment, Gérard Vié recommends oyster and shiitake mushrooms, but you can also use ordinary white button mushrooms.

1. Clean the ducklings, and season inside and out with thyme, bay leaves, unpeeled garlic cloves, salt and pepper. Place in an ovenproof pan and brown on all sides over medium heat. Remove from the pan.

2. Braise the diced carrots and onions with thyme and bay leaves in the same pan and deglaze with Madeira. Add the chicken stock, return the ducklings and roast on all sides in the oven for 45 minutes, basting frequently. Keep warm. Reduce the roasting juices until the consistency of a sauce, and strain.

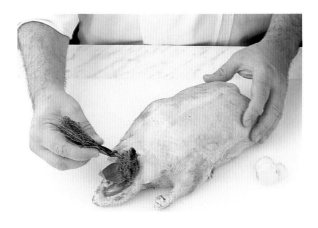

Madeira and Ham

3. Cut the turnips into ¼ in/½ cm thick slices, add butter and sugar, and after half the cooking time add the finely chopped mushrooms. Brown the ham in a skillet. Place the ducklings on a serving dish. Hold the ham with a fork or tongs; flambé it and let the fat drip onto the ducklings.

4. Carve the duck, saving the legs for another meal. Cut the breasts in thin slices. Put duck breast slices on each plate with the garnish of turnips and mushrooms, and pour sauce over. Serve the rest of the sauce in a sauceboat.

Fondant of Beef with

Preparation time: 1 hour 30 minutes
Cooking time: 7 hours
Difficulty: ★★

Serves 4

3⅓ lb/1½ kg beef cheek
1 duck foie gras
2 pork cauls (see note on page 32)
5 carrots
2 shallots
1 onion studded with cloves
diced carrots and onions
2 garlic cloves

1 bouquet garni
8 cups/2 l Burgundy or other dry red wine
10 cups/2½ l veal stock
oil
coarse salt
salt and pepper

For the purée:
3⅓ lb/1½ kg potatoes
13 tbsp/200 g butter
4 cups/1 l milk
7 oz/200 g smoked bacon
salt and pepper

Here Gérard Vié is making an allusion to the classic *grande cuisine* dish, hare "à la royale", for which he has created a variation using beef. Since game is not available all year round, a substitute needs to be found, and in this case it is beef cheek, which is delicate and meltingly tender.

The preparation is somewhat tedious, and so you should start a couple of days in advance. Prepare the stock two days ahead, and be careful in measuring out the seasoning, since an excessively strong stock could overpower the fla-

vor of the meat. Take the opportunity to stew other cuts of beef along with the cheek, because you can use then later for salads or pies.

The fondants are wrapped in pork caul, which you should first soak in cold water. When you shape the fondants in a ladle or small bowl, press the meat a little, because beef cheek contains gelatin, and the fondants will hold together better if their structure is uniform. The meat should braise slowly in the oven—this was one of the secrets of chefs of the old school.

1. Trim the rind from the beef cheek. Boil the rind with 2 carrots, the onion studded with cloves and the bouquet garni for 2 hours in 8 cups/2 l of salted water. Boil the potatoes, drain, purée and stir in butter and milk. Dice the bacon finely and fry without additional fat and add to the purée.

2. Season the beef cheek and brown in oil, chop the remaining vegetables coarsely, add to the meat and brown. Add wine and veal stock, reserving ⅔ cup/150 ml of each. Cook in a covered pan for 4 hours over low heat. Dice the meat. Reduce the cooking liquid until the consistency of a sauce. Strain.

Burgundy and Potato Purée

3. Slice the foie gras and brown. Line a medium-sized ladle or small bowl with pork caul, half-fill with diced meat, add a slice of foie gras, and fill with more diced meat. Press well, then close up the pork caul. Repeat for 3 more portions.

4. Put the diced carrots and onions in a baking dish, then lay the fondants on top, and add ⅔ cup/150 ml stock and ⅔ cup/150 ml wine. Cook for 40 minutes at 320 °F/160 °C, basting frequently. Place a fondant in the center of each plate, adding a mound of potato purée on each side. Add sauce and serve.

Calf's Head with

Preparation time: 1 hour 30 minutes
Cooking time: 2 hours
Difficulty: ★★

Serves 4

1 calf's head with tongue and brain
8 carrots
1 onion studded with cloves
2 generous lbs/1 kg potatoes
6 small leeks
1 lemon
15 juniper berries
3½ tbsp/50 g flour
parsley
thyme
bay leaves

peppercorns
coarse salt

For the sauce ravigote:
4 hard-boiled eggs
2 shallots
1 onion
3½ oz/100 g capers
3½ oz/100 g cornichons
2 cups/500 ml peanut oil
1¼ cup/300 ml brandy vinegar
3½ tbsp/50 ml sherry vinegar
1 tbsp mustard
1 bunch of flat-leaf parsley
1 bunch of chives
salt and pepper

Calf's head has been eaten for many years with traditional sauces: with sauce gribiche or sauce ravigote, and sometimes with both at once. The calf's head is white in color. What with the crunchy ears, the lean cheek and the rest of the gelatinous meat, there is something for everyone to enjoy. Some people find calf's head rather bland, which is why many cooks serve it with a highly seasoned accompaniment.

If possible, get a whole head complete with brain and tongue, whose flavor will enrich it. Don't forget to rub lemon juice into the head before cooking, to preserve its whiteness until served. Jean-Pierre Vigato sometimes presents

calf's head divided into its various parts, but sometimes he likes to keep it whole (in accordance with tradition), and still steaming. This dish does not keep, so it must be eaten in one sitting.

The vegetables (carrots, leeks, trimmed potatoes) are served hot, and the powerful sauce ravigote adds dignity to the meat. The name of the sauce comes from the French *ravigoter*, that is, to strengthen or enliven, which is quite understandable, because the vinegar, mustard and capers are very stimulating. This very satisfying dish is best served on cold winter evenings.

1. For the sauce ravigote, chop the hard-boiled eggs, onions, shallots, capers and cornichons, chop the herbs finely and mix all together.

2. Prepare a vinaigrette, mixing mustard, vinegar, salt, pepper and oil. Add all the chopped ingredients.

Sauce Ravigote

3. Trim the potatoes and boil in salted water with 7 carrots and 4 leeks. Blanch the calf's head, singe and rub all over with lemon juice so that it will remain white after cooking.

4. Put the calf's head together with 1 carrot, parsley and onion in a large pan, and cover with cold water, in which 3½ tbsp/50 g flour has been dispersed. Bring to boil, skim and season. Cook for 2 hours over low heat. Twenty minutes before the end of cooking time, add the remaining leeks. Serve with sauce ravigote and coarse salt.

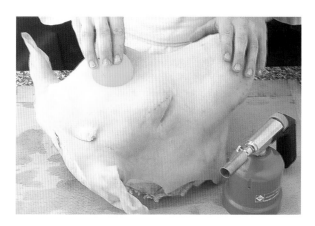

Rack of Lamb

Preparation time: 1 hour
Cooking time: 4 hours
Difficulty: ★★

Serves 4

2 racks of lamb, about 1¾ lb/800 g each
11 oz/300 g lamb shoulder
2 eggplants
1 large tomato, diced
2 pearl onions
2 garlic cloves
1 celery rib
1 sprig of thyme

1 bay leaf
1 sprig of rosemary
1 bunch of chives
1 bunch of flat-leaf parsley
1 egg
1 cup/250 ml white veal stock
6½ tbsp/100 ml olive oil
¾ cup/200 ml white wine
1 stick of cinnamon
5 cloves
10 juniper berries
40 white and black peppercorns
salt

Innumerable ways of preparing lamb are found on the menus of the great restaurants of Europe. Among the many breeds of lamb available to him, our chef prefers Pauillac lamb, which is slaughtered when it is 65 days old and whose flesh is famous for its tenderness. The leanest ribs are selected for the rack.

Lamb shoulder can be roasted the same way as a leg. Here, however, it is important to stick strictly to the preparation time given (braise for about 3 hours), because only then will it be fork-tender. The exquisite taste of lamb can be underlined by herbs and spices, but should not be disguised by them. So measure them out with care.

For the moussaka you need very fresh eggplants with firm flesh and smooth, glossy skins. The eggplant is an ingredient in countless dishes containing olive oil, such as ratatouille, and it is often combined with tomatoes and zucchini.

1. Braise the shoulder with the onions, garlic, celery, herbs, and spices, adding water and white wine. Cook for 3–4 hours over low heat. Remove the meat and break it up with a fork. Pour the fat from the pan, then reduce the stock to intensify its color and flavor.

2. Cut the 2 eggplants in half lengthwise, place in an ovenproof dish, season with coarse salt, and roast at 300 °F/150 °C on the middle rack of the oven for 40 minutes. Sauté the diced tomatoes briskly in olive oil. Mix the flesh of the eggplants with the lamb shoulder. Add the egg, chives, and chopped parsley.

with Spicy Sauce

3. Line small molds with the eggplant skins and fill with the eggplant mixture. Then bake at 340 °F/170 °C on the middle rack of the oven for 20 minutes.

4. Brown the racks of lamb on all sides in hot oil and continue to cook until medium-rare. Let rest for 5 minutes, then cut in half. Put a stuffed eggplant skin in the center of each plate, place the pieces of lamb on top, and pour the sauce around.

Preparation time: 30 minutes
Cooking time: 3 hours 30 minutes
Difficulty: ✶✶

Serves 4

2 calves' tails
1 eggplant
2 small zucchini
1 red (bell) pepper
5 celery ribs
3 carrots

finely diced celery, carrot, onion
1 generous lb/500 g peeled tomatoes
1 tsp pine nuts
4 garlic cloves
20 purple basil leaves
3 bay leaves
1 tsp cocoa powder
12 cups/3 l meat stock, unsalted
6½ tbsp/100 ml white wine
extra virgin olive oil
salt and pepper

This recipe would be entirely Roman if it were not for the typically Sicilian *caponata* that goes with it. Once beef and veal were reserved for the wealthy, so it was very rare in the region around Rome. The slaughterhouse workers (*vaccinari*) of Rome were paid in *naturalia*, that is, the less sought-after parts of the animals, such as the tripe, ears or tails. This historical circumstance explains the Italian name of this dish, *coda alla vaccinara*.

The calves' tails should not be boned before cooking, because they would lose some of their flavor. It is impor-

tant that it should cook for a long time over very low heat. This gives you time to prepare the *caponata* with the care it deserves. This is a sophisticated medley of flavors and colors, combining zucchini, peppers and pine nuts. The vegetables must be cut into very small dice.

The celery enhances this dish with its delicate but crisp freshness. Take care that the stems are firm and glossy, with healthy-looking leaves. The powerful taste of basil will be enough on its own with no further herbs and spices.

1. Cut the calves' tails in 1³/₄ in/3½ cm pieces. Put the finely diced vegetables, the 2 unpeeled garlic cloves and the bay leaves in a deep pan with some olive oil. Braise over low heat. Add the meat and brown, still over low heat, for about 20 minutes. Add white wine and reduce completely.

2. Sprinkle with cocoa powder, season with salt and pepper and add the stock. Cover and simmer for 3 hours. At the end of this time, add to the meat the peeled, finely chopped tomatoes, 3 carrots and 3 ribs of celery cut into thin strips. Cook for 20 minutes. Remove from the heat and take the meat out of the sauce.

3. Put the celery and carrot strips in a bowl and keep warm. Strain the sauce. Julienne the remaining 2 ribs of celery and braise in a pan in olive oil, finally adding the purple basil leaves. Toast the pine nuts in a pan.

4. For the caponata, dice the eggplant, zucchini and red pepper, and braise for 3 minutes in olive oil, without browning. Place pieces of calves' tail in the center of each plate, pour on sauce and garnish with celery and carrot strips. Lay the celery julienne on top of the meat and garnish the plate with caponata and some olive oil.

Beef Tenderloin

Preparation time: 15 minutes
Cooking time: 15 minutes
Difficulty: ✷

Serves 4

1 beef tenderloin, about 1⅓ lb/600 g
red wine
1 celery rib
1 shallot
1 bay leaf
thyme
rosemary
5 peppercorns

salt and pepper

For the vegetables:
6 carrots
1 zucchini
15 small onions

For the sauce:
4 cups/1 l red wine
3½ tbsp/100 ml port
1 cup/250 ml veal stock
4 shallots
1 cup plus 3½ tbsp/300 g butter
salt and pepper

This dish is one for connoisseurs who can distinguish Charolais from Angus beef at a glance!

It is a light dish, whose gentle preparation brings out the flavor and character of the meat. It is only for those who like rare beef.

Heinz Winkler refuses to serve a dish unless he knows the ingredients are fresh and from an impeccable source. His passion for the white Charolais breed is a tribute to French cattle breeding.

Nevertheless one cannot deny that the Charolais has formidable competition in the Scottish Angus, a breed of black cattle that are, with justification, the pride of Scotland. Of course, American beef of many breeds, including the Angus, has earned a global reputation for its high quality.

1. For the vegetable stock, peel the shallot, cut into coarse dice and cook with red wine and salt. Add herbs, celery and pepper. Cut the beef into 4 thick slices.

2. Clean the carrots, zucchini and onions. Cut the carrots and zucchini into large olive shapes, and cook separately in salted water with a dash of sugar, until just cooked.

3. For the sauce, bring the red wine and port to a boil with the chopped shallots, reduce by two thirds, let cool slightly and add the butter in small pieces, stirring constantly. Strain and add the veal stock. Reheat and season to taste.

4. Bring stock, red wine and herbs to the boil. Add the meat slices and simmer, gently, for 8 minutes. Put the sauce on heated plates, with one slice of meat on top, and surround with the garnish of vegetables.

Guinea Fowl

Preparation time: 30 minutes
Cooking time: 45 minutes
Difficulty: ★★★

Serves 4

1 guinea fowl
1 chicken or guinea fowl carcass
salt pork fatback to cover the guinea fowl
4½ lb/2 kg clay (not plastic-based)
1 onion
1 celery rib
2 large potatoes
8¾ oz/250 g leek

12 egg yolks
⅔ cup/150 ml cream
6½ tbsp/100 g butter
3½ oz/100 g puff pastry
3½ tbsp/100 ml truffle juice
3½ tbsp/50 ml chicken roasting juices
1 cup/250 ml chicken stock
2 cups/500 ml white wine
oil
rosemary
tarragon
basil
salt and pepper

For Heinz Winkler, the guinea fowl is typically French, and rosemary has the robust flavor of the Mediterranean south. This, of course, is flattering to French national pride, but it is not quite correct: the guinea fowl is esteemed throughout the Mediterranean, and the method of preparation described here, in a coat of clay, comes from North Africa. In any case, the dish is quite delicious.

Winkler originally tried this recipe with pheasant and chicken, but was disappointed by the results and eventually decided in favor of the guinea fowl, which always remains juicy, tender and full of flavor in its clay covering. The rosemary, for its part, imparts an additional exquisite aroma to the bird.

Place a few sprigs of rosemary inside the guinea fowl, along with some tarragon and a couple of basil leaves. Do not overdo the herbs; the various flavors, of which rosemary is the dominant one, complement each other well, but their combined effect could easily cover up the flavor of the guinea fowl.

Finally, you must transform yourself into a potter, so as to be able to manage the clay. This is not particularly difficult, if enough water is added to make it smooth and easy to spread out. This method ensures even cooking and an intensification of the flavors, and gives you the opportunity for a spectacular presentation for your guests – the breaking of the clay covering with a hammer.

1. Place the clay on a damp kitchen towel, cover with another cloth and roll out. Prepare the sauce: cut up the carcass and brown the bones with the rosemary and the diced onions and celery. Deglaze with white wine, reduce, add chicken stock and juices, reduce again, and strain.

2. Clean the guinea fowl, wash and dry, and season inside and out. Stuff with herbs (basil, tarragon and rosemary), cover with fatback, enclose in the clay and bake for 45 minutes in a 355 °F/180 °C oven. Remove from the oven and allow to rest for 15 minutes.

with Rosemary

3. For the potato-leek tart, peel the potatoes, slice, dab dry and season. Cover the bottom of a pan with oil, heat and add the potatoes in 1 thick layer. Cook until golden brown, turning once. Cut the white of leek diagonally and cook in cream. Add white wine and truffle juice. Season.

4. Place a ¼ in/½ cm thick layer of leek on top of the potatoes. Roll out the puff pastry and cut out circles of the same diameter as the potatoes. Cover the leeks with the pastry, brush with egg yolk and bake for 5–8 minutes in a 430 °F/220 °C oven. Break the clay covering, remove the guinea fowl and cut slices from the breast. Serve on heated plates with the sauce and portions of the quartered potato-leek tart.

Quail Breasts in

Preparation time: 40 minutes
Cooking time: 20 minutes
Difficulty: ★★

Serves 4

4 quails
3 large potatoes
1 egg yolk

13 tbsp/200 g butter
salt and pepper

For the rosemary sauce:
sprigs of rosemary
poultry bones
diced onion, celery and carrot
6½ tbsp/100 ml white wine
1 cup/250 ml poultry stock

As far as Heinz Winkler is concerned, a dish can be prepared only with the correct ingredients, and for this dish he insists on a Vigneron quail and Nicola potatoes (although you will use your favorite local variety). Choose high-quality farm-raised quail; the flavor is somewhat weaker than wild quail, but it can be boosted with rosemary. Wild quail are rare, and unavailable outside of the hunting season. If you like, you can substitute squab in this recipe.

For the mantle of potatoes, you must slice the potatoes very thinly, after which they should not be washed, so they will not lose their starch content. The thin slices will become beautifully crisp and golden brown when cooked.

Green beans are a good accompaniment, but ratatouille, whose Mediterranean character corresponds to that of the rosemary, will underline the fine flavor of the quail clothed in its mantle of potato.

1. Skin the quail, remove the breasts and legs. Season with salt and pepper.

2. For the rosemary sauce, crush the poultry bones and quail carcasses and brown with the diced vegetables and the sprigs of rosemary in a pan. Deglaze with white wine and reduce. Add the stock, reduce, and strain.

a Mantle of Potatoes

3. Peel the potatoes, wash and slice very thinly. On a kitchen towel, arrange 8 rectangles in fish-scale formation, season with salt and pepper, and brush with egg yolk.

4. Carefully wrap the quail breasts and legs in the potato slices, then brown in melted butter over medium heat. Lower the heat and continue to cook until the potatoes and quail are done. Place on warmed plates and pour the sauce around, and garnish with green beans or ratatouille as preferred.

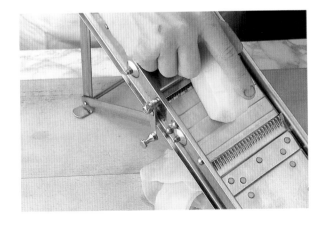

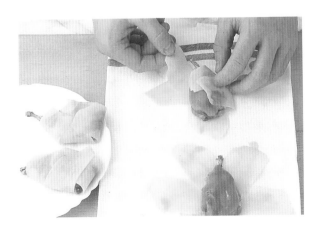

Medallions of Wild Hare

Preparation time: 2 hours
Cooking time: 40 minutes
Difficulty: ★★

Serves 4

12 loin medallions of wild hare, 1½ oz/40 g
each
1¼ cup/300 ml vegetable oil
salt and ground pepper

For the mushroom crust:
12 small cèpes, caps only
5½ oz/150 g chanterelles
5½ oz/150 g whole cèpes
1 shallot, 3½ tbsp/50 g butter
salt and ground pepper

For the quince compote:
2 large quinces, ¾ cup/200 ml red wine
¾ cup/200 ml port, 1 tbsp sugar
6½ tbsp/100 ml crème de cassis

For the sauce:
bones and trimmings of the hare
5½ oz/150 g carrot, shallot and celery
6½ tbsp/100 ml game stock
3½ tbsp/50 ml Madeira, 3½ tbsp/50 ml port
4 tsp/20 ml cognac
1 cup/250 ml cream, 2 tsp/10 ml gin
rosemary, ½ bay leaf, thyme
4 juniper berries, crushed
salt and ground pepper

For the chartreuse:
2 small carrots
1 celeriac, 3½ oz/100 g thin green beans
2 leaves Savoy cabbage
2 tsp/10 ml truffle juice
2 tsp/10 ml port, 5½ oz/150 g raw foie gras
salt and pepper

The combination of game with sweet and fruity flavors is one of the great traditions of German cuisine. Harald Wohlfahrt proves himself a worthy heir of this tradition in presenting to us here a dish of hare with quinces.

The mushrooms recommended here are chanterelles and cèpes, which are very plentiful in the Black Forest. Try to mold the foot of a cèpe with the finely chopped mushrooms, on which the cèpe cap will then be placed, to give the impression of a whole cèpe. The quince is a yellow fruit with hard flesh, whose medicinal qualities have long been recognized.

The hare can be replaced by venison in this recipe, and the quince by apples or pears. Cauliflower also goes very well with this dish.

1. For the compote of quince, peel and core the fruit. Poach in red wine, port, sugar and cassis. Leave in the poaching liquid for at least 24 hours. Finally purée the quince pieces in a food processor. Cook the liquid down until it becomes a syrup, then add the quince purée and simmer until it has reached the desired consistency.

2. For the chartreuse, cut carrots, celery and beans into 1¼ x ¼ in/ 3 x ½ cm strips. Blanch and refresh. Cut the foie gras into ¼ in/½ cm thick slices, 2¼ in/5 cm in diameter, and then marinate for 1 hour in salt, port, pepper and truffle juice. Blanch the cabbage. Line the sides of small round baking pans alternately with the vegetable strips, line the bottoms with cabbage, place a slice of foie gras on top, and finish with another layer of cabbage. Heat in the oven for 12 minutes.

with Quince Compote

3. Season the hare medallions with salt and pepper, brown on each side for 2 minutes, and keep warm. Clean the mushrooms well, and cut into small dice. Heat the butter in a pan until foaming, add the shallot, season with salt and pepper and set aside. Prepare the cèpe caps the same way.

4. Add the finely chopped bones and trimmings of the hare to the medallions and brown nicely. Deglaze with port and Madeira, and reduce. Add the game stock and the cream, reduce again, strain, and add cognac and gin. On each medallion, place finely chopped mushrooms and place the cèpe caps on top. Heat through in the oven. Arrange on plates with the quince compote and the sauce.

Variations on Wild Boar

Preparation time: 2 hours 30 minutes
Cooking time: 3 hours 15 minutes
Difficulty: ★★★

Serves 4

2 tenderloins of wild boar, 1 loin of wild boar
1 pork caul (see note on page 32)
4 Savoy cabbage leaves
5½ oz/150 g each chanterelles and cèpes
1 tbsp finely chopped chervil
3½ tbsp/50 g butter
1 shallot 4½ oz/120 g game stuffing
oil, salt and ground pepper

For the sauce:
bones and trimmings of wild boar

5½ oz/150 g carrot, celery and shallot
3½ oz/100 g mushrooms oil
2 tbsp tomato paste 2 cups/500 ml red wine

6½ tbsp/100 ml port
3½ tbsp/50 ml Madeira
10 juniper berries

For the garnish
2 apples (such as Granny Smith)
5½ oz/150 g cèpes
5½ oz/150 g chanterelles
1 tbsp finely chopped chervil
1 chopped shallot, 2 cloves
⅓ cup/80 g butter
1 tsp confectioners' sugar
4 sheets filo pastry
2 thyme leaves 1 bay leaf
6½ tbsp/100 ml heavy cream
¾ cup/200 ml white wine
salt and ground pepper

At Harald Wohlfahrt's restaurant, the Schwarzwald-stube, on the edge of the Black Forest, the visitor has the opportunity to become acquainted with the wealth of game in the region. The wild boar must take first place here; all hunters have an equal admiration for it and the recipes in which it features are delicious.

The young boar follows the sow with the rest of the litter, and communicates with his family by grunting. It should be no more than 6 months old when bought. At this age its flesh has practically no fat, and should be cut up carefully. It is suitable for the simplest as well as the most complicated methods of preparation.

Here our chef recommends the use of the loin, which is generally regarded as the finest cut, and whose slightly sweet taste distinguishes it from the powerful flavors of other types of game.

Accompanied, according to season, by red or green cabbage and wild mushrooms (Harald Wohlfahrt is especially fond of *trompettes de la mort*), young boar is a great success at the table. The delicious caramelized apples are in accordance with the German tradition of combining game with fruit. If you cannot get wild boar, you can prepare venison in the same way.

1. For the sauce, chop up the bones and brown them with the mirepoix of vegetables. Deglaze with wine, port and Madeira, add tomato paste and the seasonings. Reduce, add water, and simmer for about 3 hours. Strain. For the garnish, peel and quarter the apples. Caramelize the butter and sugar, and add the white wine and the apples.

2. Cut 4 medallions from the loin, cover with slices of cèpes and wrap in a pork caul, or brush all over with oil. Dice the rest of the cèpes and the chanterelles, and brown briskly with the shallot and chervil. Mix with the game stuffing. Make little baskets with sheets of filo pastry 6 in/15 cm in diameter with the help of a champagne cork.

with Pepper Sauce

3. Clean the mushrooms for the garnish, and cut in thin slices. Braise the chopped shallot and mushrooms, and season to taste with cream and chervil. Blanch the savoy cabbage, refresh, dry, press flat and spread a fine layer of stuffing on each leaf. Season the tenderloins with salt and pepper, wrap in cabbage leaves and then in pork caul (if used).

4. Put both meats in a 430 °F/220 °C oven for 3–8 minutes, according to size, then allow to rest. Add the roasting juices to the sauce and reduce to the desired consistency. Finally, add pepper and stir in butter; season to taste. Fill the little pastry baskets with mushrooms and serve with the caramelized apples, the meat and the sauce.

Saddle of Venison

Preparation time: 15 minutes
Cooking time: 2 hours
Difficulty: ★★

Serves 4

1¾ lb/800 g loin of venison, boned
¼ cup pine nuts
4 cups/1 l red wine
½ cup marsala
¼ cup cognac
4 cups/1 l stock
2 cups/500 ml peanut oil
1 tbsp flour
1 tbsp sugar

For the polenta:
1¼ lb/500 g corn meal
1 tbsp olive oil
4 cups/1 l water
salt

For the marinade:
4 cups/1 l red wine
1 onion
2 carrots
2 celery ribs
3 bay leaves
rosemary
20 juniper berries
10 cloves
½ stick cinnamon

Armando Zanetti himself is fond of hunting small game, but here he gives us his method of preparing venison. As a chef he has often had the opportunity to do so, as many of his customers own hunting grounds. Venison is one of the noblest meats; its qualities are best realized when it is cooked rare. Our chef recommends using the meat of a young animal. The description "Monviso" recalls the forests of that name, where venison is traditionally prepared in this way.

The marinade contains many of the spices which Marco Polo claimed to have brought back from India. That tireless traveler, or others who followed him, exercised a permanent influence on European cuisine. Be careful with the quantities, to avoid making the marinade too robust. By the way, Armando Zanetti would not forgive you if you did not use a tannin-rich wine, such as a good Bordeaux.

Now we come to the polenta, which is prepared in many ways in northern Italy. Resist the temptation to use instant polenta. Just before serving, the little polenta triangles should be reheated under the broiler.

1. A day ahead, marinate the saddle of venison in 4 cups/1 l of red wine. Add the finely chopped vegetables and the marinade herbs and spices. Next day, take out the meat and strain the marinade.

2. For the polenta, bring water to a boil with salt and oil. Slowly sprinkle in the corn meal, constantly stirring with a whisk. Cook for about 45 minutes over low heat, stirring constantly.

Monviso

3. In a pan, brown the marinade vegetables in oil. In another pan, briskly brown the loin of venison for a few minutes in a little oil, and then remove. Put the venison in the pan with the vegetables, and dust with flour. Add sugar, and flambé with cognac and marsala.

4. Add 4 cups/1 l red wine and reduce. Slowly add the stock and gently simmer for 1 hour. Remove the venison and strain the sauce. Slice the meat and serve with the polenta, which has been cut into triangles and reheated under the broiler. Garnish with a few pine nuts.

Stuffed Lamb with

Preparation time: 40 minutes
Cooking time: 2 hours 30 minutes
Difficulty: ★★★

Serves 4

2¼ lb/1 kg racks of lamb
1 lamb's head
6 lambs' feet
2 cups/500 ml lamb's blood
1 lamb's brain

1 sprig of thyme
1 bay leaf
1 bouquet garni
3 eggs
toasting bread, crusts removed
salt and white pepper

For the garnish:
12 green asparagus tips
7 oz/200 g small fresh fava beans

So many parts of the lamb are used for this dish: the gelatin of the lambs' feet, the tongue, the fat of the cheeks, the tender brain. and even the blood, which is used to thicken the sauce. The variety meats, called *tripochas* in the Basque country, are cooked twice—first alone, and then with the boned rack of lamb. This gives the rack additional fine subtleties of flavor.

The famous food writer Curnonsky gave the name of "lamb boudin noir" to this specialty. In the French Basque country it is served with potatoes, like traditional blood sausages. In the Spanish areas of the Basque country, however, it is combined with green asparagus. In spring, too, the first fava beans are available; these are shelled and cooked in boiling salted water.

1. Bone the racks of lamb. Cook the lambs' feet and head with thyme and bay leaf in salted water for 90 minutes. Let cool, then chop all the meat very finely. Mix with the crustless bread and the eggs. Add the poached and chopped brain.

2. Stuff the racks with this mixture, roll up, wrap in cheesecloth, seal well, and tie at both ends and in the middle.

Beans and Asparagus

3. Brown the lamb bones with the bouquet garni, add the stuffed rack of lamb, and cook for 1 hour over low heat, adding some water if necessary. Unwrap the meat and let cool, then tie it in the cheesecloth to keep its shape.

4. Reduce the meat juices, while repeatedly skimming off the scum, and finally thicken with the blood. Take the meat out of the cloth, reheat in the oven, and slice. Arrange on plates with the sauce, and add the asparagus and shelled and skinned fava beans, which have been cooked in salted water and tossed in melted butter.

Pigs' Feet with

Preparation time: *1 hour 30 minutes*
Cooling time: *24 hours*
Cooking time: *2 hours*
Difficulty: ★★

Serves 4

6 pigs' feet
12 dried red peppers
3 onions

1 leek
1 head of garlic
parsley
bay leaf
2 cups/200 g bread crumbs
flour
2 eggs
1 cup/250 ml olive oil
salt and white pepper

In Spanish the front extremities of the pig are called "hands," while we say "feet" for both front and back. For this recipe you should use *manitas*, that is, "little hands," as the Spanish call them.

The saying "with the swine, everything's fine" describes the special quality of the pig, all parts of which are eaten. However, pigs' feet demand quite special attention. First they must be carefully cleaned and then cooked for a long time. Afterwards they must be boned, scraping off all the gelatin in the process. Finally, the sliced meat must be coated twice in flour and egg, so that the coating stands up well to deep-frying. Incidentally the gelatin will be better if the pigs' feet are prepared the day before. The dried red peppers, frequently used in Spanish and Basque cuisine, have been grown since the 16th century, when Christopher Columbus brought them to Europe. Today Spain leads the world in their production. They are harvested from April to October, and after being dried can be used throughout the following year.

As an accompaniment, lentils, beans and chick peas are equally suitable. If you prefer, you can use calves' feet instead, but use the cheeks as well, as they have a higher gelatin content than the feet.

1. Cook the pigs' feet in unsalted water, together with the garlic, leek, onions, bay leaf and white pepper. Bone the cooked pigs' feet and chop finely. Season, pack into a terrine and refrigerate for 24 hours.

2. For the sauce, blanch the dried peppers three times. Scrape out the flesh. In another pan, reduce by three quarters the cooking water from the pigs' feet with the flesh of the dried peppers. Season to taste, purée and strain the sauce.

Pimento Sauce

3. Next day, take the terrine out of the refrigerator and cut the gelled meat carefully into ½ in/1 cm thick slices.

4. Coat the slices in flour, egg and then bread crumbs mixed with chopped parsley. Deep-fry in hot oil. Arrange on plates with the sauce.

Basic recipes

Bigarade sauce

Recipe: Duck with preserved figs à la Virgil
by Freddy Van Decasserie

Ingredients:
4 cups/1 l duck stock; 2 oranges; 1 lemon; $^3/_4$ oz/20 g sugar; 1 tsp cornstarch; 1 tbsp port; 8 cups/2 l vinegar; butter.

Preparation:
Prepare a light caramel in a deep saucepan with the sugar and vinegar. Deglaze with orange and lemon juice and allow to boil for a couple of minutes. Add duck stock, and reduce to two-thirds over a low heat.

Stir the cornstarch into the port and thicken the sauce with this mixture. Strain the sauce, and season to taste. Top with 3–4 small pats of butter to prevent the formation of a skin.

Puff pastry

Recipes: Squab and foie gras tourte with truffles
by Michel Haquin
Squab in puff pastry by Roger Jaloux
Medallions of veal with duck fois gras by Émile Tabourdiau

Ingredients:
1 generous lb/500 g flour; 1 tbsp/15 g salt; 1 cup/250 ml water; 2 cups/500 g butter.

Preparation:
Sift the flour onto the work surface and form a well. Add salt and water in the center, and quickly knead into a ball of pastry. Set aside to rest for 20 minutes, then roll out into a rectangle on a marble surface. Place all 2 cups/500 g of butter in the center. Wrap up the butter with the ends of the pastry to make a square. Roll out.

Turning: Give the pastry a quarter turn and roll out again. Refrigerate for 20 minutes. Turn and roll out again, refrigerate for a further 20 minutes, and repeat at least once more. Refrigerate until needed.

Coconut and curry sauce

Recipe: Pork tenderloin with coconut and curry sauce by Philippe Groult

Ingredients:
$^1/_2$ onion; $^1/_2$ apple; $^1/_2$ banana; 1 coconut; $^1/_3$ cup plus 1$^1/_2$ tbsp /100 ml chicken stock; 1 tbsp/15 g Madras curry powder; 3$^1/_2$ tbsp/50 ml olive oil; $^1/_4$ cup/60 g butter; salt and pepper.

Preparation:
Heat oil in a saucepan, and braise onion, apple and banana in it. Add curry powder. Mix the coconut milk with the chicken stock and boil for 5 minutes. Purée all ingredients in a blender, then strain and stir in butter. Season to taste.

Polenta

Recipe: Pigs' feet "cassoëula" by Nadia Santini

Ingredients:
1$^1/_4$ cup/300 ml water or chicken stock; 7 oz/200 g corn meal; $^1/_3$ cup plus 1$^1/_2$ tbsp/100 ml olive oil; salt and pepper.

Preparation:
Bring water (salted) or stock to boil. Gradually add corn meal, stirring constantly. Then simmer over low heat for about 45 minutes, stirring constantly. Pour onto an oiled surface. Allow to cool, then cut into pieces.

Tapenade

Recipe: Roast lamb with tapenade by Laurent Tarridec

Ingredients:
1 oz/35 g pitted olives; 1 anchovy fillet; 1 finely chopped shallot; a few capers; pepper.

Preparation:
Mix all ingredients and finely chop in the food processor.

Cumberland sauce

Recipe: Venison with Cumberland sauce and winter fruits by Freddy Van Decasserie

Ingredients:
2 generous lb/1 kg bones and trimmings of game; $^1/_3$ cup plus 1$^1/_2$ tbsp /100 ml peanut oil; 1$^1/_4$ cup/300 ml wine vinegar; 4 cups/1 l thickened veal stock; 2 tbsp red currant jelly.
Ingredients for marinating the bones:
1 carrot; 1 onion; 1 bay leaf; 1 sprig of thyme; 12 peppercorns; parsley; 3 cups/750 ml red wine; 3$^1/_2$ tbsp/50 ml peanut oil; salt and pepper.

Preparation:
The day before, marinate the bones and trimmings with finely chopped onion and carrot, thyme, bay leaf, peppercorns, parsley and oil. Season with salt and pepper, add red wine to cover, and refrigerate overnight. Strain, reserving the wine. In a large saucepan, brown the bones and the finely chopped vegetables; add wine vinegar and reduce until no liquid remains. Add the red wine from the marinade and reduce by one quarter. Add 4 cups/1 l thickened veal stock and reduce by half over low heat, then strain and stir in 2 tbsp red currant jelly. Season to taste.

Introducing the chefs

Fernando Adría

born May 14, 1962

Restaurant: **El Bulli**
Address: 30, Apartado de Correos Cala Montjoi
17480 Rosas, Spain
Tel. (9)72 15 04 57; Fax (9)72-15 07 17

As a talented 21-year-old back in 1983, Fernando Adría received two Michelin stars for his culinary achievements in **El Bulli**, his restaurant on the Costa Brava whose kitchens had previously been run by his friend Jean-Louis Neichel. Awarded 19 points and four red chef's hats by Gault-Millau, Adría has also fared well with the Spanish restaurant guides: four stars in Campsa and 9.5/10 in Gourmetour. A winner of the Spanish National Gastronomy Award, Fernando Adría also received the European Culinary Grand Prix in 1994. When his work leaves him time, this chef is a great supporter of the Barcelona soccer team.

Hilario Arbelaitz

born May 27, 1951

Restaurant: **Zuberoa**
Address: Barrio Iturrioz, 8
20180 Oyarzun, Spain
Tel. (9)43 49 12 28; Fax (9)43 49 26 79

Born in the heart of the Spanish Basque Country, whose gourmet traditions form the emphasis of his cooking, Hilario Arbelaitz began his career in 1970 at **Zuberoa**, where he became chef in 1982. Since then, he has received numerous French and Spanish awards: two Michelin stars, three red chef's hats, and 17 points in Gault-Millau, as well as four Campsa stars. In 1993 he was named Best Chef in Euzkadi (the Basque Country), after being named Best Chef in Spain in 1991. He brings equal measures of enthusiasm to the Basque game of *pelota* and family life, and is very interested in the history and future of his profession.

Firmin Arrambide

born September 16, 1946

Restaurant: **Les Pyrénées**
Address: 19, place du Général de Gaulle
64220 Saint-Jean-Pied-de-Port, France
Tel. (0)5 59 37 01 01; Fax (0)5 59 37 18 97

Firmin Arrambide has been at the helm of this restaurant, not far from his place of birth, since 1986, garnering two Michelin stars, three red chef's hats, and 18 points in Gault-Millau for **Les Pyrénées**. His regionally inspired cuisine won him second place in the 1978 *Taittinger* awards and carried him to the finals of the *Meilleur Ouvrier de France* competition in 1982. True to his Basque origins, Arrambide hunts woodpigeon and woodsnipe in the fall, and also loves mountain climbing; occasionally, though, he enjoys simply soaking up the sun by the pool.

Jean Bardet

born September 27, 1941

Restaurant: **Jean Bardet**
Address: 57, rue Groison
37000 Tours, France
Tel. (0)3 47 41 41 11; Fax (0)3 47 51 68 72

Before opening a restaurant in Tours under his own name in 1987, Jean Bardet traveled throughout Europe, working mainly as a sauce chef at the **Savoy** in London. A member of *Relais et Châteaux*, *Relais Gourmands*, and the Auguste Escoffier Foundation, he was awarded four red chef's hats in Gault-Millau (19.5) and two Michelin stars. In 1982 he had the honor of preparing dinner for the heads of state at the Versailles Summit. Jean Bardet is an enthusiastic cigar smoker (American Express awarded him the title of Greatest Smoker in the World in 1984) and in the fall indulges his passion for hunting, together with friends.

Michel Blanchet

born June 16, 1949

Restaurant: **Le Tastevin**
Address: 9, avenue Eglé
78600 Maisons-Laffitte, France
Tel. (0)139 62 11 67; Fax (0)1 39 62 73 09

After a topnotch training in 1967–71 at **Maxim's**, **Lutétia**, and **Ledoyen**, Michel Blanchet took over the reins at **Tastevin** in 1972; today, the restaurant boasts two Michelin stars. Blanchet's talents have more than once carried him through to the final rounds of prestigious competitions: the *Prosper Montagné* prize (1970 and 1972); the *Taittinger* prize (1974), and the *Meilleur Ouvrier de France* competition in 1979. Michel Blanchet is a *Maître Cuisinier de France* and a member of the Culinary Academy of France. A great nature-lover, he enjoys rambling through the woods—sometimes collecting mushrooms—as well as cycling and hiking.

Michel Bourdin

born June 6, 1942

Restaurant: **The Connaught**
Address: Carlos Place, Mayfair
London W1Y 6AL, England
Tel. (0)171 491-0668; Fax (0)171 495-3262

One of the old and distinguished line of French chefs in Great Britain, Michel Bourdin has been delighting London diners at the **Connaught** since 1975. The recipient of numerous prizes (*Prosper Montagné*, *Taittinger*) since training at **Ledoyen** and under Alex Humbert at **Maxim's**, he has been Chairman of the British branch of the Culinary Academy of France since 1980. In addition, he is a member of the 100 Club, and, like Paul Haeberlin, is also an honorary member of the *Chefs des Chefs* association. His pastry-chef colleagues, the twins Carolyn and Deborah Power, have made the Connaught famous for its desserts.

Christian Bouvarel

born April 26, 1954

Restaurant: **Paul Bocuse**
Address: 69660 Collonges-au-Mont-d'Or, France
Tel. (0)4 72 42 90 90; Fax (0)4 72 27 85 87

The youngest chef at **Paul Bocuse** had famous teachers, training under Raymond Thuillier at **Oustau de Baumanière** in Baux-de-Provence in 1971 and Paul Haeberlin at the **Auberge de l'Ill** in Illhaeusern in 1972, before coming to work at this celebrated restaurant in Collonges in 1975. Christian Bouvarel has played his part in the success story of this restaurant, with its three Michelin stars, four red chef's hats in Gault-Millau (19), and four stars in the Bottin Gourmand guide, and was named *Meilleur Ouvrier de France* in 1993. A native of Lyons, he is an enthusiastic nature-lover and spends his scarce leisure hours mountain climbing whenever possible.

Carlo Brovelli

born May 23, 1938

Restaurant: **Il Sole di Ranco**
Address: 5, Piazza Venezia
21020 Ranco, Italy
Tel. (0)3 31 97 65 07; Fax (0)3 31 97 66 20

It was only fitting that the Italian restaurant guide Veronelli should pay tribute to this restaurant with the sun in its name by awarding it one sun. Looking back on a 120-year-old family tradition, **Il Sole di Ranco** is run in a masterly fashion by Carlo Brovelli, who took over the reins in 1968 after training at the College of Hotel Management in La Stresa. A member of the *Le Soste*, *Relais et Châteaux* and *Relais Gourmands* chains, the restaurant has received many accolades: two Michelin stars, three chef's hats in Gault-Millau, (18), 84/100 in the Italian Gambero Rosso. Carlo Brovelli loves cycling and soccer, as well as his favorite sport, hunting.

Jean-Pierre Bruneau

born September 18, 1943

Restaurant **Bruneau**
Address: 73-75, avenue Broustin
1080 Brussels, Belgium
Tel. (0)24 27 69 78; Fax (0)24 25 97 26

For over 20 years, Jean-Pierre Bruneau has run the restaurant bearing his name which stands in the shadow of the imposing Koekelberg Basilica in the center of Brussels. The sophisticated creations of this Belgian *Maître Cuisinier* have won him many distinctions: three Michelin stars, four chef's hats in Gault-Millau, three stars in Bottin Gourmand, and 94/100 in the Belgian restaurant guide Henri Lemaire. He is also a member of *Traditions et Qualité*. Outside of the kitchen, he enjoys hunting and motor racing (first hand), and also collects old automobiles.

Michel Bruneau

born February 11, 1949

Restaurant **La Bourride**
Address: 15–17, rue du Vaugueux
14000 Caen, France
Tel. (0)2 31 93 50 76; Fax (0)2 31 93 29 63

"Normandy is proud of herself"—this is the motto of Michel Bruneau, who never tires of enumerating the sumptuous produce of the Calvados region on his extensive, tempting menu. Starting off his career in the midst of the plantations in Ecrécy, on the banks of the Guigne (1972–82), he then moved to **La Bourride** in Caen, where he has been since 1982. There he continues to delight gourmets with his inventive cooking, steeped in regional traditions, which has also impressed the critics: two Michelin stars and three red chef's hats in Gault-Millau (18).
In his spare time, Michel Bruneau enjoys cooking for friends. He plays soccer and sometimes accompanies his son to the skating rink.

Alain Burnel

born January 26, 1949

Restaurant **Oustau de Baumanière**
Address: Val d'Enfer
13520 Les Baux-de-Provence, France
Tel. (0)4 90 54 33 07; Fax (0)4 90 54 40 46

Alain Burnel served his apprenticeship in Beaulieu at **La Réserve de Beaulieu** (1969–73), in Nantes at the **Frantel** under Roger Jaloux, in Marseilles at **Sofitel**, and in Saint-Romain de Lerps at the **Château du Besset**, where he served as chef in 1978–82 before taking over the reins from the famous Raymond Thuillier in Baux, whose restaurant is now owned by the Charial family. Alain Burnel has earned two Michelin stars and three white chef's hats in Gault-Millau (18), and is a member of *Traditions et Qualité*, *Relais et Châteaux*, and *Relais Gourmands*. In his free time this chef is a keen cyclist, and was even once a participant in the Tour de France.

Jan Buytaert

born October 16, 1946

Restaurant **De Bellefleur**
Address: 253 Chaussée d'Anvers
2950 Kapellen, Belgium
Tel. (0)3 664 6719; Fax (0)3 665 0201

Despite being a dyed-in-the-wool Belgian who has spent a large part of his career in his native country—first at the **Villa Lorraine** in Brussels from 1973–4—Jan Buytaert worked for two years in the kitchens of **Prés et Sources d'Eugénie** in Eugénie-les-Bains under Michel Guérard (1974–5). In 1975, after this French interlude, he opened his current restaurant, which has earned him two Michelin stars and is one of the best in the region.
This Belgian *Maître Cuisinier* loves gentle activities, such as hiking and horseback riding, and also enjoys gardening.

Jacques Cagna

born August 24, 1942

Restaurant **Jacques Cagna**
Address: 14, rue des Grands Augustins
75006 Paris, France
Tel. (0)1 43 26 49 39; Fax (0)1 43 54 54 48

This distinguished chef has worked in the most famous restaurants of the French capital—1960 at **Lucas Carton**, 1961 at **Maxim's**, and 1964 at **La Ficelle**—and was even Chef to the French National Assembly (1961–62) before opening a restaurant under his own name in 1975, for which he has received high honors: two Michelin stars, two red chef's hats in Gault-Millau (18), and three stars in Bottin Gourmand. Jacques Cagna is a Knight of the *Mérite Nationale des Arts et des Lettres*. He knows his way around Asia, speaks fluent Japanese, and is a fan of classical music, opera, and jazz.

Stewart Cameron

born September 16, 1945

Restaurant **Turnberry Hotel & Golf Courses**
Turnberry KA26 9LT, Scotland
Tel. (0)1655 331 000; Fax (0)1655 331 706

Since 1981, the kitchens of the Turnberry Hotel—one of only two 5-star Scottish restaurants—have had a real Scot at the helm: Stewart Cameron, who previously worked at **Malmaison**, the restaurant of the Central Hotel in Glasgow. This chef is also a member of the Taste of Scotland and of the British branch of the Culinary Academy of France. In 1986 and 1994 he was privileged to play host to the participants of the British Golf Open in his restaurant. When he gets the chance, Stewart Cameron goes hunting or fishing. A rugby fan, of course, he is one of the Scottish XV's most faithful supporters.

Marco Cavallucci

born May 20, 1959

Restaurant **La Frasca**
Address: 38, Via Matteoti
47011 Castrocaro Terme, Italy
Tel. (0)543 76 74 71; Fax (0)543 76 66 25

Two Michelin stars, four chef's hats in Gault-Millau (19), one sun in Veronelli, 89/100 in Gambero Rosso: what more could Mario Cavallucci want? Working in perfect harmony with the restaurant's proprietor and sommelier, Gianfranco Bolognesi, this young, energetic chef has already received many accolades. A member of the *Le Soste* restaurant chain since 1978, he has vigorously supported Italy's great culinary tradition.
This extraordinarily busy chef still manages to find a little spare time for fishing, reading, seeing the occasional movie, and playing cards, soccer, and billiards.

Francis Chauveau

Born: September 15, 1947

Restaurant: **La Belle Otéro**
Address: Hôtel Carlton (7th floor)
58, La Croisette
Cannes 06400, France
Tel. (0)4 93 69 39 39; Fax (0)4 93 39 09 06

Although born in Berry in the northwest of France, Francis Chauveau's encounter with Provençal cooking has led to outstanding results, which visitors to the legendary Palace-Hotel in Cannes—holder of two Michelin stars—have been enjoying since 1989. Francis Chauveau gained his first experience as a chef in the **Hôtel d'Espagne** in Valençay, continuing his career at the **Auberge de Noves** in 1965. Later, he worked in restaurants such as the **Auberge du Père Bise**, the **Réserve de Beaulieu**, the **Terrasse** in the Hotel Juana in Juan-les Pins, and in the famous **L'Amandier** in Mougins in 1980–89. In his free time he enjoys traveling.

Jacques Chibois

Born: July 22, 1952

Restaurant: **La Bastide St-Antoine**
Address: 45, avenue Henri Dunant
06130 Grasse, France
Tel. (0)4 92 42 04 42; Fax (0)4 92 42 03 42

During the course of a career involving many moves, Jacques Chibois has met numerous famous names in French gastronomy: Jean Delaveyne in Bougival, Louis Outhier in La Napoule, Roger Vergé in Mougins, and the famous pastry chef Gaston Lenôtre. Since 1980 he has often worked under Michel Guérard, and was awarded two Michelin stars during his time at **Gray d'Albion** in Cannes (1981–95). He opened **La Bastide Saint-Antoine** in Grasse in 1995. In his spare time, Jacques Chibois is an enthusiastic cyclist and nature-lover, as well as an avid hunter and angler.

Serge Courville

Born: December 9, 1935

Restaurant: **La Cote 108**
Address: Rue Colonel Vergezac
02190 Berry-au-Bac, France
Tel. (0)3 23 79 95 04; Fax (03) 23 79 83 50

Serge Courville mentions his three teachers—Roger Petit, Robert Morizot and Jean-Louis Lelaurain—with warmth. Although not much interested in accolades, he has nonetheless reached the finals of numerous culinary competitions (*Prosper Montagné* prize, 1971, *Trophée National de l'Académie Culinaire*, 1972, *Taitinger* prize, 1973). Since 1972, he and his wife have run *La Cote 108*, which in 1982 received one Michelin star.
When not working, Serge Courville enjoys cooking for friends. He is also a passionate reader and cyclist, and spends a lot of time in the wilds, fishing or gathering mushrooms.

Bernard Coussau

Born: September 15, 1917

Restaurant: **Relais de la Poste**
Address: 40140 Magescq, France
Tel. (0)5 58 47 70 25; Fax (0)5 58 47 76 17

Bernard Coussau's name is synonymous with the characteristic cuisine of the Landes region in southwest France. At the **Relais de la Poste**, opened in 1954 and the continuous holder of two Michelin stars since 1969, this Honorary Chairman of the *Maîtres Cuisiniers de France* offers diners fine regional cuisine in the surroundings of a superbly preserved old coaching inn. At the summit of an extraordinary career, this chef is an officer of the *Mérite Agricole*, a Knight of the Legion of Honor, and of the *Palmes Académiques*. An old rugby fan, he supports the Dax team, and is also an automobile enthusiast.

Jean Coussau

Born: May 6, 1949

Restaurant: **Relais de la Poste**
Address: 40140 Magescq, France
Tel. (0)5 58 47 70 25; Fax (0)5 58 47 76 17

A worthy heir to the mantel of his father Bernard, Jean Coussau is a *Maître Cuisinier de France*, and a member of the J.R.E. (Young Restaurateurs of Europe) and of the French *Haute Cuisine* association. Following an exemplary Franco-Spanish career at the **Café de Paris** in Biarritz, the **Plaza-Athénée** in Paris, and the **Ritz** in Madrid, since 1970 he has worked with his father in the kitchens of the **Relais de la Poste** in Magescq. In 1976 he reached the finals of the Best Sommelier in France competition. Jean Coussau shares his father's passion for hunting and is also an enthusiastic golfer.

Richard Coutanceau

Born: February 25, 1949

Restaurant: **Richard Coutanceau**
Address: Place de la Concurrence
17000 La Rochelle, France
Tel. (0)5 46 41 48 19; Fax (0)5 46 41 99 45

Richard Coutanceau, whose restaurant boasts a marvelous location in "green Venice" between Marais Poitevin and the Côte Sauvage, started his career in Paris at **L'Orée du Bois** in 1968. He moved to La Rochelle and the **Hôtel de France et d'Angleterre**, where he worked in 1968–82. This native of Charentais has received many distinctions: two stars in Michelin, three stars in Bottin Gourmand, and three red chef's hats and 17 points in Gault-Millau. His restaurant belongs to the *Relais Gourmands* chain, and he is also a member of the Young Restaurateurs of Europe. Richard Coutanceau is an enthusiastic tennis player and an avid fisherman, who has the good fortune to live on the coast.

Jean Crotet

Born: January 26, 1943

Restaurant: **Hostellerie de Levernois**
Address: Route de Combertault
21200 Levernois, France
Tel. (0)3 80 24 73 68; Fax (0)3 80 22 78 00

Amid a splendid park of Louisiana cedar, willow, and ash, through which a small river flows, Jean Crotet offers discerning diners a sophisticated cuisine which has been awarded two Michelin stars and three stars in Bottin Gourmand. He is a *Maître Cuisinier de France*, as well as a member of the *Relais et Châteaux* and *Relais Gourmands* chains. In 1988, after working for 15 years at the **Côte d'Or** in Nuits-Saint Georges, he settled down in Levernois, near Beaune. In his spare time Jean Crotet enjoys fishing, flying a helicopter, playing tennis, hunting, and gardening.

Michel Del Burgo

Born: June 21, 1962

Restaurant: **La Barbacane**
Address: Place de l'Église
11000 Carcassonne-La Cité, France
Tel. (0)4 68 25 03 34; Fax (0)4 68 71 50 15

This young man from the northern province of Picardy has worked in the kitchens of Alain Ducasse in Courchevel, Raymond Thuillier in Baux-de-Provence, and Michel Guérard in Eugénie-les-Bains, all in the south of France. After a short stay in the Rhône valley and Avignon (1987–90), in 1991 Michel Del Burgo was appointed chef of **La Barbacane** in the center of Carcassonne by Jean-Michel Signoles. In 1995 he was awarded his second Michelin star, the Lily of the Restaurant Trade, and the Gault-Millau Golden Key, as well as three red chef's hats and 18 points in the Gault-Millau guide. Michel Del Burgo appreciates the cooking of his fellow chefs in the Land of the Cathars and is also fond of music, motor sport, and hiking.

Joseph Delphin

Born: September 4, 1932

Restaurant: **La Châtaigneraie**
Address: 156, route de Carquefou
44240 Sucé-sur-Erdre, France
Tel. (0)2 40 77 90 95; Fax (0)2 40 77 90 08

A Maître Cuisinier de France and member of the Culinary Academy of France, Joseph Delphin delights gourmets from the Nantes area with his culinary skills. A Knight of the Mérite Agricole, this chef has also received the Vase de Sèvres award from the French President. His restaurant, La Châtaigneraie (one Michelin star), is located on the banks of the Erdre, and can be reached by road, river, or helicopter. You are sure to be won over by the warmth of the welcome from the Delphin family, as Jean-Louis, a member of the Young Restaurateurs of Europe, works here with his father. Joseph Delphin enjoys cycling and takes part in the Tour de France.

Philippe Dorange

born: May 27, 1963

Restaurant: **Fouquet's**
Address: 99, avenue des Champs Élysées
75008 Paris, France
Tel (0)1 47 23 70 60; Fax (0)1 47 20 08 69

Is it actually necessary to introduce the legendary **Fouquet's** in these pages? Surely not, nor the prestigious restaurants in which Philippe Dorange has worked in the past: Roger Vergé's **Le Moulin de Mougins** (1977–81), Jacques Maximin's **Negresco** in Nice (1981–88), and **Ledoyen** in Paris, where he was chef in 1988–92. All in all, a fine career path for a young chef whose Mediterranean origins are reflected in his culinary preferences, a fact which is particularly esteemed by his Champs-Elysées clientele. When not in the kitchen, Philippe Dorange likes to box, drive sports cars, or play soccer.

Claude Dupont

born: June 7, 1938

Restaurant: **Claude Dupont**
Address: 46, avenue Vital Riethuisen
1080 Brussels, Belgium
Tel (0)2 426 0000; Fax (0)2 426 6540

The Belgian and French gourmet restaurant guides have positively showered awards on Claude Dupont's cooking: two Michelin stars since 1976, three stars in Bottin Gourmand, three white chef's hats in Gault-Millau (17), and 92/100 points in the Belgian Henri Lemaire guide. In 1967 he was awarded the *Prosper Montagné* prize, and in 1973 the Oscar of Gastronomy. In addition, this chef ran the Belgian Pavillion at the 1970 World Fair in Osaka, before opening a restaurant under his own name in Brussels. In his leisure time Claude Dupont occupies himself by making things with his hands, gardening, playing tennis, and swimming.

Éric Dupont

born: April 16, 1966

Restaurant: **Claude Dupont**
Address: 46, avenue Vital Riethuisen
1080 Brussels, Belgium
Tel (0)2 426 0000; Fax (0)2 426 6540

Éric Dupont has had a truly star-studded training, serving successive apprenticeships with the Brussels Masterchef Freddy Van Decasserie (*Villa Lorraine*), Pierre Wynants (*Comme Chez Soi*), and Willy Vermeulen (*De Bijgaarden*). Nowadays he works with his father Claude Dupont in the family business. The apple never falls far from the tree, and it does not seem unreasonable to place high hopes on this young chef who founded the Brussels college of hotel management C.E.R.I.A.
Éric Dupont is an ardent traveler and loves sports, such as swimming, tennis, and horseback riding.

Lothar Eiermann

born: March 2, 1945

Restaurant: **Wald- & Schloßhotel Friedrichsruhe**
Address: 74639 Friedrichsruhe, Germany
Tel (0)7941 60870; Fax (0)7941 61468

For over 20 years Lothar Eiermann has worked at Friedrichsruhe, the summer residence of the Prince von Hohenlohe-Öhringen which belongs to the *Relais et Châteaux* chain. Before this, he traveled throughout Europe, working as a chef in Switzerland in 1964–72 in the **Grappe d'Or** in Lausanne and in the **Hotel Victoria** in Glion. He then worked in the **Gleneagles Hotel** in Scotland, traveled south to England, and returned to Scotland, where he managed a hotel in 1972–3. This Bordeaux-wine enthusiast also has a degree in economics from the University of Heidelberg, and depending on the season, enjoys skiing, cycling, or playing tennis. He is also a fan of the American author Philip Roth.

Jean Fleury

born: April 22, 1948

Restaurant: **Paul Bocuse**
Address: 69660 Collonges-au-Mont-d'Or, France
Tel (0)4 72 42 90 90; Fax (0)4 72 27 85 87

After a highly promising début in his hometown of Bourg-en-Bresse—the chief town of Bresse, a region renowned for its outstanding produce—Jean Fleury achieved fame as a chef in the **Hotel Royal** in Évian (1968–9) and in the Brussels **Hilton** (1971–78). Winner of the *Prosper Montagné* prize in 1976, he was named Best Chef in Belgium in the same year, and won the Meilleur Ouvrier de France competition in 1979. In 1985 he left the kitchens of the **Arc-en-ciel** in Lyons, following Paul Bocuse to his famous restaurant in Collonges. Jean Fleury loves traveling and hiking and collects antique cookbooks, from which he enjoys drawing inspiration.

Constant Fonk

born: September 1, 1947

Restaurant: **De Oude Rosmolen**
Address: Duinsteeg 1
1621 Hoorn, the Netherlands
Tel (0)229 014752; Fax (0)229 014938

Thanks to Constant Fonk, the town of Hoorn in north Holland has had a two-Michelin-starred restaurant since 1990. After his first highly promising steps in the Amsterdam **Hilton** (1965–6), and the **Amstel Hotel** (1966–7), he returned to his hometown, where in 1967 he began work in **De Oude Rosmolen**, finally taking over the reins of the kitchen in 1976. A lover of fine cuisine and good wines, he especially enjoys partaking of both with like-minded people. As far as sport is concerned, golf is his favorite form of exercise, and makes a change from the kitchen.

Louis Grondard

born: September 20, 1948

Restaurant: **Drouant**
Address: 16-18, rue Gaillon
75002 Paris, France
Tel (0)1 42 65 15 16; Fax (0)1 49 24 02 15

Louis Grondard has catered for the jury of the prestigious *Goncourt* literary prize since 1990. He was named *Meilleur Ouvrier de France* in 1979. Grondard served his apprenticeship at **Taillevent** and at **Maxim's**, first in Orly, then in Roissy. He then achieved his first successes in the Eiffel Tower restaurant and in the famous **Jules Vernes**, which opened in the Tower in 1983. To quote Michel Tournier, "The stars [two in Michelin] fall as his due from heaven." Louis Grondard has also been favored with three white chef's hats and 17 points in Gault-Millau. He loves literature, Baroque music and opera, and enjoys scuba diving when on vacation.

Philippe Groult

born: November 17, 1953

Restaurant: **Amphyclès**
Address: 78, avenue des Ternes
75017 Paris, France
Tel (0)1 40 68 01 01; Fax (0)1 40 68 91 88

A devoted pupil and colleague of Joël Robuchon at **Jamin** in 1974–85, this native Norman now runs his own restaurant, to the satisfaction of diners and critics alike. Named *Meilleur Ouvrier de France* in 1982, today Philippe Groult has two Michelin stars and three red chef's hats (18) in Gault-Millau. In 1988 he was a contender in the "Culinary Olympics" in Tokyo, and one year later took over the reins in the kitchen at **Amphyclès**. He has been a member of *Devoirs Unis* since 1978. Philippe Groult is an ardent traveler, a connoisseur of the Far East, and an enthusiastic martial arts practitioner.

Marc Haeberlin

born: November 28, 1954

Restaurant: **Auberge de L'Ill**
Address: 2, rue de Collonges-au-Mont-d'Or
68970 Illhaeusern, France
Tel. (0)3 89 71 89 00; Fax (0)3 89 71 82 83

This worthy heir to the Haeberlin dynasty will certainly not disappoint the gourmets who, once lured by the success of his father Paul, return to this temple of Alsatian cuisine. Three Michelin stars, four red chef's hats (19.5) in Gault-Millau, and four stars in Bottin Gourmand are the impressive distinctions garnered by this former student at the College of Hotel Management in Illkirch. Completing his training with Paul Bocuse and the Troisgros brothers, he proved his skills in Paris at the *Lasserre* in 1976. When time allows, Mark Haeberlin occupies himself with painting and automobiles. In winter he skis on the slopes of the Vosges.

Michel Haquin

born: September 27, 1940

Restaurant: **Le Trèfle à 4**
Address: 87, avenue de Lac
1332 Genval, Belgium
Tel. (0)2 654 0798; Fax (0)2 653 3131

Not far from Brussels, on the shores of Lake Genval, Michel Haquin successfully pursues a culinary career which began in 1961 in the Belgian capital. There, in 1977–85, he ran a restaurant under his own name. As a Belgian *Maître Cuisinier* and member of the Culinary Academy of France, this chef was admitted to the Order of the Thirty-three Masterchefs and was awarded the Oscar of Gastronomy. The guidebooks have showered him with honors: two Michelin stars, three red chef's hats in Bottin Gourmand, and 91/100 in the Belgian guide Henri Lemaire. In his leisure time, Michel Haquin enjoys reading and traveling.

Paul Heathcote

born: October 3, 1960

Restaurant: **Paul Heathcote's**
Address: 104–106 Higher Road,
Longridge PR3 3SY, England
Tel. (0)1772 784969; Fax (0)1772 - 785713

This young British chef is very open to culinary influences from the other side of the English Channel. After working with Michel Bourdin at the **Connaught**, he spent two years with Raymond Blanc at the **Manoir au Quatr' Saisons** in Oxfordshire and worked at the **Broughton Park Hotel** in Preston, before finally opening his own restaurant (two Michelin stars) in 1990. In 1994, the Egon Ronay guidebook awarded him the enviable title of Best Chef of the Year. An enthusiastic sportsman, Paul Heathcote loves soccer, squash, and skiing.

Eyvind Hellstrøm

born: December 2, 1948

Restaurant: **Bagatelle**
Address: Bygdøy Allé 3
0257 Oslo, Norway
Tel. 22 44 63 97; Fax 22 43 64 20

No other chef in Scandinavia has received as many accolades as Eyvind Hellstrøm. He is strongly influenced by French gastronomy, with which he became familiar in the course of his training under famous chefs, such as Guy Savoy, Alain Senderens, Bernard Loiseau, and Fredy Girardet. A member of *Eurotoques* and *Traditions et Qualité*, Eyvind Hellstrøm was awarded two Michelin stars for his restaurant in 1982. A passionate wine connoisseur and a lover of Burgundies in particular, this chef often visits the wine cellars of Beaune and the surrounding area. He enjoys traveling and skiing, and is a fan of the Swedish skier Ingmar Stenmark.

Alfonso Iaccarino

born: January 9, 1947

Restaurant: **Don Alfonso 1890**
Address: Piazza Sant'Agata,
80064 Sant'Agata sui due Golfi, Italy
Tel. (0)81 878 0026; Fax (0)81 533 0226

In 1973, Alfonso Iaccarino named his restaurant, with its marvelous view of the Gulf of Naples and Salerno, after his grandfather. A member of the *Le Soste*, *Relais Gourmands*, and *Traditions et Qualité* chains, this chef has garnered numerous honors: two Michelin stars, four chef's hats in Espresso/Gault-Millau, one sun in Veronelli, and 92/100 in Gambero Rosso. In 1989 he was awarded the title Best Wine Cellar in Italy for his collection of superb Italian and French wines. In his private life, Alfonso Iaccarino is a true sportsman and particularly enjoys racing and cycling. He also loves nature, painting, and traveling.

André Jaeger

born: February 12, 1947

Restaurant: **Rheinhotel Fischerzunft**
Address:Rheinquai 8,
8200 Schaffhausen, Switzerland
Tel. (0)52 625 3281; Fax (0)52 624 3285

André Jaeger can proudly claim to have successfully inspired Swiss and even European gastronomy with an eastern flavor. His restaurant, which he opened in 1975, boasts two Michelin stars and four red chef's hats in Gault-Millau (19). Named 1995 Chef of the Year by Gault-Millau, he was awarded the Golden Key of Gastronomy in 1988 and appointed Chairman of the *Grandes Tables* in Switzerland. He is also a member of *Relais et Châteaux* and *Relais Gourmands*. A connoisseur of wines from around the world, André Jaeger is also very interested in contemporary art and collects automobiles.

Roger Jaloux

born: May 20, 1942

Restaurant: **Paul Bocuse**
Address: 69660 Collonges-au-Mont-d'Or, France
Tel. (0)4 72 42 90 90; Fax (0)4 72 27 85 87

As the most loyal of the loyal pupils of Paul Bocuse, Roger Jaloux joined his mentor in his restaurant in 1965, which incidentally received its third Michelin star in the same year. Everything there is to say about this celebrated restaurant in Collonges and the accolades it has received has already been said: it was here that Roger Jaloux prepared for the competition for the prestigious title of *Meilleur Ouvrier de France*, which he won in 1976. In his spare time, Roger Jaloux enjoys the arts, such as painting and singing, and numerous sports, including tennis, cycling, and skiing.

Patrick Jeffroy

born: January 25, 1952

Restaurant: **Patrick Jeffroy**
Address: 11, rue du Bon Voyage
22780 Plounérin, France
Tel. (0)2 96 38 61 80; Fax (0)2 96 38 66 29

A Breton with a penchant for solitude, Patrick Jeffroy settled down in a village in the Côtes-d'Armor *département*, where he serves innovative, delicious food in his restaurant, established in 1988 and now boasting one Michelin star and three red chef's hats in Gault-Millau (17). The earlier part of his career was spent in Abidjan in the Ivory Coast (1972) and the **Hôtel de l'Europe** in Morlaix back in France (1977–87). Patrick Jeffroy has had his Michelin star since 1984. He is also a *Maître Cuisinier de France*, and a recipient of the *Mandarine Impériale* first prize. Out of working hours, he enjoys going to the theater and the movies.

Émile Jung

born: April 2, 1941

Restaurant: **Le Crocodile**
Address: 10, rue de l'Outre
67000 Strasbourg, France
Tel. (0)3 88 32 13 02; Fax (0)3 88 75 72 01

Behind the sign of the crocodile—an allusion to Napoleon's Egyptian campaign—is Émile Jung's restaurant, highly rated by food lovers and a veritable temple of Alsatian cuisine, boasting no fewer than three Michelin stars, three white chef's hats in Gault-Millau (18), and three stars in Bottin Gourmand. The awards hardly come as a surprise, considering that this chef's career took him from **La Mère Guy** in Lyons to **Fouquet's** (1965) and **Ledoyen** (1966) in Paris. Émile Jung is a *Maître Cuisinier de France* and member of *Relais Gourmands* and *Traditions et Qualité*. A passionate oenologist, he is particularly well versed in Alsatian wines.

Dieter Kaufmann

born: June 28, 1937

Restaurant: **Zur Traube**
Address: Bahnstraße 47,
41515 Grevenbroich, Germany
Tel. (0)2181 68767; Fax (0)2181 61122

Dieter Kaufmann harbors a great love of France, and that country knows how to repay him: with two Michelin stars and four red chef's hats in Gault-Millau (19.5) he figures among the most highly esteemed non-French chefs, and was named Gault-Millau 1994 Chef of the Year. He is a member of the prestigious *Traditions et Qualité*, *Relais et Châteaux*, and *Relais Gourmands* chains. With over 30,000 bottles and some remarkable vintages, his restaurant, which he has run since 1962, boasts what is without a doubt the most important wine cellar in Germany. A bibliophile and polyglot, Dieter Kaufmann is also an enthusiastic traveler.

Örjan Klein

born: May 15, 1945

Restaurant: **K.B.**
Address: Smalandsgatan, 7
11146 Stockholm, Sweden
Tel. 86 79 60 32; Fax 86 11 82 83

At the pinnacle of a career based largely in the Swedish capital (**Berns** in 1966–7 and **Maxim's** of Stockholm in 1971–9), Örjan Klein joined forces with Ake Hakansson in 1980 to open **K.B.**, which boasts one Michelin star. Named Chef of the Year in 1993, Örjan Klein is also a *Nordfishing* Trondheim and Swedish Academy of Gastronomy gold-medallist (1976 and 1983, respectively). A nature-lover, he enjoys gardening and hiking. He also writes (cook)books and keeps fit by playing tennis and skiing.

Robert Kranenborg

born: October 12, 1950

Restaurant: **La Rive/Hotel Amstel Inter-Continental**
Address: Prof. Tulpplein, 1
1018 GX Amsterdam, the Netherlands
Tel. (0)20 622 6060; Fax (0)20 520 3277

No one becomes chef of **La Rive** (one Michelin star)—the restaurant of the Inter-Continental, the most prestigious hotel in Amsterdam—overnight. In fact, Robert Kranenborg had a string of successes as glowing references when he began work there in 1987: **Oustau de Baumanière** in Baux-de Provence (1972–4), **Le Grand Véfour** in Paris (1975–7), and **La Cravache d'Or** in Brussels (1979–86). In 1994, Robert Kranenborg was named Chef of the Year. When he is able to escape from the kitchen, he enjoys playing the drums and sports—golf being his favorite.

Étienne Krebs

born: August 15, 1956

Restaurant: **L'Ermitage**
Address: 75, rue du Lac
1815 Clarens-Montreux, Switzerland
Tel (0)21 964 4411; Fax (0)21 964 7002

As chef-proprietor of a magnificent house on the shores of Lake Geneva, Étienne Krebs is a happy man: a member of the Young Restaurateurs of Europe and *Grandes Tables Suisses*, he boasts one Michelin star and three red chef's hats in Gault-Millau (18), as well as the title of Chef of the Year 1995 for French-speaking Switzerland. After training with the greatest Swiss chefs—Fredy Girardet in Crissier and Hans Stucki in Basel—he ran the **Auberge de la Couronne** in Cossonay in 1984–90, before finally opening **L'Ermitage** in Montreux. Étienne Krebs enjoys walking and cycling around the lake, as well as cooking for his family.

Jacques Lameloise

born: April 6, 1947

Restaurant: **Lameloise**
Address: 36, place d'Armes
71150 Chagny, France
Tel. (0)3 85 87 08 85; Fax (0)3 85 87 03 57

The third generation of his family to bear the name, Jacques Lameloise has, since 1971, also carried on the tradition of running the family restaurant. Cutting his professional teeth at Ogier's in Pontchartrain, in 1965–9 he worked at the Parisian temples of gastronomy **Lucas Carton**, **Fouquet's**, **Ledoyen**, and **Lasserre**, not forgetting the **Savoy** in London. The **Lameloise** can boast three stars in both Michelin and Bottin Gourmand, as well as three red chef's hats in Gault-Millau (18), and is a member of the *Relais et Châteaux*, *Relais Gourmands*, and *Traditions et Qualité* chains. Jacques Lameloise is especially interested in antiques and old automobiles, and enjoys golf and occasionally skiing.

Erwin Lauterbach

born March 21, 1949

Restaurant: **Saison**
Address: Strandvejen, 203
2900 Hellerup, Denmark
Tel. 39 62 48 42; Fax 39 62 56 57

In 1972–3, Erwin Lauterbach served the cuisine of his native Denmark at the **Maison du Danemark** in Paris—a time of which he has many fond memories. In 1977–81 he cooked in Malmö, Sweden at **Primeur**, after which he returned to Denmark. Opened in 1981, **Saison** boasts one Michelin star. Erwin Lauterbach is also a member of the Danish Academy of Gastronomy, and a virtuoso proponent of Danish culinary traditions. An admirer of naive painting, he is an ardent visitor of museums and exhibitions. Of all the sports, he most enjoys playing soccer.

Dominique Le Stanc

born December 7, 1958

Restaurant: **Chanteclerc—Hôtel Negresco**
Address: 37, Promenade des Anglais
06000 Nice, France
Tel. (0)4 93 16 64 00; Fax (0)4 93 88 35 68

Some of the biggest names in the world of gastronomy have watched over the early stages of Dominique Le Stanc's career. After serving an apprenticeship with Paul Haeberlin, he worked with Gaston Lenôtre, Alain Senderens, and Alain Chapel, and became *chef de partie* under the latter before putting out his own shingle, first at the **Bristol** in Niederbronn-les-Bains (1982–84), then in Monaco and Eze. A member of the Italian chain *Le Soste*, he has been head chef of **Negresco** since 1989, earning this celebrated establishment two Michelin stars and three red chef's hats in Gault-Millau (18). An enthusiastic athlete, he takes part in triathlons and water-skis.

Michel Libotte

born May 1, 1949

Restaurant: **Au Gastronome**
Address: 2, rue de Bouillon
6850 Paliseul, Belgium
Tel. (0)61 53 30 64; Fax (0)61 53 38 91

Since 1978, Michel Libotte has presided over the kitchens of **Au Gastronome**, rated 94/100 in the Belgian restaurant guide Henri Lemaire. French critics have also been unstinting in their praise, awarding his establishment two Michelin stars and three stars in Bottin Gourmand. Michel Libotte has won the title of Best Cook in Belgium, and is a member of *Eurotoques* and the Culinary Academy of France. His restaurant, which lies close to the Franco-Belgian border, serves a highly individual, imaginative cuisine. Michel Libotte collects firearms as a hobby, and keeps fit by swimming and playing tennis regularly.

Léa Linster

born April 27, 1955

Restaurant: **Léa Linster**
Address: 17, route de Luxembourg
5752 Frisange, Luxembourg
Tel. 66 84 11; Fax 67 64 47

Léa Linster is the first, and to date the only, woman to receive the highest gastronomic accolade, the *Bocuse d'Or*, awarded to her in Lyons in 1989 by the master himself in well-earned recognition of her daily efforts to make the generous cuisine of Luxembourg better known to the dining public. Converting her parents' inn into an *haute cuisine* restaurant in 1982, this chef received her master craftsman's diploma in 1987. In addition to her obvious enthusiasm for fine cuisine, Léa Lister enjoys walks in the wild and stimulating conversations with diners in her restaurant.

Régis Marcon

born June 14, 1956

Restaurant: **Auberge et Clos des Cimes**
Address: 43290 Saint-Bonnet-le-Froid, France
Tel. (0)4 71 59 93 72; Fax (0)4 71 59 93 40

In 1995, at only 39 years of age, Régis Marcon was awarded the *Bocuse d'Or*, with his neighbor Michel Troisgros serving as godfather—just one more glowing distinction in a career already crowned with accolades: the *Taittinger* prize in 1989, the *Brillat-Savarin* prize in 1992, and several-time finalist in the *Meilleur Ouvrier de France* competition (1985, 1991, 1993). In 1979 he opened a restaurant in his village, which was designed to resemble "a cloister bathed in light." It has earned him three red chef's hats in Gault-Millau (17). The eye of a painter is apparent in the restaurant, and this is what Régis Marcon, a great sportsman and medal-winning skier, as well as a passionate lover of nature, once hoped to become.

Guy Martin

born February 3, 1957

Restaurant: **Le Grand Véfour**
Address: 17, rue de Beaujolais
75001 Paris, France
Tel. (0)1 42 96 56 27; Fax (0)1 42 86 80 71

It would be impossible to summarize Guy Martin's career in just a couple of sentences—two Michelin stars, three white chef's hats in Gault-Millau (18), three stars in the Bottin Gourmand, and 18.5/20 in Champérard. This young prodigy of gastronomy studied first with Troisgros, then in his native region, chiefly in Divonne. In 1991 he took over the reins of **Le Grand Véfour**, that jewel among Parisian restaurants at which the *litterati* of the French metropolis have rubbed shoulders for over 200 years, made famous by Raymond Oliver. Guy Martin remains true to the memory of his mother and to his native region of Savoy, of whose culinary history he is a fervent devotee. He also loves music, painting, and Gothic art.

Maria Ligia Medeiros

born August 9, 1946

Restaurant: **Casa de Comida**
Address: 1, Travessa das Amoreiras
1200 Lisbon, Portugal
Tel. (0)1 388 5376; Fax (0)1 387 5132

Since 1978, Maria Ligia Medeiros has run the kitchens of a cozy restaurant owned by Jorge Vales, a former actor of the *Casa de Comedia* theater—hence the pun of the restaurant's name (*comida* means food). There, in the heart of the historic Old Town of the capital, she serves traditional Portuguese dishes with skill and flair, for which she was awarded a Michelin star several years ago. In addition to *haute cuisine*, she loves classical music and spends a large part of her leisure hours reading.

Dieter Müller

born July 28, 1948

Restaurant: **Dieter Müller**
Address: Lerbacher Weg,
51469 Bergisch Gladbach, Germany
Tel. (0)2202 2040; Fax (0)2202 204940

Dieter Müller had already beaten a career path across several countries and continents by the time he settled down in his native Germany in 1992. From 1973 onward he served as head chef of various establishments in Switzerland, Australia (Sydney), Japan, and Hawaii, collecting numerous awards along the way, including the title of Chef of the Year in the Krug guidebook in 1982 and in Gault-Millau in 1988. Today, he boasts two Michelin stars and four red chef's hats (19.5), as well as a National Gastronomy prize. A member of *Relais et Châteaux* and *Relais Gourmands*, his hobbies are photography and collecting old recipes, as well as playing ice hockey and soccer.

Jean-Louis Neichel

born February 17, 1948

Restaurant: **Neichel**
Address: Beltran i Rózpide, 16 bis
08034 Barcelona, Spain
Tel. (9)3 203 8408; Fax (9)3 205 6369

Thanks to his training under such culinary celebrities as Gaston Lenôtre, Alain Chapel, and Georges Blanc, Jean-Louis Neichel is a European chef *par excellence*. For 10 years he brought his invaluable experience to bear while running **El Bulli** in Rosas, where Fernando Adría is now head chef, before opening his own restaurant in Barcelona in 1981, esteemed in particular for its collection of old armagnacs and cognacs. Awarded two Michelin stars and 9/10 in Gourmetour, Jean-Louis Neichel is also a member of *Relais Gourmands*. His leisure hours are devoted to oil painting (landscapes), his family, and sports (tennis, cycling, skiing).

Pierre Orsi

born July 12, 1939

Restaurant: **Pierre Orsi**
Address: 3, place Kléber
69006 Lyons, France
Tel. (0)4 78 89 57 68; Fax (0)4 72 44 93 34

Pierre Orsi's career reads like a dream. Named *Meilleur Ouvrier de France* in 1972, he has worked with the culinary greats of his generation: with Bocuse in 1955–8, then at **Lucas Carton**, with Alex Humbert at **Maxim's**, and at **Lapérouse** in Paris. There followed a stint in the United States from 1967–71, after which he returned to Lyons and put out his shingle at the edge of the *Tête d'Or* quarter. His superb restaurant, which boasts one Michelin star and three stars in Bottin Gourmand, is a mecca for gourmets. A member of *Relais Gourmands* and *Traditions et Qualité*, Pierre Orsi is also interested in table decoration and collects *objets d'art* and antiques.

Georges Paineau

born April 16, 1939

Restaurant: **Le Bretagne**
Address: 13, rue Saint-Michel
56230 Questembert, France
Tel. (0)2 97 26 11 12; Fax (0)2 97 26 12 37

Georges Paineau had the unusual good fortune to start off his career under Fernand Point at **La Pyramide** in 1960. Since then, he drew ever closer to Brittany, stopping off in La Baule (1962) and Nantes (1963), before settling at **Le Bretagne** in Questembert, close to the Gulf of Morbihan, where he now collects stars (two in Michelin and four in Bottin Gourmand) and Gault-Millau chef's hats (four red, 19 points). He works with his son-in-law, Claude Corlouer. His restaurant, an old coaching inn, is a member of *Relais Gourmands* and *Relais et Châteaux*. A gifted painter, Georges Paineau also loves literature and rugby.

Paul Pauvert

born July 25, 1950

Restaurant: **Les Jardins de la Forge**
Address: 1, place des Piliers
49270 Champtoceaux, France
Tel. (0)2 40 83 56 23; Fax (0)2 40 83 59 80

Professionally speaking, Paul Pauvert took his first steps at the **Café de la Paix** in Paris. In 1972–4 he served a stint in the kitchens of the Transatlantic Shipping Company's famous ocean liner *Grasse*, after which he worked at the hotel *Frantel* in Nantes at the invitation of Roger Jaloux. In 1980 he opened his own restaurant in his home town, at the site where his ancestors had once run a forge. The holder of one Michelin star, Paul Pauvert is also a member of the Culinary Academy of France and the Young Restaurateurs of Europe. The border area between Anjou and Nantes where he lives offers ample opportunity for the hunting, fishing, and horseback riding which he enjoys.

Horst Petermann

born May 18, 1944

Restaurant: **Petermann's Kunststuben**
Address: Seestraße 160,
8700 Küsnacht, Switzerland
Tel. (0)1 910 0715; Fax (0)1 910 0495

After serving his apprenticeship in Hamburg, Horst Petermann continued his career in Switzerland, in Saint Moritz, Lucerne and Geneva. He cooked in the kitchens of Émile Jung at **Le Crocodile** in Strasbourg, and at the Culinary Olympics in Tokyo in 1985, where he figured among the prizewinners. Further accolades received were the Golden Key of Gastronomy in 1987, Chef of the Year in 1991, four red chef's hats in Gault-Millau (19), and two Michelin stars. The success of his restaurant is also ensured by his master pastry chef, Rico Zandonella. As well as being a keen sportsman, Horst Petermann is passionate about his work and enjoys cultivating the friendships he has made through it.

Roland Pierroz

born August 26, 1942

Restaurant: **Hôtel Rosalp-Restaurant Pierroz**
Address: Route de Médran,
1936 Verbier, Switzerland
Tel. (0)27 771 6323; Fax (0)27 771 1059

Since 1962, Roland Pierroz has worked in this popular winter-sports resort in an equally popular restaurant. The holder of one Michelin star, four red chef's hats and 19 points in Gault-Millau, and three stars in Bottin Gourmand, he was awarded the Golden Key of Gastronomy in 1980 and named Chef of the Year in 1992. Roland Pierroz trained in Lausanne (Switzerland) and London, and is a member of *Relais et Châteaux* and *Relais Gourmands*, as well as vice-chairman of the *Grandes Tables Suisses*. A native of the Valais, he enjoys hunting and playing golf.

Jacques & Laurent Pourcel

born September 13, 1964

Restaurant: **Le Jardin des Sens**
Address: 11, avenue Saint Lazare
34000 Montpellier, France
Tel. (0)4 67 79 63 38; Fax (0)4 67 72 13 05

Although specializing in different areas, these inseparable twins underwent the same training, serving apprenticeships with Alain Chapel, Marc Meneau, Pierre Gagnaire, Michel Bras, Michel Trama, and Marc Veyrat. Together with their business partner, Olivier Château, they opened the **Jardin des Sens** in a house made of glass and stone in 1988, and have since collected stars in various guides: two from Michelin and three red chef's hats in Gault-Millau (17). Both chefs are *Maîtres Cuisiniers de France* and members of *Relais Gourmands*.

Stéphane Raimbault

born May 17, 1956

Restaurant: **L'Oasis**
Address: rue Honoré Carle,
06210 La Napoule, France
Tel. (0)4 93 49 95 52; Fax (0)4 93 49 64 13

After working for several years in Paris under the watchful eye of Émile Tabourdiau at **La Grande Cascade**, followed by a stint with Gérard Pangaud, Stéphane Raimbault spent nine years in Japan, where he ran the **Rendez-vous** restaurant in the Hotel Plaza d'Osaka in Osaka. After returning to France in 1991, he took over **L'Oasis** in La Napoule, with his brother as pastry chef. The recipient of two Michelin stars and three red chef's hats in Gault-Millau (18), he was also a finalist for the title of *Meilleur Ouvrier de France*. In addition, he is a *Maître Cuisinier de France* and a member of *Traditions et Qualité*.

Paul Rankin

born October 1, 1959

Restaurant: **Roscoff**
Address: 7, Lesley House, Shaftesbury Square
Belfast BT2 7DB, Northern Ireland
Tel. (0)1232 331 532; Fax (0)1232 312 093

Paul Rankin has had an international career, working first in London with Albert Roux in **Le Gavroche**, then in California and Canada. It was not, however, in Canada, but on a cruise in Greece that he met his Canadian wife Jeanne, whose skills as a pastry chef have delighted diners at **Roscoff** since 1989. Named Best Restaurant in the United Kingdom by the Courvoisier guidebook in 1994–5, it is only a wonder that **Roscoff** has just one Michelin star. Paul Rankin also presents the BBC television program *Gourmet Ireland*. He loves traveling and wine, plays soccer and rugby, and practices yoga.

Jean-Claude Rigollet

born September 27, 1946

Restaurant: **Au Plaisir Gourmand**
Address: 2, rue Parmentier
37500 Chinon, France
Tel. (0)2 47 93 20 48; Fax (0)2 47 93 05 66

Jean-Claude Rigollet began his career at **Maxim's** under Alex Humbert, then arrived in the Loire valley, working first at **Domaine de la Tortinière** in Montbazon (1971–7), then at the famous **Auberge des Templiers** of the Bézards (1978–82), not far from Montargis. In 1983 he became chef at **Plaisir Gourmand** in Chinon in the Touraine, the home of Rabelais. He received one Michelin star in 1985. Although he comes from the Sologne, Jean-Claude Rigollet also cooks in the style of the Touraine, and his wine cellar is a testament to his extensive knowledge of regional wines.

Michel Rochedy

born July 15, 1936

Restaurant: **Le Chabichou**
Address: Quartier Les Chenus,
73120 Courchevel 1850, France
Tel. (0)2 47 93 20 48; Fax (0)2 47 93 05 66

Michel Rochedy received his earliest professional instruction from André Pic, the celebrated chef from Valence, in 1954–6. Originally from the Ardèche, Rochedy arrived in Savoy in 1963 and succumbed to the charms of the region. His restaurant **Chabichou**, which specializes in Savoy cuisine, has earned him two Michelin stars and three red chef's hats in Gault-Millau (17). A *Maître Cuisinier de France* and member of *Eurotoques*, he is also the chairman of the tourist information board of Courchevel. In his spare time, Michel Rochedy enjoys art and literature, fishes, and plays soccer and rugby.

Joël Roy

born November 28, 1951

Restaurant: **Le Prieuré**
Address: 3, rue du Prieuré,
54630 Flavigny-sur-Moselle, France
Tel. (0)3 79 26 70 45; Fax (0)3 86 26 75 51

In 1979, while still in the employ of Jacques Maximin at the **Hôtel Negresco** in Nice, Joël Roy won the *Meilleur Ouvrier de France* competition. Shortly afterwards, he became head chef at the **Frantel** in Nancy. In 1983 he opened **Le Prieuré**, which looks like a modern cloister with its arcades and garden. His one-Michelin-starred establishment is in the Lorraine, a region he loves for its traditions and natural beauty.
An expert on fish, he is especially fond of river angling, and also enjoys cycling in his spare time.

Santi Santamaria

born July 26, 1957

Restaurant: **El Racó de Can Fabes**
Address: Carrer Sant Joan, 6
08470 San Celoni, Spain
Tel. (9)3 867 2851; Fax (9)3 867 3861

Since 1981, Santi Santamaria has taken great pleasure in serving specialties from his native Catalonia to his discerning clientele. His restaurant, which is just a stone's throw away from Barcelona, at the foot of Montseny National Park, has been awarded three Michelin stars and 8/10 in Gourmetour. In addition, Santi Santamaria is a member of *Relais Gourmands* and *Traditions et Qualité*. He also organizes gastronomic seminars, on herbs in the spring and on mushrooms in the fall. These gourmet workshops are always a great success. In his free time, Santi Santamaria enjoys reading.

Nadia Santini

born July 19, 1954

Restaurant: **Dal Pescatore**
Address: 46013 Runate Canneto sull'Oglio, Italy
Tel. (0)376 72 30 01; Fax (0)376 70304

Since 1974 Nadia Santini has presided over the kitchens of **Dal Pescatore**, which was opened in 1920 by her husband's grandfather. The outstanding reputation of this restaurant is impressively documented in both Italian and French restaurant guides: two Michelin stars, four red chef's hats in L'Espresso/Gault-Millau (19), one sun in Veronelli, and 94/100 in Gambero Rosso. A member of *Le Soste*, *Relais Gourmands*, and *Traditions et Qualité*, she was awarded the prize for the Best Wine Cellar of the Year by L'Espresso/Gault-Millau in 1993. Nadia Santini is interested in history, especially the history of the culinary arts, from which she draws inspiration. She also loves hiking in the mountains.

Maria Santos Gomes

born August 10, 1962

Restaurant: **Conventual**
Address: Praça das Flores, 45
1200 Lisbon, Portugal
Tel. (0)1 60 91 96; Fax (0)1 387 5132

The **Conventual** is located in the historic Old Town of Lisbon, right by the Parliament. There, in 1982, Dina Marquez engaged the young chef Maria Santos Gomes—to the great delight of Lisbon politicians, who dine there regularly. Much of the restaurant's decor comes from the former cloister of Igreja (hence the restaurant's name). Maria Santos Gomes' inventive cuisine already earned her one Michelin star. In 1993, she won first prize in the Portuguese Gastronomy Competition, which always takes place in Lisbon. In addition to cooking, she loves literature, going on walks, and traveling.

Nikolaos Sarantos

born December 5, 1945

Restaurant: **Hôtel Athenaeum Inter-Continental**
Address: 89-93, Syngrou Avenue
117 45 Athens, Greece
Tel. (0)1 902 3666; Fax (0)1 924 3000

From 1971-88, Nikolaos Sarantos traveled around the Mediterranean and the Middle East, honing his culinary skills in the various Hilton Hotels in Teheran, Athens, Corfu, Kuwait City, and Cairo before finally settling down at the **Athenaeum Inter-Continental** in 1988. Nikolaos Sarantos is a member of the jury at international cooking competitions in San Francisco, Copenhagen, and Bordeaux. Chairman of the Chef's Association of Greece, he is also a great sports fan, and an avid tennis, soccer, and basketball player.

Fritz Schilling

born June 8, 1951

Restaurant: **Schweizer Stuben**
Address: Geiselbrunnweg 11,
97877 Wertheim, Germany
Tel. (0)9342 30 70; Fax (0)9342 30 71 55

A chef since 1972, Fritz Schilling opened his restaurant in the Main valley near the romantic little town of Wertheim in 1990. His refined and versatile cuisine, which cultivates the best German gastronomic traditions, has already earned him two Michelin stars and four red chef's hats in Gault-Millau (19.5). A member of *Relais et Châteaux* and *Relais Gourmands*, his restaurant is one of the best in Germany. In his spare time, Fritz Schilling loves listening to pop music. He is a passionate driver, enjoys playing golf, and likes most beach sports.

Jean Schillinger

born January 31, 1934
died December 27, 1995

This former Chairman of the *Maîtres Cuisiniers de France* was a symbol of Alsatian gastronomy: The well-known restaurant **Schillinger** in Colmar, France (1957-95) boasted two Michelin stars, three red stars in Gault-Millau (17), and three stars in Bottin Gourmand. Jean Schillinger, a Knight of the *Mérite* Order, was the third generation of a family which had been in the restaurant business since1893. For over 20 years he worked to heighten the profile of French cuisine throughout the world, from Japan to Brazil and Australia.

Jean-Yves Schillinger

born March 23, 1963

Succession in the Schillinger culinary dynasty is guaranteed thanks to this brilliant young chef, who has shown himself in all respects worthy of his predecessors. In 1988–95 he worked with his father in Colmar. Prior to this he had worked in prestigious restaurants, such as the **Crillon** in Paris, in **Jamin**, where he was Joël Robuchon's sous chef, and even at **La Côte Basque** in New York. He is also a member of the Young Restaurateurs of Europe, as well as of the *Prosper Montagné* and the French *Haute Cuisine*associations. Jean-Yves Schillinger is very active and especially enjoys golf, skiing, and motorcycling.

Rudolf Sodamin

born April 6, 1958

Restaurant: **Passenger vessel *Queen Elizabeth 2***
Home port: Southampton, England

The Austrian Rudolf Sodamin (pictured standing next to his colleague Jonathan Wicks) currently works for the Cunard Line shipping company, which owns several other magnificent liners besides the QE2. This *chef de cuisine*/pastry chef has attracted much favorable attention in numerous restaurants in Austria, France, Switzerland, and the United States. In New York, he worked in the kitchens of the famous **Waldorf-Astoria**. He is a member of the *Prosper Montagné* and *Chefs des Chefs* associations. Although Sodamin enjoys jogging, his favorite sport is still skiing in his home town of Kitzbühel.

Roger Souvereyns

born December 2, 1938

Restaurant: **Scholteshof**
Address: Kermstraat, 130
3512 Stevoort-Hasselt, Belgium
Tel. (0)11 25 02 02; Fax (0)11 25 43 28

Roger Souvereyns has presided over the **Scholteshof** since 1983. This eighteenth-century farmstead has a large vegetable garden, which used to be tended by his friend and gardener Clément, and which is the source of the wonderful fresh fruit and vegetables used in his cooking. Roger Souvereyns has two Michelin stars, four red chef's hats in Gault-Millau (19.5), three stars in Bottin Gourmand, and 95/100 in the Belgian restaurant guide Henri Lemaire. A member of *Relais et Châteaux*, *Relais Gourmands*, and *Traditions et Qualité*, he is a collector of antiques and old paintings. He also loves opera and enjoys swimming and cycling.

Pedro Subijana

born November 5, 1948

Restaurant **Akelaré**
Address: 56, Paseo del Padre Orcolaga
20008 San Sebastián, Spain
Tel. (9)43 21 20 52; Fax (9)43 21 92 68

Since 1981, Pedro Subijana has had his own restaurant overlooking the Bay of Biscay. Awarded two stars in Michelin and 9/10 in Gourmetour, he was named Best Cook in Spain in 1982. Subijana underwent a traditional training at the College of Hotel Management in Madrid and at Euromar College in Zarauz, and became a cooking teacher in 1970. In 1986 he became Commissioner General of the European Association of Chefs, whose headquarters is in Brussels. He presents food programs on Basque Television and on *Tele-Madrid*. Pedro Subijana loves music and the movies.

Émile Tabourdiau

born November 25, 1943

Restaurant **Le Bristol**
Address: 112, rue du Faubourg Saint-Honoré
75008 Paris, France
Tel. (0)1 53 43 43 00; Fax (0)1 53 43 43 01

Since 1964, Émile Tabourdiau has worked in only the most famous of restaurants: First at **Ledoyen**, then at **La Grande Cascade**, and finally, since 1980, at **Le Bristol**, located in the immediate vicinity of the Élysée Palace and boasting magnificent large gardens. A former pupil of Auguste Escoffier, Émile Tabourdiau is a member of the Culinary Academy of France, and was the winner of the *Prosper Montagné* prize in 1970, as well as *Meilleur Ouvrier de France* in 1976. His restaurant has one Michelin star. In his spare time he loves painting, and enjoys playing tennis and spending time in his garden.

Romano Tamani

born April 30, 1943

Restaurant: **Ambasciata**
Address: 33, Via Martiri di Belfiore
46026 Quistello, Italy
Tel. (0)376 61 90 03; Fax (0)376 61 82 55

Romano Tamani is the only one of our chefs to hold the coveted title of *Commendatore della Repubblica Italiana*, a distinction conferred on him by his native Italy in 1992. This Lombardian, who learned his craft in London and Switzerland, is one of the most skillful representatives of Italian gastronomy. Together, he and his brother Francesco have run the **Ambasciata** since 1978. Accolades received include two Michelin stars, three chef's hats in Espresso/Gault-Millau, one Veronelli sun, and 90/100 in Gambero Rosso, as well as membership of the prestigious Italian chain *Le Soste*. Cooking is Tamani's consuming passion, but he also loves the sea and maritime life on the coast.

Laurent Tarridec

born May 26, 1956

Restaurant: **Le Restaurant du Bistrot des Lices**
Address: Place des Lices,
83990 Saint-Tropez, France
Tel. (0)4 94 97 29 00; Fax (0)4 94 97 76 39

That this Breton, a pupil of Michel Rochedy, could set himself up on the Côte d'Azur of all places, and after only one year (1995) walk off with one Michelin star and three red chef's hats in Gault-Millau (18), is testimony to his extraordinary adaptability. Before this, he honed his skills in Brittany at the **Lion d'Or**, in Paris, and in the Rhone valley at the **Beau Rivage**. Laurent Tarridec is interested in politics, as well as anything related to the sea. He also skis, rides a motorcycle, and, since living in Saint-Tropez, has discovered the game of *boules*.

Dominique Toulousy

born August 19, 1952

Restaurant: **Les Jardins de l'Opéra**
Address: 1, place du Capitole
31000 Toulouse, France
Tel. (0)5 61 23 07 76; Fax (0)5 61 23 63 00

Dominique Toulousy has lived in Toulouse only since 1984. Hanging out his shingle on the Place du Capitole, he reaped accolades by the dozen: Golden Key of Gastronomy (1986), three red chef's hats in Gault-Millau (18), and two Michelin stars, as well as the title of *Meilleur Ouvrier de France* (1993). Before this, he had his first successes in Gers, a region known for its generous cuisine. Dominique Toulousy is a member of the Young Restaurateurs of Europe, the *Prosper Montagné* association, *Eurotoques*, and *Traditions et Qualité*. He enjoys poring over old cookbooks and loves gardening, tennis, and swimming.

Gilles Tournadre

born June 29, 1955

Restaurant **Gill**
Address: 8 & 9, quai de la Bourse
76000 Rouen, France
Tel. (0)2 35 71 16 14; Fax (0)2 35 71 96 91

Even a Norman can occasionally be persuaded to leave his native region in order to learn his craft: Gilles Tournadre started out his career at **Lucas Carton**, followed by the **Auberge des Templiers** of the Bézards and **Taillevent**, before ending up—on his own two feet—in Bayeux, and in 1984, back in his hometown. His career successes have justified all these changes: the young gastronome can boast two Michelin stars and three red chef's hats (17 points) for his restaurant near Rouen cathedral. A member of the Young Restaurateurs of Europe, this enthusiastic sportsman loves judo, golf, and motor sports, and is also a passionate conservationist.

Luisa Valazza

born December 20, 1950

Restaurant: **Al Sorriso**
Address: Via Roma, 18
28018 Soriso, Italy
Tel. (0)322 98 32 28; Fax (0)322 98 33 28

Taking their cue from the name of the restaurant that she and her husband Angelo have run since 1981 in their hometown in the Piedmont region, the food critics have all "smiled" on Luisa Valazza, awarding **Al Sorriso** two Michelin stars, four chef's hats in Espresso/Gault-Millau (19.2), one sun in Veronelli, and 90/100 in Gambero Rosso. Luisa Valazza, who is also a member of the *Le Soste* chain, remains modest in the midst of this praise, carefully cooking the recipes she has amassed since 1971 in the **Europa** in Borgomanero. She is passionately interested in the arts, especially painting and literature. She frequently visits museums and is also an enthusiastic practitioner of winter sports.

Guy Van Cauteren

born May 8, 1950

Restaurant: **T'Laurierblad**
Address: Dorp, 4
9290 Berlare, Belgium
Tel. (0)52 42 48 01; Fax (0)52 42 59 97

Before opening his restaurant **T'Laurierblad** (The Bay Leaf) in 1979, Guy Van Cauteren was taught by some of France's most outstanding chefs: Alain Senderens at **Archestrate** in Paris, and the Allégriers at **Lucas Carton** (1972–4). He then spent several years cooking at the French Embassy in Brussels (1974–9). Since then, he has acquired two Michelin stars, three red chef's hats in Gault-Millau (17), and 89/100 in the Belgian restaurant guide Henri Lemaire. In addition, he was the fortunate recipient of the bronze **Bocuse** in 1993, and holds the title of *Maître Cuisinier de Belgique*. Guy Van Cauteren collects old books and enjoys traveling. In his spare time, he relaxes by cycling.

Freddy Van Decasserie

born October 10, 1943

Restaurant: **La Villa Lorraine**
Address: 75, avenue du Vivier d'Oie
1180 Brussels, Belgium
Tel. (0)2 374 3163; Fax (0)2 372 0195

Freddy Van Decasserie started off at **La Villa Lorraine** in 1963 as a kitchen boy and worked his way up the hierarchy until he became head chef and the recipient of numerous awards: two Michelin stars, three red chef's hats in Gault-Millau (18), three stars in Bottin Gourmand, and 92/100 in Henri Lemaire. He is a *Maître Cuisinier de Belgique* and a member of the Culinary Academy of France and *Traditions et Qualité*. In his spare time, he stays fit by being a training partner to the racing cyclist Eddy Merckx. He also swims and goes to the occasional soccer match.

Geert Van Hecke

born July 20, 1956

Restaurant: **De Karmeliet**
Address: Langestraat, 19
8000 Bruges, Belgium
Tel. (0)50 33 82 59; Fax (0)50 33 10 11

Geert Van Hecke was introduced to his craft by Freddy Van Decasserie at the **Villa Lorraine** in 1977, then served a stint with Alain Chapel at the famous **Cravache d'Or** in Brussels, finally opening his own restaurant in an historic house in the heart of Bruges. To date, his cooking has earned him two Michelin stars, three stars in the Bottin Gourmand, three red chef's hats in Gault-Millau (18), and 92/100 in Henri Lemaire. A winner of the Best Chef in Belgium award, he is also a member of **Traditions et Qualité**. It was not coincidence which led him to settle in Bruges, a well-preserved medieval town and popular tourist destination, as he is interested in art and enjoys visiting museums.

Gérad Vié

born April 11, 1943

Restaurant: **Les Trois Marches (Trianon Palace)**
Address: 1 boulevard de la Reine
78000 Versailles, France
Tel. (0)1 39 50 13 21; Fax (0)1 30 21 01 25

The chef of the **Trois Marches** (since 1970) started his career at the age of 13 at **Lapérouse**. There followed stints at **Lucas Carton** and the **Plaza-Athénée** in Paris and **Crillon Tower's** in London, as well as three years with the Compagnie des Wagons-Lits (1967–70). Today, Gérard Vié can boast two Michelin stars and three red chef's hats (18). Recipient of the Silver Table award from Gault-Millau in 1984, he was presented with the Golden Key of Gastronomy in 1993. An enthusiastic fan of the theater, opera, and movies, he collects paintings and is a *Chevalier des Arts et Lettres*. He also loves hiking and swimming.

Jean-Pierre Vigato

born March 20, 1952

Restaurant **Apicius**
Address: 122, avenue de Villiers
75017 Paris, France
Tel. (0)1 43 80 19 66; Fax (0)1 44 40 09 57

Jean Pierre Vigato started off as a sommelier and served an apprenticeship in various restaurants before his first major successes at **Grandgousier** in Paris in 1980–3. In 1984 he set up on his own, opening **Apicius** in his native Paris. The restaurant, named after a famous Roman epicure, was awarded its first Michelin star in 1985, and its second two years later. It also boasts three red chef's hats in Gault-Millau (18). A member of *Relais Gourmands*, Jean-Pierre Vigato was Gault-Millau Best Chef of the Year in 1988, and chef at the French Pavillion at the 1992 World's Fair in Seville, Spain.

Gianfranco Vissani

born November 22, 1951

Restaurant **Vissani**
Address: 05020 Civitella del Lago, Italy
Tel. (0)744 95 03 96; Fax (0)744 95 03 96

With a rating of 19.6 and four chef's hats, Gianfranco Vissani got a near-perfect report card from Espresso/Gault-Millau—the best in all Italy. Two Michelin stars, one Veronelli sun, and 87/100 in Gambero Rosso complete the guidebook honors showered on the restaurant run by Vissani since 1980 as a family concern with his wife, mother, and sister. One of the selling points of his establishment is his own-production olive oil, an indispensable flavor in his Mediterranean cooking. In his spare time, this gourmet collects clocks and relaxes by listening to classical music or reading. In addition, he is a fan of the AC Milan soccer club.

Jonathan F. Wicks

born June 14, 1962

Restaurant: **Passenger vessel** *Queen Elizabeth 2*
Home port: Southampton, England

In 1980–7, Jonathan Wicks (pictured seated next to his colleague Rudolf Sodamin) worked at a number of prestigious London restaurants, including the **Mayfair Intercontinental**, the **Grosvenor House** in Park Lane, and the **Méridien** in Picadilly, where he made his way up the ranks to sous chef. In 1987 he became chef aboard the luxury ocean liner QE2. The home port of the vessel is Southampton, but the constant change of scenery suits this travel-loving gourmet. Although rugby is the main sport in his hometown of Bath in England, Jonathan Wicks plays football and sails in his spare time. He also collects porcelain plates and loves having breakfast in bed.

Heinz Winkler

born July 17, 1949

Restaurant: **Residenz Heinz Winkler**
Address: Kirchplatz 1,
83229 Aschau im Chiemgau, Germany
Tel. (0)8052 17990; Fax (0)8052 179 966

At only 31 years of age, Heinz Winkler already boasted three Michelin stars—how on earth did he do it? Perhaps by training at the **Victoria** in Interlaken, under Paul Bocuse, and at **Tantris** in Munich, before opening the **Residenz Heinz Winkler** in 1991. To crown it all, this gastronome has three white chef's hats (18) and was Chef of the Year in 1979, as well as Restaurateur of the Year in 1994 in Gault-Millau. Heinz Winkler is a member of *Relais et Châteaux*, *Relais Gourmands*, *Traditions et Qualité*, and the Italian chain *Le Soste*. He enjoys poring over old cookbooks, playing golf, and skiing.

Harald Wohlfahrt

born November 7, 1955

Restaurant: **Schwarzwaldstube**
Address: Tonbachstrasse 237,
72270 Baiersbronn, Germany
Tel. (0)7442 49 26 65; Fax (0)7442 49 26 92

Harald Wohlfahrt started work at the **Schwarzwaldstube**, the restaurant of the Hotel Trauben-Tonbach in the heart of the Black Forest, in 1976, and has been chef there since 1980. He learned his trade at **Stahlbad** in Baden-Baden and **Tantris** in Munich. Voted Chef of the Year in 1991 by Gault-Millau, he currently boasts three Michelin stars and four red chef's hats (19.5). He is also a member of *Relais Gourmands* and *Traditions et Qualité*. While his main interests, unsurprisingly, are the traditions of eating and cooking, Harald Wohlfahrt is also an outstanding athlete, with swimming, soccer, and cycling being his favorite sports.

Armando Zanetti

born December 11, 1926

Restaurant: **Vecchia Lanterna**
Address: Corso Re Umberto, 21
10128 Turin, Italy
Tel. (0)11 53 70 47; Fax (0)11 53 03 91

A native Venetian, Armando Zanetti ran the **Rosa d'Oro** in Turin in 1955–69 before opening the evocatively named **Vecchia Lanterna** (Old Lantern) restaurant in the same city in 1970. Today, our chef, who devotes himself chiefly to the traditional cuisine of his native country, now proudly boasts two Michelin stars and four chef's hats in Espresso/Gault-Millau (19.2/20). In his spare time, Armando Zanetti tirelessly researches European cuisine of the past. He derives special pleasure from trying new dishes, both his own and those of his fellow chefs.

Alberto Zuluaga

born March 31, 1960

Restaurant: **Lopez de Haro y Club Nutico**
Address: Obispo Orueta, 2
48009 Bilbao, Spain
Tel. (9)4 423 5500; Fax (9)4 423 4500

As a Basque from the Spanish province of Vizcaya on the Bay of Biscay, Alberto Zuluaga is especially proud to be able to exercise his profession in the true capital of his native province. He has been chef of the five-star luxury restaurant **Club Nautico** in the banking district of Bilbao since 1991. Before this, in 1987–91, he cultivated his love of Basque cuisine and culinary traditions at the **Bermeo** in the same city, earning the title of Best Cook in *Euzkadi* (the Basque Country) in 1988. It goes without saying that he enjoys playing Basque *boules* in his spare time, but he also likes motor racing, and is an enthusiastic mushroom hunter when time allows.

Glossary

AIOLI: Provençal garlic mayonnaise (Fr. *ail*, garlic), served with poached fish, hard-boiled (hard-cooked) eggs and vegetables.

BAIN-MARIE: Gentle cooking in a heat-proof container placed over a pan containing hot water, or in a special double boiler, so as to avoid overheating.

BARBECUE: To cook over hot coals, under a hot broiler (grill) or on a spit (see also GRILL).

BASTE: To pour hot cooking juices over roasting meat, such as beef, duck or pork, so that the meat does not dry out but becomes appetizingly brown and crisp.

BECHAMEL SAUCE: Creamy white sauce made from flour, butter and milk, and served hot. Named after the Marquis de Béchamel, the majordomo of Louis XIV.

BLANCH: To cook foods, particularly vegetables, very briefly in boiling water in order to remove a strong taste or smell, or to fix a bright color. This term is also used to mean pouring hot water over fruit or nuts, in order to loosen the shells or skins before removing.

BLINI: Small Russian pancakes made with buckwheat flour, usually garnished with sour cream, caviar or smoked salmon.

BROIL see GRILL

BOUQUET GARNI: A bunch of herbs tied together for seasoning soups, stews and casseroles. Usually consists of thyme, bay leaf and parsley, but according to the dish and the region, may also include leek greens, rosemary, marjoram, lovage, fennel, chives or celery.

BRAISE: Braised ingredients are cooked in a combination of fat, liquid and steam. You first brown the ingredients slightly, then add a little liquid (water, stock or wine), cover tightly and cook slowly.

BROWN: To sauté meat or other ingredients in a little hot fat or oil until golden brown.

CARPACCIO: A dish made from very finely sliced raw meat, usually beef, dressed with oil and lemon juice, or a vinaigrette sauce made with olive oil, and served as a first course.

CARVE: To cut meat, poultry or fish into slices or serving pieces before serving. This calls for a large, very sharp knife and a wooden carving board.

CHANTILLY: Dishes à la Chantilly, usually desserts, are always accompanied by whipped cream or mixed with it.

CHARLOTTE: Dessert prepared from pureed fruit or cream, used as a filling for a mold lined with sponge fingers (lady fingers), wafers or slices of buttered bread.

CHARTREUSE: Soufflé of meat cut in small pieces, vegetables and bacon, cooked in a bain-marie and served warm.

CLARIFY: The removal of solids from soups and sauces by stirring in lightly beaten egg white and careful heating, followed by straining.

COCKLES: Shellfish with brown-striped, grooved shells, found in the shallow coastal waters of the Atlantic and Mediterranean, eaten raw with lemon juice, fried or in stews.

CONSOMMÉ: (Fr. *consommer*, to complete) Strong broth made from meat or poultry, cooked until reduced and then strained. May be served hot or cold.

CORAL: Roe of shellfish, such as lobster, considered a great delicacy.

CROUTONS: Fried or baked slices or cubes of bread, served with soups, casseroles or salads.

crudités: (Fr.) Raw vegetables, usually cut into sticks, served with dips and cold sauces as a first course..

CUSTARD: Dessert or sauce for desserts made from sugar, egg yolks, milk or cream and a little salt.

DEEP-FRYING: To cook or brown foods in a deep pan of very hot fat or oil, resulting in a crust that seals in taste and moisture.

DEGLAZE: To loosen the rich meat sediment from the bottom of the roasting pan (tin) or frying pan (skillet) by adding liquid such as wine or meat broth while stirring over heat.

DIJONNAISE: Fr. term for dishes prepared with light Dijon mustard—a special, creamy mustard made with mustard seeds softened in the sour, fermented juice of unripe grapes. Dijonnaise is also the name given to a mustard-flavored mayonnaise that is served with cold meat.

DRESS: To prepare pieces of meat or fish for cooking, for example removing skin and sinews.

FARCE: (Fr. stuffing) A finely chopped mixture of meat or fish with herbs and spices for stuffing vol-au-vents or poultry. Mushrooms, other vegetables, rice, bread crumbs or egg are also mixed with meat or offal (variety meats) for use as a stuffing.

FILO PASTRY: A pastry made from wheat flour, water and oil or fat, rolled out until paper-thin and then cut into sheets, brushed with fat and used in several layers. Frequently used in the cuisine of the Middle East, Turkey, Greece, Austria and Hungary. Puff pastry or strudel dough may be used as a replacement in recipes calling for filo.

FLAMBÉ: To pour high-proof spirits over a dish and set it alight in order to improve the flavor.

FOLD IN: To add ingredients to beaten egg whites or whipped cream and mix it in carefully, without vigorous stirring, to avoid losing volume.

FOND: (Fr.) Juices remaining after the cooking of meat or fish, which form the basis for a sauce.

FUMET: Term for concentrated liquid, usually produced by thickening.

GALANTINE: Roulade cooked while rolled in a cloth or in thin strips of bacon or fat, or an equivalent.

GARNISH:(verb) To prepare trimmings for the main dish or to decorate the dish. (noun) Decorative addition to a dish, or solid ingredient (such as dumplings) added to soups and sauces.

GAZPACHO: Cold vegetable soup of Spanish origin, made with ripe tomatoes, red bell peppers, cucumbers, olive oil, bread and garlic.

GELEE: Clear or semi-clear jelled mixture prepared with pectin or gelatin, or jellied meat juices.

GLAZE: To produce a glossy effect by covering a dish with its own juice, jelly or sugar.

GRATIN: Dishes *au gratin* are cooked and then, before serving, sprinkled with bread crumbs or grated cheese and dotted with butter, and briefly baked in the oven under a strong heat from above, or broiled (grilled), so that a crisp topping is formed.

GRILL (BROIL): To cook foods by exposing them to close dry heat, which makes them brown and crisp.

HOISIN SAUCE: Piquant reddish-brown sauce made from a paste of fermented soy beans, flour, salt, sugar and red rice. A natural coloring that gives color to many Chinese dishes.

JULIENNE: Vegetables cut into uniform thin strips and added to soup or used to accompany the main dish.

LARD (verb): To interleave lean meat with strips of bacon to prevent it from drying out, or with slices of truffle or garlic cloves to impart additional flavor.

MARINATE: To soak meat, fish or poultry in a mixture often of oil, vinegar or lemon juice as well as herbs and spices. This tenderizes the food and adds flavor.

MOUSSE: (Fr. foam) Rich, sweetened or savory dish that derives its delicate, foamy texture from stiffly beaten egg whites, whipped cream or both.

PARFAIT: (Fr. perfect, complete) A cold dish made from a fine stuffing, bound with egg white or gelatin, placed in molds and turned out after chilling. A sweet parfait is a chilled dessert made from custard, jelly, ice cream and cream, and served in a tall glass.

PERSILLADE: (Fr. *persil*, parsley) Mixture of finely chopped parsley and garlic, or cold beef slices in a dressing of vinegar, oil and a large amount of parsley.

POACH: To cook ingredients at a low temperature in liquid.

PRAWN (SHRIMP): Small shellfish without claws, with long antennae, slim legs and a long, plump body. The color depends on the variety, but most of them turn reddish orange when cooked. They are found in both fresh and salt water. Their firm, moist flesh forms the basis of various dishes in many countries.

PUREE: Process of converting soft ingredients into a uniform texture by means of chopping or mashing.

REDUCE: To thicken a sauce or juices from roast meat so that water evaporates, the sauce becomes more concentrated and the aroma stronger.

REFRESH: To dip a hot foodstuff in cold water, or hold it under running cold water, in order to lower the temperature quickly and preserve a color.

REMOULADE: A herb mayonnaise with chopped tarragon, chervil, parsley, pickled gherkins (cornichons) and capers, served with cold meat, fish and shellfish.

ROUX: A combination of cooked fat and flour used to thicken sauces.

SABAYON: Light, airy sauce made from egg yolk, sugar and white wine or champagne. Served warm or cold with desserts.

SAFFRON: The dried stigmas of a species of crocus. Because the little threads of saffron have to be gathered by hand, genuine saffron is the most expensive spice in the world. However, only tiny amounts are required for the flavoring and coloring of various dishes such as fish and rice dishes, curries, casseroles and desserts.

SAUCE AMERICAINE: Sauce made from aromatic vegetables, white wine, butter and tomatoes with crushed lobster shells, flambéed with brandy. Served with fish and shellfish.

sauté: (Fr. *sauter*, jump, or fry quickly in butter) To fry gently or brown ingredients in a little hot butter or oil.

SCALLOP: Mollusk with characteristic fan-shaped shell. Its white muscle and the orange-colored coral can be eaten.

SEASON: To add salt, pepper, herbs or spices to a dish in order to improve the flavor.

SHRIMP see PRAWN

SIMMER: To cook foods in liquid just below the boiling point, or to heat a liquid until bubbles begin to appear on the surface.

SKIM: To remove the fat floating on top of sauces or soups by straining or another method.

SLASH: To make decorative cuts on both sides of a piece of fish or meat, so that the food does not break apart while cooking, but swells up evenly.

SOUFFLE: (Fr. *souffler*, to blow) Light, airy egg dish, sweet or savory, served hot or cold. A hot soufflé is made from stiffly beaten egg whites, folded into a warm sauce or puree.

STEAK TARTARE: Raw ground steak seasoned with chopped onions, gherkins (cornichons), capers or parsley, and salt and pepper.

STEAM: To cook foods above steam, in a steamer containing a sieve or in a special multi-layered metal or bamboo container.

STEW: To cook foods in their own juices or with additional liquid and usually also a little fat.

STOCK: A flavored broth for cooking fish or meat or making soup.

STRAIN: To pass a soup, sauce or other liquid through a strainer or cloth to remove everything but the liquid.

TERRINE: A preparation of finely chopped meat, poultry, game, fish or vegetables, cooked in a deep straight-sided mold and then served chilled.

THICKEN: To condense or bind a simmering sauce by stirring in egg yolk and cream, milk or butter, or flour, cornstarch (cornflour) or arrowroot.

TURN (Fr. to turn) To cut vegetables such as mushrooms, potatoes or carrots into uniform, decorative shapes.

TRUFFLE: Large edible fungus that grows wild, found in autumn near the roots of oak and chestnut trees, particularly in France.

VELOUTE: (Fr. *velours*, velvet) A thick white basic sauce made from butter, flour, and meat or poultry juices, seasoned with salt and pepper.

VINAIGRETTE: Salad dressing based on vinegar (Fr. *vinaigre*) and oil, and often Dijon mustard.

Index